EFFICIENCY IN UNIVERSITIES: The La Paz Papers

EFFICIENCY IN
UNIVERSITIES: The La Paz Papers

edited by

KEITH G. LUMSDEN

Heriot-Watt University and Stanford University

Elsevier Scientific Publishing Company
Amsterdam · London · New York 1974

ELSEVIER SCIENTIFIC PUBLISHING COMPANY
335 JAN VAN GALENSTRAAT
P.O. BOX 211, AMSTERDAM, THE NETHERLANDS

AMERICAN ELSEVIER PUBLISHING COMPANY, INC.
52 VANDERBILT AVENUE
NEW YORK, NEW YORK 10017

Studies on Education

Lady Bracknell . . . *I have always been of the opinion that a man who desires to get married should know either everything or nothing. Which do you know?*
Jack: (After some hesitation) *I know nothing, Lady Bracknell.*
Lady Bracknell: *I am pleased to hear it. I do not approve of anything that tampers with natural ignorance. Ignorance is like a delicate exotic fruit; touch it and the bloom is gone. The whole theory of modern education is radically unsound. Fortunately, in England, at any rate, education produces no effect whatsoever. If it did, it would prove a serious danger to the upper classes, and probably lead to acts of violence in Grosvenor Square . . .*

Act I *The Importance of Being Earnest*, Oscar Wilde

Contents

V. FINANCING UNIVERSITY EDUCATION

List of books from the Higher Education Research Unit

Preface

This book is concerned with the crucial question of how university efficiency can be improved. The papers tackle the issue from many angles, but they share the economic framework of analysis. They were originally discussed when their authors met for a week at La Paz, Mexico, in June 1972. In the light of the discussion which took place at the conference the papers were revised and are being published because of their obvious interest to university administrators, public policymakers, economists, other academics and members of the public at large.

The conference was organized by the Esmée Fairbairn Economics Research Centre (TEFERC), Heriot-Watt University, Edinburgh. TEFERC was founded in 1970 and grew out of the United Kingdom Economics Education Project (EEP) which was started under a grant from the Esmée Fairbairn Charitable Trust in 1968. The purpose of the Centre is to undertake research in the economics of education and related aspects of human resource development. While its principal research activity has been and still is the EEP, a report on 'Efficiency in Higher Education' was completed for the U.S. Department of Health, Education and Welfare in 1971–72 (Contract HEW-OS-71-169). The La Paz conference was partially financed by that Contract and the authors were all staff or consultants of TEFERC.

It seemed eminently appropriate that this volume should appear in Studies in Education, a series closely linked to another research unit concerned with the economics of education, the Higher Education Research Unit of the London School of Economics. This Unit was established in 1964 following the work of the Robbins Committee on Higher Education and the present volume was prepared for publication in the Unit by Jennifer Pinney. We hope this enterprise will be the first of many collaborative ventures between the two groups.

Keith G. Lumsden
Claus A. Moser

IX

Contributors

G.C. ARCHIBALD
University of British Columbia

KENNETH J. ARROW
Harvard University

RICHARD ATTIYEH
University of California, San Diego

DONALD V.T. BEAR
University of California, San Diego

WILLIAM C. BRAINARD
Yale University

PAUL H. COOTNER
Stanford University

HARRY G. JOHNSON
*London School of Economics and Political Science
and the University of Chicago*

RICHARD LAYARD
London School of Economics and Political Science

KEITH G. LUMSDEN
Heriot-Watt University and Stanford University

MELVIN W. REDER
City University of New York

To Paul M. Stobart
planter of acorns

Part I

1. Survey of the Issues

by Richard Attiyeh

Until recently research on the economics of higher education has been confined mainly to an inquiry into the proper allocation of resources between higher education and alternative uses. It asked: given the system of public and private education, should society increase, decrease or leave unchanged the share of its scarce resources allocated to university education? This question has been approached from several points of view, each of which provides at best an ambiguous answer and none of which examines the internal efficiency of the higher education system.

The most widely adopted approach has been to estimate from differences in individual incomes and educational attainments the rate of return on investment in additional years of higher education. Whether society would make better use of its resources by allocating more or less of them to higher education would depend on whether the rate of return on investment in higher education exceeded or fell short of that on alternative opportunities for investment.

Another approach has been to measure the aggregate educational investment embodied in the labour force for different years and to infer from time-series data on aggregate output, labour, physical capital and the stock of educational capital, the contribution which a marginal addition to the stock of educational capital would make in the national product. Again, given the costs of adding to educational capital, it is possible to calculate a rate of return to educational investment to be compared to the rates of return on alternative forms of investment with obvious implications for the allocation of resources.

A third approach has been to calculate average educational attainments of employees in different occupational categories and, on the basis of forecasts in manpower requirements, to determine the amount of resources which must be devoted to higher education if the required numbers of employees with the required qualifications are to be trained. Clearly, if the resources available to higher education fall short of the needs calculated in this way, then according to the model it would be desirable to eliminate the gap.

Each of these three lines of enquiry has been marked by serious limitations resulting from the inadequacy of the available data and the untested and restrictive assumptions of the theory. But quite apart from these shortcomings these kinds of analyses would provide only a limited basis for educational policy, since they fail to suggest how resources allocated to higher education could be most effectively used. The complexity of what is involved in the rational planning of higher education is apparent only when the problems of allocation of resources between higher education and other economic activities are considered jointly with those relating to internal efficiency. It is unwise to consider the first set of problems and ignore the second, when the elimination of substantial internal misallocations would have a profound influence on the optimal share of resources to be devoted to higher education.

The inadequacy of the results of past economic analyses of higher education has become very evident during the past decade. Hit by the dissatisfaction of taxpayers and the antagonism of students, together with rising costs and dwindling resources, those who have had to make decisions on the scale of support for higher education have been handicapped by the absence of a model of higher education which could form a basis for rational planning. It is against this background that economists, dissatisfied with their own accomplishments and more acutely aware of the problems of colleges and universities, have begun to re-examine the economics of education.

Problems in planning the university

Research in the economics of higher education must find a way to deal with the fact that the output produced by the contemporary university includes numerous and diverse components, the quantities and prices of which are difficult to measure. The present lack of valid quantitative information creates serious difficulties. Unless techniques for measuring these variables can be found or methods of

4

rational decision-making which do not depend on this information can be devised, the prospects for significant increases in efficiency will remain poor.

A list of the various components of the output of the universities would include at least the following broad categories: (i) educational output – increases in students' knowledge and skills, both cognitive and social, which increase their productivity and therewith their ability to earn income; (ii) informational output – the reporting of students' attributes and educational attainments to students themselves and to prospective employers, which may facilitate more rational career choices and hiring decisions; and (iii) research output – increases in empirical knowledge, development of new logical concepts and creation of new works of art, which may directly or indirectly increase the economy's productive capacity.

The fact that university output is so variegated is not in itself the source of the analytical difficulty. If the components of university output were like other goods, it would be a relatively straightforward matter to apply the calculus of optimization behaviour to the problem of allocation and to find a reasonably adequate solution. In order for an educational planner to determine the optimal amounts of the different components of university output, it would be necessary for him to have information about both technology and preferences. Technology can be described in terms of production relations which indicate the amounts of each good which can be obtained from different combinations of diverse resources. Given the costs of acquiring various inputs, technology determines the cost of producing an extra unit of each good. Preferences, on the other hand, indicate the terms on which consumers would be willing to exchange one good for another. Given total income, preferences determine the price consumers would be willing to pay for an extra unit of each good. Clearly, as long as consumers value an extra unit of any particular element of what the university produces more highly than it costs to be produced, then the university should expand production of that element.

The fact that those who have authority over universities do not have reliable measures of the quantities and prices of the outputs of a university is the principal reason why they cannot readily apply this simple model. To clarify this point it is useful to raise an issue which has been much discussed recently, namely, whether resources should

5

be shifted from research to undergraduate education. To assess the benefits of such a reallocation, it would first be necessary to determine what the results in education and research would be. Consider some of the difficulties involved in making such a determination.

The concept of educational output refers to many different elements the measurement of which varies in difficulty. Three of these elements are: (i) increases in the students' familiarity with the basic literature and historical development of a discipline; (ii) increases in the students' ability to analyze problems of the real world by applying generalized knowledge; (iii) increases in the students' ability to perceive and formulate problems independently and to develop new methods of their solution. Outstanding results in one of these elements certainly does not indicate equally high achievement in the other types. Furthermore, all three are difficult to measure directly and each is more difficult than the one which precedes it on this list. As a result, misleading inferences could be made as a consequence of measuring teaching effectiveness primarily in terms of increases in students' knowledge of the literature, the most readily measured component of output.

The measurement of achievement in research is even less tractable than the measurement of the effectiveness of teaching. The number of pages of published research reports or the number of patents applied for or any other simple measure does not tell anything about the quality of the research done in a university. Consequently, we do not know how the quality of research would be affected. It is not obvious how the quantity of an ideal measure of research output would change by the amount of resources allocated to research. But even if it could be assumed that research output is proportional to the amount of resources used in research, the possibility that a shift in resources from research to teaching might reduce both research and educational achievements cannot be ruled out. The usual implicit assumption that a smaller allocation of resources to research and a larger allocation to teaching will lead to higher educational output, might be erroneous for several reasons.

First, there may be effects of the time teachers spend doing research on the quality of their teaching. Research at the frontiers of a discipline might change the perspective of a teacher. The topics and approaches he emphasizes while teaching and the literature he draws upon might be affected by his research. Second, the amount of research a teacher does might affect his understanding of his subject and, consequently, his ability to increase his students' ability to analyze problems of the real world, discern problems on their own and to discover their solution. Third, an awareness of the research being conducted in a university might in itself be an educational advantage for advanced undergraduates. Finally, improvement in course content is largely attributable to the advances in knowledge made possible by research done in universities. In sum, the outputs of research might be inputs into the teaching process and it is entirely possible, in shifting resources from research to teaching, that the loss in educational output as a result of the decline in research might outweigh the gain in educational output made possible by the increase in resources provided for teaching.

It is clear, from this example, that existing knowledge of the processes of production in universities and their resultant outputs is so limited that an accurate assessment of the consequences of the reallocation of resources cannot be made. If we ask how consumers would value the resulting changes in output, the deficiencies in our knowledge become even greater. Even if the effect on the quantities of the various outputs of a university could be accurately measured, there would be enormous problems involved in measuring the price of each component.

Our ignorance of the nature of the educational process is made evident too when we consider another problem. Two of the general types of output of universities listed above are educational output and informational output. What is their relative importance? The traditional view of university education is that it provides students with additional human capital in the form of increased knowledge and skill which lead to increased productivity. An alternative view is that university education consists of a series of trials which provide information on the students' capacities to perform certain tasks. These two views are not mutually exclusive, but it is important for educational policy to know which view is more appropriate.

The organization of universities which would be most effective in the formation of human capital would be less than optimal for providing information for the labour market regarding students' capacities. The recent discussions about the 'grading' or 'classing' of students illustrates this. It has been asserted that educational output would be increased if students were not classed or graded. The elimination of such procedures, however, might well be detrimental to the university's supply of information to the labour market. Even if the argument about the effect of changes from traditional policies of grading or classing improving the students' acquisition of knowledge is correct, whether these policies should be abandoned would depend in large part on the relative importance of these two components of university output.

In general, it is clear that what seems appropriate for increasing efficiency from one extreme point of view can reduce efficiency from the other extreme point of view. A proper combination of these two types of output can be selected only when it becomes possible to estimate both the extent to which university education adds to human capital and the extent to which university selection and assessment procedures provide useful information about those characteristics of students which are thought to be determinants of productivity. The principal reason why it is difficult to make these assessments at present is that it is practically impossible to determine from the available data how much of the difference between the incomes of persons with and without a university education is attributable to what graduates gained from having attended a university and how much is attributable to the greater ambition and ability of those who are admitted to and graduate from a university. Until data are collected which make it possible to control statistically for other factors which influence productivity and which are correlated with educational attainment, there is no point to making calculations of the rate of return based on the assumption that most or all of the difference in the average income of graduates and non-graduates is attributable to the additional human capital which is provided to graduates by a university education.

Reorganizing higher education

For a variety of reasons, universities in English-speaking countries have been organized as non-profit public or private institutions, the aims of which have not been clearly defined nor their behaviour well understood. In practice, the management of universities is carried out by administrators who depend largely on government financial support and private gifts and who are subject to various forms of pressure applied by diverse groups which try to use the university as a means to further their particular objectives. Each group attempts to persuade the administrators that what it desires is best for the university. Teachers advocate low student/staff ratios and substantial support for their own research, students demand less stringent standards and low fees, and both teachers and students seek to increase their own power in the making of decisions within the university – all purportedly in the best interests of the university. Outside of the university, ethnic, economic and political groups see the university as an ideal instrument for social policy of one kind or another, irrespective of the benefits and costs of using the university for these purposes. And, cutting across all these particular interests, within the university there is a demand for higher quality regardless of the effect on costs, while outside the university there is a general demand for lower cost regardless of the effect on quality.

The difficulty is not that these demands on the university are in any sense illegitimate, but that there is no mechanism under existing arrangements for reconciling these different demands in a rational way. The political process is not really adequate for so complex an allocation problem. The question that immediately occurs to economists is whether putting greater reliance on a market system, with all of its inadequacies, might not result in considerably greater efficiency in higher education. Consideration of the advantages and disadvantages of using the market to allocate resources in universities provides insight into the problem of efficiency in higher education which might prove useful in developing an entirely different type of solution.

Some of the advantages of making higher education more responsive to market forces can be seen in the following oversimplified scheme. Each university is conceived as a firm which hires resources to produce educational informational and research services which it sells to interested buyers. Its aim is simply the maximization of social profit which would be achieved when each of the components of output is produced to the point where the value (i.e., the market price) of an additional unit of output just equals the cost of producing it. Supposing, for the moment, that the market price of each university service accurately reflects its value to society, there would be a number of advantages to this arrangement compared to the present form of university organization.

The use of profit as a criterion would make it possible to judge the allocation of resources by means of a single measure which would take into account all of the university's operations. At present, there are no satisfactory means of measuring the economic efficiency of any activity of the university, let alone a good measure of its efficiency as a whole. If those who make decisions were to be rewarded on the basis of university's profits, they would have strong incentives to find more efficient allocations of resources and new techniques to increase the quality and reduce the cost of university services. In the absence of a good measure of efficiency, the incentives provided by the existing system are based on criteria which sometimes encourage inefficiency. For example, where new teaching posts are granted to departments on the basis of the need for teaching, there is little incentive to finding less expensive methods of instruction which would economize on teaching time; this explains the remarkably low rate of technological progress in the teaching profession. Furthermore, if the continued existence of a university depended on meeting its costs from the sales of its services, universities which produce output of greater value than its costs would expand or be imitated while those which run at a loss would be forced to contract and eventually cease to exist. Under the system of political planning guiding higher education to-day, even the least efficient university is able to maintain its existence because there is no basis for judging its efficiency as a whole. If universities operated under the forces of the market, they would be considerably more responsive to the preferences of the consumers of their services. If students — or their parents or other benefactors — desire a particular form of education and are willing to pay its cost, they would have no problem in bringing universities to provide it. Similarly, if the government wishes to purchase more research services, it can persuade the universities to supply them simply by offering to pay enough to make it profitable for resourees to switch from alternative uses. While universities are to some extent responsive to consumers' demands under the present system — students do have an influence when they decide where to enroll and governmental funds for research do pay for the time of teachers who are released from their obligations as teachers in order to do research — the result is unsatisfactory since political pressures prevent universities from responding fully to dimly perceived economic forces.

10

If universities were to operate as firms which seek to maximize their profits and which are subject to market prices, significant reorganization within universities would have to be made so that internal decisions would be evaluated in accordance with their effects on profits. A number of the possible internal arrangements which would be appropriate to operation in a market are of interest because they could be adapted for use by universities which do not explicitly seek to maximize profits. One scheme involves the setting of prices in accordance with the marginal cost of the educational services purchased by students. In a system wholly organized in the form of a market this might involve charging a separate fee for each course taken, so that the total tuition fee paid by a student would depend on whether he purchased services which were more or less expensive to produce. Under the present system, where tuition fees do not generally correspond to costs of production, the internal allocation of resources could be improved by adopting a voucher system. Each student could be given the same number of vouchers which he could spend as he wished for different educational services. Higher voucher prices for higher cost services, such as small seminars, courses entailing work in laboratories and courses offered at much demanded times, would increase the efficiency with which existing facilities would be used by providing more highly priced services to those students who value them more highly.

Another proposal is intended to encourage teachers to develop and adopt techniques which would result in higher productivity. At present, there are incentives, i.e. rewards, for teachers to maximize their output of research (as judged by their peers) and to teach adequately (as judged by their students), both regardless of cost. What is required is a system which rewards the individual or group (e.g. an academic department) for increased productivity, whether it takes the form of improvements in quality which are not offset by increases in cost or reductions in cost which are not offset by reductions in quality.

Problems in the market approach

The advantages of reorganizing universities in a market framework would be substantial. Nevertheless, there does not appear to be any significant movement in this direction. The lack of enthusiasm for this reform results in part from a vague but prevalent distrust of the market mechanism as a way of allocating resources for "socially important" services. Another partial explanation for the unchanging persistence of the present system is that the groups with a large stake in higher education — teachers, students and administrators — are subtle but effective lobbyists for the *status quo*, even when they appear to be advocating change. This results from the fact that most proposals for reform which are made within the university are designed to enhance the power and real income of their proponents. Teachers wish to increase their control over the educational process at the expense of administrative control; they say they are protecting academic freedom. Students demand more influence over the decisions made in universities on the grounds that this will improve the quality of education. Administrators demand more university autonomy to protect the university from 'undesirable' political interference. Yet each of these is a form of self-aggrandisement which serves to reinforce the present form of organization in higher education.

I do not imply that there are only self-serving arguments for doubting the desirability of moving toward a market-type arrangement in higher education. A number of serious problems would arise if the mechanisms of the market alone were relied on to promote efficiency in universities. Most of these problems arise from the failure of market prices for university services to reflect accurately the value to society of additional units of these services.

One such problem arises because the university's output of research is a public good in the sense that one person or group can consume the output without depriving other persons or groups of the opportunity to consume it. Knowledge, unlike a loaf of bread or electrical power, can be used again and again without destroying it. As a result, no individual consumer is likely to take into account the full value to society of his purchase of research. Thus, in the absence of any collective action — through governments or foundations, for example — the market price for additional research would be less than its value to society. As a result universities which sought to make a profit would produce less than the optimal amount of research.

Historically, the concentration of research in universities arose in

12

consequence of the apparent complementarity of teaching and research. Direct support for research by governments was not common when the idea of the unity of teaching and research was put forward. General acceptance of the need for government policy and programmes in support of research implies that there is no longer a need for universities to support research from their general funds, except to the extent that research beyond that paid for by external bodies is required as an input into teaching. The university would then simply sell its research services to the government – and other purchasers – whose responsibility it would be to determine the social value of additional research and to increase support for research as long as the additional benefits from it exceeded the cost. To the extent that research really is complementary to teaching, universities would be able to supply research services at a lower price than would research institutes and they could continue to be significant research centres.

It is sometimes argued that a similar problem arises in connection with educational output of universities. If there is a benefit which results from a student's education, over and above the return to the student, then students would be willing to pay a price for educational services that would fall short of their value to society as a whole. As a consequence of the belief that the public has a stake in the higher education of the individual, universities have been pressed by their supporters to charge less than the full cost of an education. This has had the long-term effect of promoting a method of operation which is totally lacking in accountability. The proposition that there are desirable external effects from higher education is based on the belief that a person, by obtaining a university degree, becomes a more intelligent voter, a more responsible citizen, a better neighbour. Whether this view has any factual basis need not concern an individual university operating in a market situation, since the assessment of the extent of the external effects of higher education is more properly the responsibility of the government. If externalities are deemed to exist, the government can offset the failure of the market to account for them by providing subsidies to students for attendance at university, as is already common practice.

Another major objection to the market method of allocating resources in higher education is that the market price of educational services would be the result of the consumer's valuations as they are made under the existing distribution of income. This problem assumes special significance if education is considered a means for achieving the social goal of equality of income. To achieve that goal, society has developed a whole range of policies running from the progressive income tax to specific programmes of income maintenance. One of these policies is the subsidy of higher education which is intended to provide students from lower income families with opportunities to add to their income in the future. By moving toward equality of educational opportunity, it is hoped that such programmes would reduce the inequality in the distribution of human capital and, consequently, in the distribution of income. Given this objective, financial assistance administered by individual universities, particularly in the form of tuition fees which are below the marginal cost of a student's education, is far from an ideal policy. Financial assistance of this type frequently has a perverse effect on income distribution. Taxes collected to support state universities in many cases fall heavily on families in the lower and middle range of the distribution of income, while reduced tuition fees benefit primarily students from families in the upper and middle range. Furthermore, university-administered assistance tends to bind the student to a particular university and discourages him from seeking out the university where he would be able to spend his money most effectively. It also is frequently used to seek institutional ends, such as attracting the best athletes or the brightest students, at the expense of equality of opportunity.

Far superior to the common forms of financial assistance now given, are a variety of proposals that have been designed to approximate the operations of a perfect loan market. It is really the absence of such a market — as a result of adverse selection and moral hazard which are perennial problems in the market for insurance — which prevents students from borrowing against future income and diversifying their holdings of human capital and, hence preventing potentially good students from lower income families from obtaining higher education. The most striking of these proposals, the Yale plan for the postponement of payment of tuition fees, is actually being put into practice. Under this plan a student can borrow to pay for his educational costs at an expected rate of interest which reflects the uncertainty associated with the time profile of the average income of his university class rather than with his own anticipated individual income at various stages of his career. Furthermore, the amount he

14

repays varies with the size of his income relative to that of his class-mates, so that the degree of risk associated with his investment in higher education approximates more closely that of the group as a whole. This reduces the discrepancies between private and social risk and return which arise in the absence of perfect loan markets and thereby encourages students to take into account the social benefits and costs of education in deciding whether to attend a university. If such a programme of contingent repayment loans were established by the federal government — perhaps with the amount of repayment for an individual borrower to depend on the amount of his federal income tax payment — then any individual would be able to pay for higher education at the university of his choice from the benefits which subsequently he receives, but in making his decision he would be forced to take into account whether the benefits exceeded the cost. The development of this or better programmes would com-plement the adaptation of higher education into a market frame-work. Universities would then be free, in fact they would be forced by the use of profit as a criterion of efficiency of performance, to charge students the full marginal costs of their education without hampering the realization of a policy of equality of educational opportunity. They would also be provided with greater incentive in the competition for students to keep costs down and provide good value in return for students' fees.

A different case, involving numerous philosophical and ethical issues, can be made against the use of the market to organize economic activity in higher education. The argument in favour of using market prices to guide the decisions of universities seeking to maximize profit rests on the assumption that consumers who purchase the various products of a university are rational decision-makers who know what is to their advantage. With respect to collec-tive consumption of various components of university outputs, the rationality of the political process in making public choices is often questioned. If the government is assigned the primary responsibility for purchasing research services and for providing subsidies for higher education to the extent that it produces externalities, one must examine what evidence there is for believing that actual decisions would, or even could, be in accordance with the preferences of society. Similarly, the rationality of students' choices is frequently doubted. Although universities have recently renounced the role of serving as parents where the social life of students is concerned, the notion that undergraduates are not mature enough to make their own decisions regarding investment in education is still widely accepted. According to this view, since undergraduates do not yet know what is good for them, educational decisions should be made for them by those who do. In the academic world, where distrust of the market is probably greatest, there is a widespread belief that university faculties can best decide how society should use its resources for research and teaching.

It is impossible to arrive scientifically at a conclusion as to whether collective and individual valuations of educational output are right or true. The acceptance of market prices as guides for decisions about the outputs to be produced by universities presupposes a prior decision as to whether the collective and individual decisions regarding expenditures which would determine those prices are rational. This ultimately is a matter of faith in the existing political system as a mechanism for making decisions about public expenditure and of acceptance of the individual's right to spend his income as he wishes. However uncertain one might feel about the rationality of either the existing political system or the individual student, any reasonable judgement on these matters requires that they be assessed in comparison with the feasible alternatives.

The agenda of research

I have not suggested that the problems of making higher education more efficient can be solved by adopting a particular plan of reorganization. It is rather my view that the questions of how higher education should be organized and of the degree to which reorganization should be guided by incorporating into it the various mechanisms of the market are questions on which it is most important to do research. As long as the existing gaps in our knowledge of the educational process remain, the possibility of increasing efficiency in higher education will remain limited. Those who make decisions in universities as they are presently organized have little incentive to maximize social profit, i.e. the difference between the social benefits and costs of higher education. But even if university administrators and teachers were motivated to act in the public interest — as no

16

doubt most conceive of themselves to be — they would have great difficulty in pursuing that end because the present system does not provide them with information about how their actions affect social profit. Unfortunately, the inadequacy of our knowledge of higher education would not be overcome by reorganizing the system into a perfect market. While such a reorganization would have many advantages, the efficiency of the system would depend on the rationality of decisions regarding expenditure and production; these, in turn would depend on the extent to which producers and purchasers of the educational output understand the workings of the educational process. The advantage of a market-like system of higher education is not that it requires less information, but rather that it decentralizes decision-making so that each decision-maker needs only a relatively small amount of information and himself bears the consequences of his wrong decisions. Among other things, for example, universities which maximize profit would have to know how differences among the various ways of producing educational outputs would affect their costs; students would have to know how different ways of increasing their educational attainment would affect their pecuniary and non-pecuniary income over the course of their lifetime. Such information is also needed by educational planners who make decisions under the present system. The questions which appear to be critically important include the following:

To what extent is the correlation between individual income and individual educational attainment attributable to the contribution which more education makes to higher productivity and to what extent is it attributable to the fact that those persons who obtain more education have greater ability?

To what extent does the information which is provided to employers about differences in their prospective employees' educational attainments actually lead to increases in productivity through more efficient allocation of labour?

To what extent do additions to an individual's educational attainment confer benefits on society over and above increasing that individual's productivity?

If more education adds to an individual's human capital, what are the attributes — such as the analytical and social skills — of the individual which are changed and what features of the university are most important in changing them?

What kind of academic organization will lead to more efficient allocation of resources within the university and more rapid progress in the technology by which the university produces its outputs?

Which modes of financing students in higher education will be most conducive to the equality of opportunity without causing inefficiency in the allocation of resources?

To begin to answer these and other questions, four types of research need to be carried out. First, basic research on the behaviour of organizations and social systems is needed to discover institutional forms different from the existing system of higher education and the type of market system discussed in this paper. Second, basic research on statistical methods is required to deal with non-quantifiable variables, which are characteristic features of educational processes and outcomes. Third, experiments with different techniques of production and different institutional forms are needed in order to assess the relative efficiency of alternative arrangements. Finally, detailed statistical studies of individual students over time are required to estimate the parameters of the educational process and to test alternative hypotheses about the effects of higher educafion.

Since knowledge about the processes by which educational outputs are produced and about the consequences of being educated is essential for efficiency regardless of what system of higher education is adopted, one of the proper ends of research on higher education is the discovery and diffusion of such information. Only when this is done, will it be possible to make definitive statements about how higher education should be organized. The answers to these major questions have the properties of a public good. Once the answer is attained, it is costless to society to allow everyone to benefit by knowing it.

Part II

The Role of the University

2. The University and the Social Welfare: A Taxonomic Exercise

by Harry G. Johnson

The functions of a university

The university has many different functions in the community. The most general is as a symbol and repository of "civilization," i.e. a demonstration that the community is both civilized in the sense of actively belonging to western culture, and civilized in the sense of being both able and willing to afford the support of scholarship out of the surplus of its resources over subsistence. In addition, the university is thought of as contributing in some vague sense to the advancement of civilization, through either or both setting standards of taste for the rest of the population and enabling the rest of the population to increase its productivity, income, and command over consumption goods. In this sense, a university is a public good, in a broad sense, like good weather or pleasant geography (which however cost no resources to produce), or like a forest reserve or an efficient police force or judiciary or an army (which do).

This general function is to be distinguished from the service of tangible social and economic functions, for which it is possible at least in principle to specify benefits that can be related to costs. It is an important one in relation to any discussion of efficiency in universities, because it provides justification on both sides for the support of universities by both private and public subscriptions of resources, regardless of efficiency considerations, so long as universities behave as they are traditionally expected to do and as most other universities do. In this respect, support of universities is like adherence to a religion or church — the pay-off from so doing is incalculable and problematical, but it is wise to buy insurance against unknown risks.

Second, a university is a home for research. The products of research are a public good in the strict economic sense, that once produced they can be used by anyone without precluding use by others. This poses the standard economic problem of how to finance research. It has to be financed somehow, but if it is financed by allowing those who do it a monopoly over the use of the results, the amount of it will be too small in quantity and its composition biassed towards the applied research with the maximum privately appropriable results; and the social use of it will be inefficient to the extent that a charge for private benefit is made for something that it costs society nothing for another person to use. The university, which generates research as a by-product of its scholarly activities and has a non-financial (prestige and promotion) reward system that entails the research product being made freely available to any potential user, solves the problem by the optimal *method* – public support of research allied with cost-free availability of the results – at the expense of leaving open the two questions of efficiency in deciding the *scale* of research that is optimal for society, and the efficiency of deciding the *allocation* of research effort or leaving it to be decided by individual scholars motivated by scholarly standards of what is worth doing.

A third important function of the university is information storage. In medieval times, books were expensive and scarce, and still scarcer were people who had the time to read them and the wit to understand them: knowledge was stored in both the disembodied form of collections of expensive books and the embodied form of learned men who had read all or most of the relevant ones. Nowadays, books are relatively cheap and plentiful and many people have both the capacity to read them and the normal intelligence required to understand them. But this simply creates the same problem in another form: housing a large enough collection of books in a way readily accessible to those who want or may want to use them requires both large capital and advanced technology, and knowledge either of the books relevant to a particular problem or of how to locate them quickly remains a scarce and expensive talent. (There is, further, the fact that much modern scholarship requires not published books, but data and the facilities for using them for computations.)

The fourth, and most clearly popular recognized function of the university at present, is teaching young adults. This includes two types of teaching: professional training, preparing a man for a career he has already decided to embark on, and general education, preparing a man for a future position in the upper ranks of society. Economically, general university education can be thought of as consisting in some mixture of current consumption (i.e. an enjoyable way of passing a few years before assuming adult responsibilities in the economy), formation of consumption capital (i.e. development of more sophisticated standards of taste and more discriminatory capacity for choice among consumption alternatives later), and formation of production capital ("human capital", i.e. the capacity to contribute more productive service to the economy, and hence to earn more future income, than would be possible in the absence of the university education).

In the case of professional education — medicine, law, engineering, and most of the natural and physical sciences — the human capital element predominates, though the current consumption and consumption-capital-formation elements are also present, being derived from the fact that the professional training is provided within the broader humanistically-oriented framework of the university. In the case of general education — the arts and humanities and social sciences — there is considerable room for disagreement as to which element predominates or should predominate; and such disagreement motivates much of the contemporary tensions between university spokesmen anxious to preserve their traditional independence and government spokesmen anxious to ensure that the taxpayer who foots the bill receives something tangible for his money. From an economic point of view, there are three possible conceptions of, or hypotheses about, the main economic function of general university education, each pointing in a different direction as regards public policy towards universities and university policies themselves.

The first is the maturation hypothesis: the main purpose of the university is to provide students with the opportunity to grow up to adulthood in surroundings that will broaden their minds and heighten their sensibilities. (Suitable choice of marriage partners among a wide range of prospective candidates is one aspect of this process, and from a long-range genetic point of view might well be the main contribution a modern university, or at least the vast majority with no special claim to academic teaching and research excellence, may be making to the improvement of mankind's economic and social existence — i.e., universities facilitate marriages among the intelligent, so breeding higher intelligence, though an unfortunate by-product seems to be a higher incidence of physical and mental handicaps among the resulting offspring). On the maturation hypothesis, what the university offers is a *cultural* ambience, direct contact with first-rate intellects, and the opportunity for tutored reading of books written by other first-rate minds. It does not matter much what is taught, provided the teacher knows the literature, logic, or technical apparatus of his subject and is prepared to spend enough of his time in personal contact with his students.

Research is his method of proving his competence, and also acquiring and maintaining up-to-date knowledge of his field, but it should nevertheless be secondary to and motivated by his teaching responsibilities. Both pure research motivated by idle curiosity, and even more clearly applied research undertaken for commercial gain, derogate from his responsibilities as a teacher and should not be encouraged; and if allowed should be financed otherwise than from the university's budget for teaching. (Curiosity-oriented research may also be condoned as eccentric self-indulgence, provided it is conducted in leisure time.) This hypothesis, it should be noted, is both most directly in line with the medieval conception of a university as a place where scholars researched and argued with each other and allowed students to come and listen if they were interested and could afford it, and most favourable to the "ideal" academic, since the only test of efficiency it suggests is scholarly excellence (as contrasted with the economist's and the government's test of the cost of producing educational outputs of specified characteristics). But in a university system in which parents or their children do not pay directly for the opportunity to mature in a university environment, but instead all parents pay taxes for some gifted children to be allowed that opportunity, the questions of scale, efficiency, and tangible social benefit are bound to be raised about what is clearly a luxury good for the students provided as a by-product of a luxury (and parasitic) way of living for the staff.

The second hypothesis is the "filtering" hypothesis, analyzed in rigorous theoretical terms by Kenneth J. Arrow in Chapter 3 but familar to popular thought from the Mandarin Chinese system of civil service selection by competitive examination in classical Chinese scholarship, and from much of the philosophy underlying the British university system as now organized. In broad outline, this hypothesis asserts that society has "good jobs" and "bad jobs" to offer, and that it has somehow to select those who deserve the "good jobs" out of the general population. Higher education adds nothing to a man or woman's original capacity to fill a good job; it is simply a screening device or obstacle course that contenders for the good jobs must pass through in order to qualify. Since the same number will eventually wind up in good jobs anyway, the unsuccessful candidates will have wasted their time, and the cost of the screening process (in terms of both staff and student time and real resources) can be easily increased (at least up to the point where even a candidate certain of success does not find it economically attractive to compete) without (by assumption) any effect in increasing the gross output of the economy, there is a clear-cut problem of efficiency. The problem, broadly, is to achieve a combination of probability of failure and rigour of the filtering tests that will minimize the overall cost (including the waste of time and resources and the the disappointment of the unsuccessful) while maintaining the credibility of the filter itself as an exacting obstacle course. (This suggests, incidentally, a rationale for both the recent efforts of university students everywhere to "water down" the rigour of course content, examinations, and course prerequisites, and the British government's current pressure on British universities to turn out BAs more quickly and cheaply; in both cases, the implicit presumption is that university admission constitutes the major part of the filtering process, and that the degree itself — including the final class — is primarily an official certification of what was known about the candidate at the time of admission.)

The third hypothesis is the "human capital" hypothesis: attendance at university adds value to a person's potential productive contribution to the economic system, and is to be regarded as an investment in one particular form of society's stock of productive assets or capital. This view fits the professional-school side of universities best, but runs into serious difficulty both in specifying what an arts education actually teaches that improves productivity, and in assessing the role of research activity in improving the teaching performance of university faculty members. It also has difficulty with the necessity of distinguishing between the possibilities that a student performs well on examinations because he was a good student to begin with and would have learned the relevant material without any help from the faculty, and that he performs well because he has been taught things that he otherwise would not have learned. The distinction corresponds to the economic distinction between the value of the sales of a firm — which may consist mostly of the cost of raw materials and other purchased inputs used, the extreme example being that of a dealer who sells other people's products for a small commission — and the value added by the firm to its purchased inputs (the dealer's commission for bringing producer and consumer together). As will be remarked at greater length below, universities have a marked preference for selecting the best available students, as judged by admission qualifications, rather than the most teachable poorly qualified students, so that an "excellent" university may be so with no credit due to its staff, while a "mediocre" or "backwoods" university may be doing an excellent job of teaching even though it never produces a first-class graduate qualified to go to a first-class graduate school or destined for a high business or political career. Be that as it may, the human capital approach, at least in its simplest and most naïve (though still scientifically respectable) form, raises the question of university efficiency in a direct and economically sensible form. If the function of a university is to turn out graduates armed with understanding of a particular field of specialization up to a particular level of competence (or graded according to defined levels of competence) what is the most efficient (least-cost) way of doing it? How long should it take? Is the traditional structure of the academic year, geared to a past of agricultural pursuits and slow transport between home and university, superior to the industrial practice of year-round work with one short vacation, though the work is frequently characterized by seasonal spurts and respites? What courses are really necessary as prerequisites to others in a training programme? What is the optimal mix of reading, lectures, classes, and tutorials? Should lectures be live, taped, or video-taped for minimum cost of adequate instruction? At what point does enrolment in relation to staff cost and other overheads, combined with output quality, make a course (or a whole department) uneconomic and desirable to discontinue? How many graduates of given specifications will the market absorb at remunerative prices for their services?

Once we can define the type and quantity of product desired, we can proceed to apply all the economist's techniques of cost-benefit analysis and efficiency evaluation, together with his understanding of how markets can be made to ensure social efficiency by giving the appropriate incentives to private choice, to improving the efficiency of university education. But there are three major snags.

First, many politically important groups, including both many parents and students and many university staff and administration members, do not accept the presumption that the primary function of the university is to produce graduates of clearly-defined attributes suitable for convenient insertion as well-rounded pegs into the round-hole job opportunities offered by business and government. Second (and a good reason for the contrary view), it is not clear either that the essence of a university education can be broken down into the attainment of specified levels of comprehension of either courses or subjects measured at the immediate point of completion of an examination or series of examinations, or that what pays off in future income-earning capacity is a set of specific knowledge-attainment attributes measured by conventional university standards. Rumination and reflection on the one hand, motivation or ambition on the other, may be more important. Third (especially in Britain), the price system applied to the allocation of effort by both faculty and students contains so many elements of arbitrary subsidy or tax (e.g., why should a teacher spend much time in private conversation with students when his salary is conditional only on delivering a standard number of formal teaching hours, his promotion depends on his research publications, and after a certain point his salary is quite independent of his own efforts, and why should a student study hard when his grant or fellowship is conditional only on meeting a minimum standard of examination performance?), and so many elements of non-pecuniary reward and punishment (e.g., superior teaching is hard for colleagues to evaluate while published articles are generally evaluated by journal status or number of pages rather than content, and student "swatting" is socially disapproved among students as dangerously competitive while the ability to pass examinations without apparent effort is generally admired, without reference to the difference between potential and actual performance), that it becomes virtually impossible to determine whether the introduction of more competitive pricing somewhere in the system will actually generate more rather than less efficiency. (A major problem is that academics have little or no incentive to experiment with more efficient methods of instruction, based on the exploitation of modern communications technology, because as soon as they have invested the intellectual effort required to devise means of reducing teaching costs the benefits will be removed from them by a budget cut.)

The final function of a university, and one that imposes an extremely difficult obstacle to consideration of means of increasing university efficiency, is to serve as a means of redistribution of income from the community in general towards its youthful intelligent and scholarly-inclined citizens, on the presumption that these are on the average poor and deserving, or else poor but potentially useful to society. This attitude goes back to the Middle Ages, when the church, the state, and the landed nobility needed continual recruitment of literate, numerate, and generally scholarly-rational employees for their service — and had a monopoly of the job opportunities open to un-landed students. In those circumstances, it was a good investment for the rich either to pay privately for the education of individual gifted poor children, or even (especially for the monarch) endow the education of gifted poor children in general — disregarding the moral virtue that the Christian religion conferred on such acts of charity. In modern times, however, given the availability of family resources, personal earnings, and capital markets as means of financing higher education plus near-perfect competition (or at least, absence of monopoly), it is highly questionable whether subsidization of higher education for the children of poor families who prove academically capable of attaining university admission is socially desirable, since such students are virtually guaranteed access to the high-income groups of society. It is even far more questionable whether, if the objective is the relief of undeserved poverty, the subsidy to higher education should be given without a means test, on the basis of educational qualification, through a general publically-financed subsidy to education reducing tuition fees well below the level of costs. In fact, a large body of research indicates that this particular income subsidy involves a transfer from the poor (and some of the very rich) to the middle class. Nevertheless, there prevails a strong social belief that universities ought to price the education they offer so as to subsidize the poor student (witness the facts that private American universities feel that they cannot raise

28

fees without earmarking some of the resulting revenue for increased scholarships, and that the Independent University in Britain has been obliged, at considerable risk to its financial viability, to provide generously for scholarships, though its original design was for loan finance). The implementation of this belief in governmental rules and university-accepted principles for the setting of tuition fees obviously introduces a strong element of artificiality in both student choices and faculty-responsive behaviour that makes the problem of achieving efficiency in university education extremely difficult. Why should faculty be concerned about efficiency in teaching students who do not pay the costs anyway, and why should students be concerned about the efficiency of faculty when others than themselves pay the costs of inefficiency?

Outside interest groups

The traditional university was originally a self-governing academic community of scholars, in large part self-financed and/or subsidized by the willingness of its scholars to live humbly for the sake of pursuing truth; and its outside funds, in the form of student fees or endowments, were voluntarily subscribed by students interested in learning or donors motivated by charitable and religious feelings of obligation that carried no reciprocal rights of control and management. What disputes there were lay either between students and teachers as fellow-scholars, or between the university and the church – the latter being the origin of the concept of academic freedom. The university persisted in this pattern more or less into modern times, though increasingly, especially in the United States, parental notions that a university should teach their children practically useful subjects began to be influential. In the more recent period, the medieval practice of providing subsidized university education for a few of the intellectually-talented poor, for either charitable motives or to provide recruits into the clerical service of the nobility, became gradually transformed into the generalized contemporary notions that somehow universities and especially university-educated people are good for society, over and above the tangible benefits to the university staff and students themselves; and that university education should be heavily subsidized by the state, both for this reason and as a matter of providing democratic equality of opportunity for children to whatever station born.

It is the haziness of this general conception of the university's functions, which is an uneasy compromise between the university's traditional conception of itself as superior to, because apart from, the world of material concerns and the rest of society's belief that the university provides social benefits in the form of a mixture of externalities, human capital formation, and egalitarian income redistribution, which makes it so difficult to apply the economist's concepts of the market, the producing firm, and cost-benefit and cost-efficiency analysis to the university. The purpose of this section, however, is not to dilate on the problem of such application, but to point out that the contemporary university is a matter of interest to a variety of outside groups, which differ both in their conceptions of what the university should be optimizing, and in the financial and political leverage they can exert over the management of universities in pursuit of these conceptions.

The leverage problem will be discussed only briefly, since the economics are familiar. The modern university depends typically on government for the major part of its operating expenses on the teaching side, and on foundations, private endowments, and business firms for support of its research. Hence the university is dependent on the good-will of these social institutions for its finance; parents and their student children contribute relatively little of the finance, and have to depend on political pressure directed either at government, in the case of parents, or at both government and the university itself — student protest — in the case of students. In addition, since much of a university's activities involve professional training, which usually has to be of an acceptable form and "quality" to meet the standards of organized professional associations, these associations can achieve considerable leverage over this side of the university's activities.

Turning to the conceptions of the main functions of the university held by the major outside interest groups, the crucial though elementary fact is that these conceptions vary greatly; and, as is well known, it is usually impossible to define a consistent social welfare function defining what is to be maximized subject to the relevant cost constraints in these circumstances. It may be noted in passing that the contemporary large business firm, to which economists would like to

30

analogize the university, has a problem very similar in kind, with some pressure groups demanding safer and at the same time cheaper products, others demanding higher wages and more concern for employees, others demanding the non-pollution of the environment, and still others demanding more charitable contributions to worthy causes; fortunately the corporation still has to make a profit, whereas the government-subsidized university does not. (To anticipate the next section, the large corporation also has conflicting internal interest groups, e.g., its production agencies, its marketing department, its cost accountants, and its public-figure chief executives – hence the theories of organization, and of "satisficing" as opposed to "profit-maximizing".)

Consider first the government. It has, or at least must pretend to have, a concern for the support of the university as an institution and symbol of civilization, and also for the operation of it as an instrument of (presumed) income redistribution. Since the 1950's, it has also come to be concerned with the university as a contributor to civilization in the much more specific form of contributing to the country's (or the state or province's) economic growth. But its concern has straddled the two possibilities of specific contribution through the formation of human capital (teaching) and general contribution through the formation of intellectual capital (research); and in recent years governments generally have become disillusioned with the growth potentialities of research, especially "pure" or "basic" research, and anxious to cut their expenditure on basic research and pass the costs of pure research onto foundations and applied research onto the private sector and mission-oriented departments of government. Fourth, the government is concerned on a very large scale with the recruitment of civil servants and of quasi-civil servants such as teachers, social workers, nurses, doctors, and so on. This bends its concern with universities towards professional training, the professionalization of non-professional arts and humanities courses, and emphasis on teaching rather than research. Finally, because it has to raise taxes to finance its contributions to universities, and taxable capacity is limited in the aggregate, and the proportion of it that can be used either for income redistribution or the maintenance of intangible cultural symbols restricted still further by tax-payer opinion, the government is under strong pressure to insist on economy in expenditure on universities. This implies a number of well-known observable phenomena — preference for expenditure on university buildings over expenditure on staff salaries, emphasis on the primacy of teaching over research, preference for flashy rather than fundamental research, and a tendency to side with students (and indirectly their parents) rather than with university staff and administrators in cases of student unrest. (The university can always be blamed for not delivering as much output as the politicians and public expect for their money.)

Consider, second, foundations and private donors. These are motivated by the general social belief in the university as both an element of civilization and an instrument of charity. They are also motivated, often quite legitimately, by concerns with social or scientific problems that they feel universities are not paying sufficient attention to. Unfortunately, they are also strongly influenced by current fads of opinion on these matters that then get built into the university's structure and face it later on with financial and organizational problems. There is in the process also a propensity to monument-building; a name on an institute or building for the private donor, but in some ways more dangerous to the university, the desire of the career or freshly-recruited foundation executive to make his mark by starting some kind of new research in an established university.

Third, as mentioned, professional associations often exert important influence over university professional teaching courses and standards by virtue of their control over the qualification of new members. In some cases, this may be beneficial to the teaching programme by setting professionally necessary standards; in others it may simply be a means of restricting entry to the profession in question by insisting on excessively intensive and prolonged, and inefficient, instruction. The raising of standards generally — which must be sharply distinguished from the raising of standards in a particular institution, whose main purpose is to improve its competitiveness against others — is generally defended as being in the interests of the public, attention being thereby diverted from the fact that it increases the monopoly profits of those already qualified. (Insisting that everyone must drive a Cadillac or nothing would improve the average quality of cars available to consumers, and simultaneously increase the profits of the company producing Cadillacs, but only those who already can afford Cadillacs would benefit from the resulting increase in road safety.)

Fourth, the main concern of business firms is in the university as a source of recruitment of trained professional experts and potential executives. In this connection, the three alternative hypotheses of maturation, filtering, and human capital formation are relevant. The former two give the business firm no real interest in the efficiency of the university, only in its quality as judged by the standards of the university itself; they may even give the firm an interest in the preservation of university inefficiency. The secondary concern of the business firm is with the university as a source of research talent and research facilities that can be purchased cheaply – here the business firm (like government departments) has a direct interest in university teaching inefficiency, in the sense of maintenance of a stock of underemployed teachers whose promotion depends on research performance they may lack the originality to initiate, and a stock of underemployed buildings and equipment for which the university is not prepared to charge an adequate rent. It also has an obvious interest in letting the university (or government, or foundations) pay for the discovery and incorporation in its students and staff of the basic research on which applied research is based. (This is an important and economically now well-understood problem of both national science policy and university finance – if pushed, both industry and mission-oriented government departments will pay the current and overhead costs of applied research, but who is to pay the costs of the underlying investment in basic research?)

Finally we come to households, the fundamental consumers of the university education process. Here it is necessary to recognize, in contrast to the standard theory of consumption, that the household is not an individual with a single consistent utility function but an aggregation of individuals whose choices may well be inconsistent, intransitive, etc. Moreover the household somehow (smoothly or painfully) goes through a transition from an extremely paternalistic overall utility function (young parents and their babies) to another such (the grown-up children and their babies) via a process of simultaneous aging and maturation of its members. (Even this is not the full story, due to grandparental, social, and learning-by-doing influences in the behaviour of parents.) The most important point here is that in contemporary society it is precisely at the point of prospective or actual participation of students in the university education process that the children are making the transition from child to adult status, and are moving from the role of paternalized to that of paternalists. Hence their expectations of the function of the university differ from and are frequently in sharp conflict with those of their parents. Since the parents tend to dominate the decisions while the neo-adult students have to live with the results, one major result in recent years has been student protest over their experience at universities and parental conviction that the university administration and staff, not their beloved children, are responsible for the trouble.

Many parents, of course, are interested in human capital formation in their children, either through professional schooling or through general education. Others have preconceptions about what the university will provide, whether they themselves have been to a university or not, though these preconceptions will usually vary widely between the two groups — and in either case, with respect to the contemporary university, will probably involve an out-dated over-estimation of the intellectual, cultural, or social attractions and advantages of attendance. Others will regard the university merely as a place to park their children while they mature into adulthood (and will value above all peace and quiet during the process and blame the university if such does not prevail). Still others, with pretty much the same results, will regard the university merely as a filter. Only the first group is likely to be at all concerned with the efficiency of the university as the economist conceives it.

Prospective and actual students, on the other hand, will have different motivations in significant respects. Some will accept the maturation function, and be especially interested in spending the time enjoyably. All students, however, will have a certain interest in the current consumption possibilities offered free or at subsidized prices through the university's amenities, though these may be a waste of resources from the university's own and the social point of view. Other students, in place of maturation, will regard the process of becoming social and economic adults as a process of transformation (as Buchanan and Devletoglou have well described it). The difference will correspond broadly to that between students from socially and economically well-established families and those from marginal families; also between those who have regarded their school teachers as bores to be listened to for the minimum possible time and

34

those who have been inspired, and within these groups presumably to the difference between "secure" and "insecure" children. In any case, such students are looking for inspiration and stimulation, and may conceivably get more of it from "bad" than from "good" teachers. For the maturation-motivated students, as for the human capital-motivated students discussed below, tests of efficiency in terms of least-cost achievement of a given level of educational attainment make eminent sense; for the transformation-oriented students, it is extremely difficult to define either the "product" or the methods by which it can be produced.

A further student motive is the human capital formation motive; but this has to be subdivided into consumption capital formation (becoming a superior person in knowledge, taste, and habit, so that whatever post-graduation life may hold in store will be a more enjoyable and rewarding life to live) and production capital formation (becoming a higher-income earner, so that whatever one's tastes are or may become one can indulge them more fully). The distinction corresponds very broadly to the traditional one between the arts and the sciences, but that distinction has become extremely blurred by the fact that in modern democratic, equalitarian, but competitive society one has to demonstrate one's competence in adulthood as both a superior producer and a superior consumer. The two criteria clearly indicate somewhat − but not necessarily very − different tests of efficiency in university education. The course content and emphasis, rather than comprehension of the material, becomes the differentiating factor between the two conceptions.

Finally, and especially evidently in the student troubles of recent years, many students submit to the filtering hypothesis. For them, the problem of optimization is a complex problem of weighing probable job prospects against pleasantness of period at university, which in turn involves a trade-off between consumption of university amenities (including opportunity for pseudo-adult political activities) and effort devoted to surmounting the examination obstacle course. Clearly, one very attractive short-run choice is to use the political activity to demolish the obstacle course, relying on the assumption that admission to university constitutes most of the effective screening involved in the filter process to safeguard the job prospects. From the point of view of efficiency in the longer run, it might be optimal to concentrate on improving the predictive efficiency of university admissions standards, and minimizing the staff and facility costs of having students actually in the university afterwards. (It might even be optimal to cut off the educational process at the university admissions stage, except for genuinely professional training, and announce the results of the preliminary filter to prospective employers, who would then carry out their own training programmes immediately — but this is a mischievous speculation).

Inside interest groups

The university is not only confronted by pressures from a variety of outside interest groups, varying both in their conceptions of the functions of a university and their ability to enforce these conceptions via both political pressures and direct or indirect control of university finance and hence university policy; it also contains a variety of inside interest groups that also vary both in their conceptions of what the university "product" should be and their ability to enforce these conceptions — though in this case ability to enforce is a question of the interaction of bureaucratic organization, political skill, and exploitation of the opportunities for choice and substitution that the university affords to its staff and its students. (By this last is meant on the one hand the opportunity for staff to substitute among the courses they are equipped to teach, e.g., elementary versus advanced teaching, seminars versus lectures, etc., and between teaching and research funded from either inside or outside sources; and on the other hand the ability of students to put competitive pressure on staff either downwards or upwards — the former being the more typical case — by choice among alternative sections of the same course or among optional subjects in the same degree programme.) Six major inside interest groups will be discussed, though the balance of power among them in any particular university may vary widely from what is taken here to be the norm, and there may be either more or less (in number) interest groups in any particular university.

First, there are the students. Their interests have been discussed in the preceding section, as have those of their parents, exerting influence on their behalf, and need not be discussed in great detail here. It is worthwhile, however, to call attention to two major points.

First, the students in residence have a strong interest in having the university provide subsidized housing and recreation facilities, and this interest coincides in large part with parental concerns, even though such provision may serve no educational purpose and constitute a serious drain on the university budget. The private market — which includes student co-operatives and enterprising student unions, as well as private clubs — could provide such facilities on a commercial basis if the demand warranted it, thereby sparing university funds for properly educational purposes. In this connection, one should note a recent trend respecting student housing: traditionally, both parents and the university authorities have favoured the provision of subsidized student housing on the dormitory model as a means of transferring parental moral responsibility for children to the university authorities on the one hand, and enabling the university to supervise and control its students' lives on the other, while students have accepted the moral authority for the sake of the housing subsidy; but recently students have increasingly rebelled against acceptance of the moral supervision, and sought the greater freedom of the private housing market — largely in the writer's view because they have become affluent enough not to be completely dependent on the subsidy element — with the result that either dormitories and halls of residence have been beset by protests against quality of food provided, moral restrictions imposed on student liberty, etc., or the universities have found their dormitories standing largely empty of students because the increasing desire for privacy that goes with increasing affluence makes students willing to pay more for lower-quality but less regimented and collectivized housing than the university provides. It should also be remarked that university provision of student housing on a high and subsidized standard affords a tangible talking-point for demonstrating university quality to parents and politicians who know little or nothing about what university education is about but who can appreciate a well-designed bedroom, bathroom, or pseudo-hotel when they see one.

Second, students other than those strictly interested in the formation for themselves of human capital saleable at the best possible price in the post-graduate market, have a strong interest in the watering down of the quality of the courses offered, and particularly in the lowering of failure rates and the proliferation of "soft options". Once they have surmounted the hurdles of university entry, they naturally prefer to minimize the remaining number of hurdles before graduation, unless they believe themselves capable of hurdling any examination obstacle. For a long time, this motivation has expressed itself in the quest for "soft options" and more generally for universities with not-too-high standards for the BA; much more recently it has expressed itself in demands for "relevance" of courses — i.e., easy comprehensibility to the adolescent student mind — the removal of course prerequisite stipulations, and the abolition of grading systems. In short, the student recognizes that in winning admission to the university he has already acquired a monopoly privilege in society, and one of the ways he can take advantage of it is to adulterate the product of his monopoly position. In this endeavour, he has the joint support of parental attitudes — which can more easily tolerate the idea that their children were not good enough to win admission to the mysterious university and were forced to do something else than the idea that they were good enough to get in but somehow through personal inadequacy failed to get out — and of the attitude of the university's administration, bent on both currying parental and alumni favour and winning political approval, which has a strong bias towards believing in the efficiency of its admission procedure (which selects its educational clientele) and measuring its efficiency by the proportion of its intake of students that it turns out with the BA. (It is relevant to observe, however, that if the university is forced to admit students whose qualifications for entry are determined by the secondary education system, it has a choice between deliberately enforcing a high first-year — or first and second year — failure rate — which choice simply shifts its admission procedure one or two years on — and watering down its courses to the level of comprehension of its student intake. The choice is largely one of political acceptability: American State universities have traditionally adopted the first alternative; recently, "black studies" and product adulteration have furnished a way out of the political demand for "open admission policies" in the better quality universities.

The second inside interest group is the faculty. According to the traditional concept of the university, its primary function and interest is research, in a very broad sense, and its teaching is an incidental by-product. In the contemporary university, however, its

38

prime function so far as society is concerned is teaching; but tests of the quality of its teaching are poorly defined, and the teacher is shielded from too searching an inquiry into this aspect of his behaviour by the absence of explicit training in this matter and by the tradition of respecting collegial privacy, so that teaching capacity is judged very largely by printed research output. Hence, as a teacher, the university staff member is confronted by two alternatives: to use his teaching as a means of disseminating his own ideas to inferior minds, and to use it as a means of exploiting his students in order to improve his research output. Allied with but somewhat apart from this is the question of the challenge of teaching itself: is a teacher's output and contribution to be measured by the value he adds to the raw material he starts with — i.e. is raising a student from failure to pass level as valuable (or more or less) as raising a student from a top second to a low first-class rating — or by the total value of the students he teaches? In other words, is teaching performance to be measured by the capacity to elevate low-quality students or by the capacity to attract and instruct high-quality students? The natural tendency of the teaching staff, given the emphasis of university promotion systems on research output and de-emphasis on teaching as an activity involving the improvement rather than merely the passing-through of the raw material, is to prefer the selection of high-quality students who will do them credit in terms of final grades rather than the selection of low-quality but improvable students. This is one of the major sources of conflict between the university as traditionally conceived and the current political and social emphasis on the function of the university as a leveller of social opportunity and democratizer of society; and the interest of the staff is to meet the demand for equalitarianism, not by making the teaching effort required — which has no pay-off for the ambitious in the traditional university system — but by watering down the course offerings and hiring inferior colleagues to do the teaching of them.

Turning to research, because of the prevalent use of research performance as a criterion of teaching ability, the faculty has an incentive to insist on research time and research facilities as a non-salary attraction of an academic job, and the university to offer such perquisites — one financial reason being that salaries are subject to income tax whereas research facilities are not. The university has another incentive in this direction, that its quality as a teaching institution is likely to be known only to a small local group of parents and a small group of scholars elsewhere who welcome its graduates as inputs into their own graduate teaching and research operations, whereas its published research output is clearly visible for all to see. One result of these incentives is the reiterated assertion that research is useful because it feeds back into teaching and in the long run raises the quality of teaching — a debatable proposition because the two are both substitutes and complements to an unascertainable degree. A second is the propensity of university staff to prefer institutionalized and mechanized research of a rather mundane kind, with a quick pay-off in published results, over personal research by library reading and private thought with a slow pay-off or none in impressively publishable results. A third is staff preference for senior undergraduate and graduate teaching which may pay off in research ideas or testing of research results, rather than for elementary teaching, which probably has no research pay-off.

A third aspect of faculty interest in the university is as a consumption good for themselves. This includes good public facilities for themselves — common rooms, lounges, refectories and bars, supply of current newspapers and magazines, cheap tea, coffee and pastry — and good private facilities in the form of offices, secretaries and paper reproduction facilities, and imposing buildings in which to house them. Here there is to some extent a conflict between the desire of the academic staff for munificence comparable to what they think prevails in the outside world of business affluence, and the desire of the political sphere and the university administration to house them as decently-kept servants but still as obvious servants. (This is one reason why academics are often avid to become university administrators — to obtain offices commensurate with their own opinion of their social importance.) It is questionable from the educational point of view, whether low salaries and attractive offices or high salaries and miserable offices — unless the individual chooses to spend private salary funds on office furniture and decoration — is the better enticement of good academics. Pure economic theory says the salary should be the important thing; but the nonliability of university-provided offices and facilities to income tax, together with the incentives provided by the "public good" aspect of the university to both university administrators and faculty to make the offices of the professors impressive to the non-university community, works the other way. In any case, the teaching staff, which usually does not recognize the trade-off between salaries and non-salary perquisites, has an incentive to maximize the consumption-good dimensions of university life, whether this is educationally optimal or not. (For example, professors could maintain their own studies at home, and patronize neighbouring private clubs and commercial bars, rather than expecting the university to provide office space and a subsidized faculty club. Also, the faculty could patronize commercial performances of music and drama at commercial prices, instead of subsidizing on-campus performances of artistic exercises through the use of university funds.)

A fourth aspect of faculty interest is the opportunity to invest in the formation of individual human capital at the university's expense, i.e., to improve future earning power, whether in this university or another one (the two going together in a competitive market for human talent) by being a staff member for a period of time. This has two aspects: the opportunity to earn a salary by a nominal obligation to teach, while actually doing research designed to establish a professional name and a market for the individual's talents; and the opportunity to consort with both senior and junior people who will both suggest research problems of significance and instruct one in the techniques necessary to solve them or one's own research problems. This aspect of a university improves its performance as a producer of research output, through the operation of economies of scale and agglomeration; but it may well also serve to reduce its performance as an institution obligated to efficient teaching of its undergraduate, and possibly also its graduate, students.

Finally, university teaching staff are interested in their own promotion, as a question both of academic status and of private income. Promotion to higher academic and income status may be an objective in conflict with teaching performance and with quality research output, for two reasons. First, promotion is decided by senior people who are likely both to under-value teaching as compared with research, and to judge research by their own preconceptions and pride. Second, the research output that leads to promotion is likely to be judged by quantity rather than quality — though there is a countervailing tendency to regard a man who publishes a lot in a short time as insufficiently scholarly, and a man who publishes little but that little of extremely abstruse character as a very worthy scholar whose small quantity of output is justified by its high quality — and by topicality of subject and results in relation to current research concerns rather than by scientific fundamentality. The rate of discount applied to current scholarly work promising future pay-offs in knowledge, in other words, is higher than the socially optimal, and the valuation of the social product of research reflects the immediate market valuation of a novel product rather than its long-run worth.

The third important inside interest group in a university is the administration, which serves among other things as a buffer between staff and students on the one hand, and the outside interest groups on the other. The buffer function is responsible both for the typical structure of university government, which involves the sharing of administrative and particularly decision-making functions among the formal administrative apparatus, a senate composed of senior academics, and a board of trustees or governors representing the public but selected from those sympathetic to the university, and for the standard practice of recruiting at least senior administrative staff from the ranks of successful (or at least reputable) academics — both of which are designed to ensure "independence" of the university from outside pressures and let it go its own sweet autonomous way. It may be noted that governments, as the main source of university funds, have become increasingly restive with this university government arrangement, and anxious to replace it by a more direct and subservient relationship between university management and its own civil service.

The administration has a variety of interests that may and often do conflict with those of other interest groups in the university. First, it has a strong interest in the university being and remaining popular with the community, which above all requires maintaining peace and quiet on the campus, and minimizing the extent to which the university acquires a reputation for controversial or radical ideas and activities — an objective that may easily conflict with the principle of academic freedom. This objective is a prerequisite to a second, institutional growth, which is a characteristic objective of bureaucracies, since it both demonstrates their successful management and social importance and increases their power and appropriate remuneration. Growth, especially if rapid, is not neces-

42

sarily conducive to efficient teaching, research, and staff selection or to the happiness of students and staff. Moreover, growth in response to the demands of outside interests, whether for an increase in the aggregate scale of the university or for the undertaking of new kinds of teaching and research activities, is not necessarily conducive to the maintenance of a happy academic community. A school of undertaking is surely passively, and a school of journalism frequently actively, a source of embarrassment to the traditional academic community, while in recent years defence research and military training on campus have been bones of bitter contention to both staff and students.

A third administration objective is efficient internal management of the university, though in most universities the principle of academic freedom means that the criteria of efficiency are primarily budgetary and are applied mainly to the allocation of incremental funds rather than to the spending of established fund allocations. In this respect, university efficiency is like government efficiency, and consists on the one hand in carefully checking to ensure that allocations of funds are spent for the purposes intended in the allocation, whether that purpose is still useful or not, and on the other hand in carefully scrutinizing requests for additional funds, though once the fresh funds have been allocated the allocation tends to continue automatically. A university administration can and often does deny a bad department funds for expansion; but it is almost never prepared to close it down. And if there is a budgetary squeeze, due to inflation or to a reduction in revenue, it is translated into an equi-proportionate cut in sub-budgets throughout the university (with modifications for special cases), rather than a thorough-going review of the university's activities and elimination of the marginal ones. In short, a bureaucracy's criteria of efficiency entail painstakingly honest accounting, rationality in the allocation of incremental funds, and political justice in the continuation of fair shares in the established allocation of funds, in contrast to the economic criteria of efficiency, according to which existing and incremental allocations should be considered together and existing allocations continually reviewed. (A further point is that university administrations tend to be excessively receptive to offers of fresh outside funds, regardless of the consistency of the objectives of their donors with the general purposes of the university, and as a result frequently find themselves obliged to find funds for the maintenance of the graveyards of outside donors' ideas.)

The sacrosanctity of existing budgetary allocations is in part explained by a fourth objective of university administrations, internal popularity with students, teaching staff, and library and other auxiliary staff. This objective is complementary with the first objective of external popularity, since it helps to assure peace and quiet on the campus. Its price, however, is toleration of wide margins of inefficiency in all sorts of directions, and compromises also with the principle of academic freedom. Academic freedom is the right of scholars to proclaim the conclusions of their scholarly studies without political penalty, not the right of either staff or students to use their privileged position in the university to impose their political and personal views on the rest of society, though in recent years many university administrations have tamely succumbed to the politicization of the university, i.e., its transformation into an agency for the expression and implementation of 'radical' views on the nature of education and its role in society, though it must be conceded that one reason why university administrations have been willing to do this has been that in the past they were willing to bend the rules of academic independence to discriminate against radical thinkers.

A fifth motivation of university administrations is personal consumption at public expense, expressed both in private salaries and perquisites and in the "public good" aspects of university architecture and landscaping. There is little reason to believe — aside from the consideration of impressing visitors from the outside world — that university efficiency requires that the university president, vice-chancellor, rector, or director needs three times the size of office and number of secretaries that a professor has (and a larger multiple of what an aspiring junior staff member commands), or that the administration inhabit a non-functionally-architectural building surrounded by expensively manicured grass, shrubbery, and flowering plants, or that air conditioning and central heating contribute more to the efficiency of the administration than they would to the efficiency of the teaching and research functions of the academic staff. On the contrary, it is reasonably clear that the luxury consumption that university administrations afford themselves at university expense creates a social gulf between the administration on the one hand and students and staff on the other, and so militates against the achievement of the previous objective of internal popularity.

The extreme of gratification of the desire for personal consumption by university administrations is found in the final objective in the list, the objective of monument-building. Like politicians, university administrators find a great deal of satisfaction in changing the physical appearance of the landscape by erecting new and impressive buildings for whose sponsorship they can claim the credit, whether the buildings serve any useful social purpose or not. The pyramid-building propensity militates against efficiency in two major ways. First, it prompts a quest for large outside donations to start new schools or institutes for research which may fit badly into the general structure of the university as an academic community. Second, it biasses administrative choices in the allocation of fresh funds towards expenditure on buildings and equipment and against expenditure on staff salaries and staff secretarial assistance, even though quality of staff may be far more important than quality of buildings and other plant in determining quality of educational and research effort. (This point is paralleled in recent criticisms of developed-country assistance programmes for less developed countries, which argue a bias towards large-scale expenditure on visible creation of new industries, major irrigation projects, etc., and against small-scale widely-distributed expenditures on marginal contributions to the ability of individual farmers, small-scale manufacturers, etc. to improve the efficiency and productivity of their operations.)

The fourth important interest group within the university is the library, which can be thought of mainly as library staff members but also as comprising the support of some administration and some teaching staff. In relation to the teaching and research activities of the university, the library serves two main purposes — as an accessible repository of books students have to read or should read, and as a repository of books staff may want to use for their own research. However, a university library acquires a life of its own, partly because it serves as a sort of monument to the social importance and prestige of the university, partly because its books serve the interests of scholars outside as well as inside the university (both local non-university intellectuals and scholars from other universities), and largely because its staff is specialized in the business of acquiring and warehousing books, administering their usage, and preserving them from theft and damage.

As a result, the interests of the library are not necessarily coterminous with the interests of the university as a teaching and research institution. The professional librarian naturally has an interest in building the best and most impressive library he can, according to librarian standards. This involves among other things biasses towards maximizing the number of titles he can display rather than optimizing the numbers of the same title he possesses in relation to reader demand; towards acquiring as complete as possible collections of books and papers, regardless of the interest of teaching staff and students in having such collections available or the cost-benefit ratio for the university involved, in order to enhance the local or world reputation of the library as such; and towards the acquistion of rare books, which no one in the university may want to read or even see on display, and access to which (in the case of pornographic books or very expensive collectors' items) may even be denied to students and the non-senior university teaching staff. To house these books requires an expensive building or buildings, involving special architectural features, such as reinforced flooring and rooms with closely-controlled temperature and humidity for the storage of rare ancient books, buildings whose contribution to the functions of the university, as distinct from the prestige of the library, may not be justified by the expense. The preservation of the library's stock of books in number and condition or physical quality also requires extensive policing of borrowing and reading rights, and an explicit attempt to minimize physical usage of at least the rare books, and to segregate different classes of readers into those who make heavy use of the less interesting and more dispensable books (from the point of view of the librarian: textbooks and other non-scarce books currently in print) and the few scholarly connoisseurs who can be trusted to read an ancient tome with due respect for its physical perishability. Finally, librarians are naturally interested in achieving technical efficiency in information storage, i.e., efficiency in both storage and data retrieval; but while this concern with efficiency is in general beneficial to the rest of the university in its capacity as users of the library's books, it is flawed by the library's tendency to be concerned with systems of storage and data retrieval that accord equal treatment to the rarely-used and the heavily-used books. A rational system — which some libraries approximate — would distinguish sharply between books and journals in current heavy demand, which could be made quickly accessible both by good cataloguing and ordering procedures and by the maintenance of adequate stocks of copies in the shelves, and rare and rarely-used bibliographical items, the availability of which interests only a handful of scholars who can be expected to be patient in obtaining access to them.

The fifth interest group in a university comprises the service staff, that is, the research assistants, teaching assistants, teachers of service courses (e.g., languages, or elementary mathematics), and technicians of all sorts. These people usually have little power within the university though they may occasionally be able to acquire significant power by forming coalitions with one of the first three interest groups (normally, either students or teaching and research staff.)

As people in the position of employees of the university, rather than part of it, they have the normal interest of employees in income and job security. But they have motivations and incentives to acquire the status of university teaching and research offices, including especially the privilege of tenure after a certain period of service, and a voice in university governance. The purpose of tenure, insofar as it still has a reasonable purpose, is to protect the academic freedom of the scholar against outside and inside political pressure, not to guarantee him a rental income for life regardless of his performance (within very broad limits). Similarly, the purpose of maintaining a role for the teaching and research staff of the university in university governance is to enable them to give voice to academic values, which they are presumed capable of distinguishing from personal interest, not to entitle them to run the university to suit themselves, at the expense of the public. The interests of the service staff in acquiring tenure and governance power run contrary to the requirements of university efficiency, precisely because these people provide services ancillary to the main functions of the university and their conceptions of its functions are correspondingly limited, in particular with respect to understanding of why and on what terms the political system of society is prepared to subscribe money for the support of universities. A trades union attitude towards the relation between the university and the state is conducive neither to the welfare of the university population nor to efficiency in the university; but it is attractive to some regular university staff members in the contemporary situation in which the university system has been vastly expanded at the behest of the state and the state is rapidly tending to treat university teachers like the employees that secondary and primary school teachers have long since become; and the interests of the service staff reinforce the tendency to the defensive adoption of the trades union attitude towards the university.

The final interest group in the university to be discussed is the research institute. Such institutes are not usually involved in the university as a community of scholars and students, having no formal teaching function and being divorced from the general university interest in ideas and scholarship by their missionary subject area orientation. The university simply defines their geographical location and their prestige, and virtually their sole interest in it — apart from its library and computer facilities, which are directly useful and relevant — concerns the maintenance and enhancement of its public and scholarly prestige. Otherwise, their orientation is towards the outside world of other scholars and of research markets. Their concern with the university prestige is a general and long-run interest; but it does not preclude the staff of research institutes either from undertaking types of research that undermine a university's reputation for dispassionate scholarship, or from attempting to influence university policy in directions that favour their own institutional interests at the expense of sacrificing the teaching and research obligations of the university as a whole towards its staff, students, and society in general — e.g., protests against or support of particular government policies. In short, the research institutes, like the library and the service staff, constitute only a partial sample of the university's activities, and their interests in the university are not necessarily conducive to the efficiency of the overall university operation.

Concluding remarks

This chapter has been concerned with presenting a brief and necessarily sketchy survey of the major interest groups involved in the management of the contemporary university. Its main theme has been, in technical terms, that the university is a multi-product firm, important constituents of its product line being "public goods" of one or another ill-defined kind, and that both the consumers and producers of these goods have widely divergent preference functions, so much so that it is virtually impossible to define a social welfare function containing university outputs as arguments that would be sufficiently well-behaved to be amenable to maximization subject to a cost constraint. It is, of course, always possible to impose a limited social welfare function, for example, student comprehension of course content at examination time, and maximize that function subject to a budget constraint in terms of expenditure on alternative methods of teaching. But to do so begs the fundamental question, is this what the university is all about?

To say this is not, of course, is to deny the usefulness of analysis of teaching effectiveness, or the efficiency of any other aspect of university "production". The university purportedly produces *something*, and it is useful to know how well it produces the things it claims to produce, even though it can always reject the results on the grounds that the particular product in question is a mere by-product of the process of producing a more important product, the quantity of which cannot be measured. The university system in contemporary times is under strong pressure to justify itself by its contribution to society; and any contribution that can be measured and tested for its efficiency is well worth investigating.

3. Higher Education as a Filter

by Kenneth J. Arrow[1]

This chapter sketches a model of the economic role of higher education rather different from the current human capital orthodoxy. It is designed to formalize views expressed by some sociologists (e.g. Berg, 1970) that the diploma serves primarily as an (imperfect) measure of performance ability rather than as evidence of acquired skills. I think the model is capable of illuminating certain aspects of the economic returns to higher education and gives an interpretation alternative to the conventional one.

The model certainly abstracts from aspects which have been much considered. I am not apologetic for this abstraction, but I am for the fact the model is still so primitive in form and in particular for the fact that it seems so difficult to test. I hope to work further on it and to encourage others to do the same.

The conventional view among economists is that education adds to an individual's productivity and therefore increases the market value of his labour. From the viewpoint of formal theory, it does not matter how the student's productivity is increased, but implicitly it is assumed that the student receives cognitive skills through his education. Educators, on the other hand, have long felt that the activity of education is a process of socialization; the latent content of the process, the acquisition of skills such as the carrying out of assigned tasks, getting along with others, regularity, punctuality, and the like, is at least as important as the manifest objectives of conveying information. This last doctrine is currently revived by radical economists, though with a negative rather than a positive valuation. But

---

[1] Work on this chapter was partially supported by National Science Foundation Grant GS 2874–A1 at the Institute for Mathematical Studies in the Social Sciences at Stanford University.

from the viewpoint of economic theory, the socialization hypothesis is just as much a human capital theory as the cognitive skill acquisition hypothesis. Both hypotheses imply that education supplies skills that lead to higher productivity.

I would like to present a very different view. Higher education, in this model, contributes in no way to superior economic performance; it increases neither cognition nor socialization. Instead, higher education serves as a screening device, in that it sorts out individuals of differing abilities, thereby conveying information to the purchasers of labour.

(Perhaps I should make clear that I personally do not believe that higher education performs only a screening purpose. Clearly professional schools impart real skills valued in the market and so do undergraduate courses in the sciences. The case is considerably less clear with regard to the bulk of liberal arts courses. But in any case I think it better to make a dramatic and one-sided presentation of the screening model in order to develop it than to produce a premature synthesis. It should also be understood that I am speaking only about the contribution of higher education to production; the consumption aspects are real and important, but they are irrelevant to the points being made here.)

The screening or *filter* theory of higher education, as I shall call it, is distinct from the productivity-adding human capital theory but is not in total contradiction to it. From the viewpoint of an employer, an individual certified to be more valuable *is* more valuable, to an extent which depends upon the nature of the production function. Therefore, the filtering role of education is a productivity-adding role from the private viewpoint; but as we shall see, the social productivity of higher education is more problematic.

The filter theory of education is part of a larger view about the nature of the economic system and its equilibrium. It is based on the assumption that economic agents have highly imperfect information. In particular, the purchaser of a worker's services has a very poor idea of his productivity. In this model, I assume instead that the buyer has very good *statistical* information but nothing more. That is, I assume that there are certain pieces of information about the worker, specifically whether or not he has a college diploma, which the employer can acquire costlessly. He knows, from general information or previous experience, the statistical distribution of produc-

52

tivities given the information he has, but has no way of distinguishing the productivities of individuals about whom he has the same information.

It will probably be argued that this description is valid enough at the time of hiring but that after a period of time the employer will know his workers and their productivities on an individual basis. No doubt there is something to this viewpoint but not as much as may be thought. After all, what is needed for allocative efficiency is the marginal productivity of each individual. But in a complex production process, the employer has simply no way of determining that. All he can do is act like an ideal econometrician, relating his output to the numbers of different kinds of workers (and other inputs, from which I am abstracting in this paper). Here two workers are of the same kind if the employer's information about them is the same.

The general point that information in the real world is much more limited than that assumed in our usual equilibrium models has a long history among critics of the mainstream of economic thought. In recent years, it has been especially stressed by Herbert A. Simon and his followers. The particular emphasis on lack of information concerning the productivity of workers has been argued by me in the context of racial discrimination in employment (Arrow, 1972 A and B) and, in a more general way, by A. Michael Spence in a recent Harvard dissertation (1972). The hypothesis that the actors in an uncertain world have a correct perception of the probability distribution of that uncertainty is a fairly standard one. In particular, this can be applied to lack of information about endogenous economic variables, such as prices or productivities; it becomes a condition of equilibrium that the distribution, when believed, helps generate such behaviour as to maintain the distribution.

We shall assume that each individual has three characteristics, his record before entering college, the probability of his getting through higher education, and his productivity. These have a joint distribution and presumably are positively correlated. The producers know about an individual only whether or not he is graduated from college.

The colleges serve really as a double filter, once in selecting entrants and once in passing or failing students. In admitting students, the colleges aim to maximize the expected number of graduates. Let,

y = record before college,
z = productivity,
$f(y,z)$ = joint density of the two variables.

For applicants with a record y, the college is only interested in the conditional probability of their graduating. Hence it can be assumed without loss of generality that y is the probability of graduating conditional on the pre-college record, for the conditional probability of success is the only aspect of the pre-college record relevant to admission and to the model as a whole. If the capacity of the college is limited, then choice of admission procedures to maximize the expected number of graduates implies choice of a cut-off number, y_o such that an applicant is admitted if and only if,

$$y \geqslant y_o \tag{1}$$

Let,

N_e = proportion of population admitted to college,
N_g = proportion graduating.

Since y has been transformed to be a probability, it varies from 0 to 1. The variable z is only constrained to be a non-negative variable and therefore may range from 0 to $+\infty$. From the definitions

$$N_e = \int_0^{+\infty} \int_{y_o}^{1} f(y,z)\, dy\, dz = P(y \geqslant y_o), \tag{2}$$

$$N_g = \int_0^{+\infty} \int_{y_o}^{1} y\, f(y,z)\, dy\, dz = E(y|y \geqslant y_o)P(y \geqslant y_o) = \bar{y}_e P(y \geqslant y_o), \tag{3}$$

where

$$\bar{y}_e = E(y|y \geqslant y_o) \tag{4}$$

is the probability of graduation of a random college entrant.

A detailed interpretation of productivity has not yet been given; in the sequel, two alternative interpretations will be used. However, under either interpretation, we will regard total output of the

54

appropriate commodity to be the sum of the productivities of individuals. Then the average productivity of all individuals is,

$$\bar{z} = \int_{0}^{+\infty} \int_{0}^{1} z \, f(y,z) \, dy \, dz = E(z),$$ (5)

and the total product of college graduates (per unit of total labour force) is,

$$Z_g = \int_{0}^{+\infty} \int_{y_0}^{1} zy \, f(y,z) \, dy \, dz = E(zy|y \geqslant y_0)P(y \geqslant y_0)$$ (6)

Under what conditions does college filtering convey any information? From (6) and (3), the expected productivity of a college graduate is,

$$\bar{z}_g = Z_g/N_g = E(zy|y \geqslant y_0)/E(y|y \geqslant y_0).$$ (7)

College graduation has some (positive) information content if the productivity of a randomly chosen college graduate exceeds that of a randomly chosen member of the population, i.e., if

$$\bar{z}_g > E(z).$$ (8)

The existence of the admission procedure suggests the following additional question; is it the admission or the college itself that performs the screening function? This is, after all, an important policy question, since admission procedures are much cheaper; for a first approximation we may suppose them free. Then admission procedures convey information if,

$$E(z|y \geqslant y_0) > E(z),$$ (9)

and college itself has additional informational content over simple admission, if,

$$\bar{z}_g > E(z|y \geqslant y_0).$$ (10)

Since,

$$E(z) = E(z|y \geqslant y_o)P(y \geqslant y_o) + E(z|y < y_o)P(y < y_o),$$

$$E(z|y \geqslant y_o) - E(z) = P(y < y_o)[E(z|y \geqslant y_o) - E(z|y < y_o)], \quad (11)$$

i.e., if the expected productivity of those admitted is greater than that of those rejected, then the admission procedure has predictive value.

$$\bar{z}_g - E(z|y \geqslant y_o) = \frac{E(zy|y \geqslant y_o) - E(z|y \geqslant y_o)E(y|y \geqslant y_o)}{E(y|y \geqslant y_o)}$$

$$= \frac{\sigma_{yz|y \geqslant y_o}}{E(y|y \geqslant y_o)}, \quad (12)$$

where use is made of (7), and $\sigma_{yz|y \geqslant y_o}$ means the conditional covariance of y and z, given admission to college. Thus college education conveys information about productivity beyond admission if there is a positive correlation between productivity and probability of college success among those admitted.* (See note page 73.)

The productivity advantage of college graduates over the average member of the population can be found by adding (11) and (12).

But even if college does have a positive informational value, it by no means follows that it is socially worthwhile. The filter model thus leads to a very different conclusion from the human capital model; for, as we will now see, there can easily be a divergence between social and private demands for information.

Consider the simplest model of production; all individuals are perfect substitutes in production with ratios given by their productivities. Then *there is no social value to information about productivity.* The total output of society will be $E(z) = \bar{z}$ (normalized on labour force); the more productive individuals will produce more whether or not anyone knows who they are. (I am abstracting from incentive questions here.) There will, however, be a private value to a college diploma for those most likely to get it, if we assume a competitive world. For then, the wage of an individual will be the expected value of his product conditional on the information available to the employer. Let us assume that the individual has no better information about his prospects of going through college than the

56

college has. Suppose further that anyone can go to college if he pays its cost, c. (Since education is also a consumer's good, the cost, c, is to be interpreted here empirically as the cost over and above its consumption value.) Suppose no one is going to college initially. Then a few individuals go to college; if they have selected themselves properly, then the expected value of their productivity, conditional on graduation, is greater than the overall average, $\bar{z}$. Clearly, if it is sufficiently greater and if the probability of passing is high enough, then it pays to incur the costs. But these costs are simply a social waste.

In fact, a detailed examination shows that, under certain informational assumptions, everybody would gain by prohibiting college (the following argument is really a special case of Spence's). Let us study the equilibrium. Some go to college, and some don't. The employers know the expected productivities of college graduates and of others (I assume here that employers do not distinguish between college failures and those who do not enter; such a distinction could easily be introduced if deemed realistic). Further assume that potential entrants know the overall probability of graduation among those who enter but not the probability conditional on their own record. Clearly, if it pays any individual to go, it pays an individual with a higher value of y, so we assume that there is a critical level, y_o, such that individuals go to college if and only if $y \geqslant y_o$ (the critical level here is determined by demand for college entrance, not, as before, by capacity restrictions). The employers then pay to college graduates $\bar{z}_g = \bar{z}_g(y_o)$, as defined in (7). Let $\bar{z}_n(y_o)$ be the expected productivity of the non-graduates. Then,

$$\bar{z} = \bar{z}_g(y_o)N_g + \bar{z}_n(y_o)(1 - N_g); \tag{13}$$

N_g, as defined in (3), is, of course, also a function of y_o.

If an individual goes to college, he graduates with probability $\bar{y}_e$, and fails with probability $1 - \bar{y}_e$. He incurs a cost of c in any case, so that his expected return from college is,

$$\bar{z}_g(\bar{y}_e) + \bar{z}_n(1 - \bar{y}_e) - c.$$

If he does not go to college, his return is $\bar{z}_n$ with certainty. In the absence of risk-aversion, equilibrium requires that the two returns be

57

equal; for if the expected return to going to college were the greater, individuals with records slightly less than y_o would find it profitable to go to college.

$$\bar{z}_g \bar{y}_e + \bar{z}_n (1 - \bar{y}_e) - c = \bar{z}_n,$$

or, after simplification,

$$\bar{y}_e (\bar{z}_g - \bar{z}_n) = c, \tag{14}$$

which immediately shows that $\bar{z}_g > \bar{z}_n$. But then, from (13), $\bar{z}_n < \bar{z}$. Therefore, the income of a non-graduate is lower than it was before; but since the expected income of college entrants equals that of non-graduates, the college entrants do not benefit either, at least not *ex ante*.

Hence, we have the remarkable possibility that if college is a filter, its abolition may help everyone. Not only is there no efficiency gain, but college has also created an inequality in *ex post* income where none existed before.

We are accustomed in theory to argue that information may be under-produced because its social value is greater than its private. But the opposite possibility has also been shown by Hirshleifer (1971) in a very important article. Information not used in production may merely convey a competitive advantage.

Of course, our conclusion depended on free entry to college. If college entrance is limited in some manner, then the equality in (14) becomes an inequality, and the college entrants may gain on average. The non-entrants certainly lose in any case, and further it would have paid them to bribe the entrants not to enter. The effects on equality are even worse in this case.

William Brainard has pointed out to me that the strong result found so far depends on the assumption that the potential entrant does not know the probability of graduation conditional on his own record but only the probability conditional on the fact of entrance. If the stronger informational condition holds, the expected return from college for an individual whose pre-college record is y is,

$$\bar{z}_g y + \bar{z}_n (1 - y) - c = (\bar{z}_g - \bar{z}_n) y + \bar{z}_n - c, \tag{15}$$

58

and therefore equilibrium is obtained by setting this return equal to $\bar{z}_n$ for the *marginal* man, for whom $y = y_o$. Therefore, (14) is replaced by

$$y_o(\bar{z}_g - \bar{z}_n) = c. \tag{16}$$

It remains true that $\bar{z}_g > \bar{z}_n$ and therefore $\bar{z} > \bar{z}_n$, so that the non-graduates are worse off than they would be in the absence of college education. However, individuals with sufficiently good records, i.e., sufficiently high values of y, may have expected returns (15) which are at least equal to $\bar{z}$, the expected return in the absence of college filtering. If y_1 is the smallest such value of y,

$$(\bar{z} - \bar{z}_n)y_1 + \bar{z}_n = \bar{z} + c.$$

If (13) is subtracted from this equation, we see that,

$$(\bar{z}_g - \bar{z}_n)(y_1 - N_g) = c,$$

and dividing through by (16) yields,

$$y_1 = N_g + \dot{y}_o.$$

If there are no values of y above y_1, then it remains true that everybody gains by changing from competitive equilibrium to the abolition of college. However, in any case, the fundamental point remains unaltered; there is a net gain in social output by abolishing college, and everybody could be made better off by doing so and redistributing income suitably.

(This statement may appear hard to reconcile with our usual expectation that college education is insufficient. Of course, I am abstracting from credit rationing, which has been the most powerful force working in the opposite direction. My guess is that we are moving into a period where public subsidies to higher education plus improved credit facilities are making effective credit restriction on higher education a thing of the past.)

To understand the social role of education as a filter better, one must consider more complicated production functions, in which there are complementary kinds of labour. Then education has a positive value in sorting out types of workers. For simplicity, suppose there are two kinds of labour. Everyone is capable of supplying one unit of type 1 labour, and this fact is known to all. However, there is also needed type 2 labour, of which different individuals can supply different amounts. In this model, z will be interpreted as the supply of type 2 labour, measured in efficiency-units. To emphasize the complementarity of the different types of labour, we will assume that production requires fixed proportions of the two types of labour (remembering always that type 2 labour is measured in efficiency-units). By proper choice of units, we can require without loss of generality that one unit of each type of labour is needed to produce one unit of product.

In this model, filtering is no longer useless. Suppose there are two classes of people, say A and B with expected productivities $\overline{z}_A$ and $\overline{z}_B$, respectively, $\overline{z}_A > \overline{z}_B$ (remember that "productivity" here means supply of efficiency-units of type 2 labour). Then clearly it can never be optimal to have simultaneously individuals of class A performing type 1 labour and individuals of class B performing type 2 labour. For suppose this happened. Efficiency also requires that the sum of the z's of those in type 2 labour equal the number in type 1 labour. Then remove some class A individuals from type 1 labour and replace them with an equal number of class B individuals from type 2 labour, making all selections at random. The number of type 1 labourers is unchanged, the expected number of efficiency-units of type 2 labour is increased. Output does not yet increase, since the number of type 1 labourers is a bottleneck. But then we can transfer individuals from type 2 to type 1 labour; by increasing the number of type 1 labourers, total output is increased, provided not so many are transferred that the supply of type 2 labour is reduced below that of type 1 labour.

Thus total output is increased by successful filtering, provided, of course, that the cost of the filter is not too high. We can easily calculate the gain in output due to filtering at zero cost. Let N_A and N_B be the proportions of individuals of the two classes, $N_A + N_B = 1$. Then,

$$\overline{z} = N_A \overline{z}_A + N_B \overline{z}_B$$

If the filter is not used, a fraction N_1 of the entire population is assigned to type 1 labour and the rest to type 2 labour. Since the assignment is random, the total supply of type 2 labour in efficiency units is $(1 - N_1)\bar{z}$. Efficiency requires that,

$$(1 - N_1)\bar{z} = N_1,$$

and the output is the common value of the two sides, so that,

$$N_1 = \bar{z}/(1 + \bar{z}) = \text{output without filtering.} \tag{17}$$

Now suppose for the moment that the filter is used naïvely, that is, all individuals of class A are assigned to type 2 jobs and only such. The supply of type 2 labour is then $N_A \bar{z}_A$, that of type 1 labour, N_B. Of course, these two need not be equal; if they are not, the allocation is inefficient. Suppose first that $N_B < N_A \bar{z}_A$. Then clearly some class A labour will have to be assigned to type 1 jobs. That is, $N_1 > N_B$. Clearly, efficiency requires,

$$(1 - N_1)\bar{z}_A = N_1,$$

so that,

$$N_1 = \bar{z}_A/(1 + \bar{z}_A) = \text{output with filtering and excess of} \atop \text{class A labour.} \tag{18}$$

The increase in output due to filtering is, then,

$$\frac{\bar{z}_A}{1 + \bar{z}_A} - \frac{\bar{z}}{1 + \bar{z}} = \frac{\bar{z}_A - \bar{z}}{\bar{z}(1 + \bar{z}_A)} \frac{\bar{z}}{1 + \bar{z}},$$

the first factor showing the proportionate increase in output.

If there is a deficiency of class A labour for the type 2 jobs, $N_B > N_A \bar{z}_A$, optimal allocation requires that all the class A labour be assigned to those jobs plus enough of the class B labour so that the supplies of the two types of labour are equal.

$$N_A \bar{z}_A + (N_B - N_1)\bar{z}_B = N_1,$$

so that,

$N_1 = \bar{z}/(1 + \bar{z}_B) =$ output with filtering and a deficiency
of class A labour (19)

and the increase in output is,

$$\frac{\bar{z}}{1 + \bar{z}_B} - \frac{\bar{z}}{1 + \bar{z}} = \frac{\bar{z} - \bar{z}_B}{1 + \bar{z}_B} \frac{\bar{z}}{1 + \bar{z}}.$$

Now let us identify these general classes A and B with graduates and non-graduates respectively. Then it has been shown that college education pays if it is free (in which case everyone goes to college and the screening is solely through passing or failing), and, by continuity, some college education pays if c is sufficiently small. Suppose at the optimum $N_g \bar{z}_g > 1 - N_g$. Then the output is given by (18) but from this must be subtracted the cost of education. If c is measured in terms of output, the cost is $cP(y \geqslant y_o)$, where y_o is the cut-off record for admission. Hence, the net output of society for a given y_o is,

$$[\bar{z}_g/(1 + \bar{z}_g)] - cP(y \geqslant y_o).$$

But an increase in y_o will increase $\bar{z}_g$ and therefore will increase $\bar{z}_g/(1 + z_g)$ and it will also decrease $P(y \geqslant y_o)$; hence such an allocation cannot be optimum, a contradiction.** (See note page 73.)

It has therefore been shown that the optimal amount of college education will be such that,

$$N_g \bar{z}_g \leqslant 1 - N_g. \tag{20}$$

It is interesting to note that the cost c does not enter into this condition, so it is valid even if $c = 0$. Even if education is free, it is socially optimal to restrict it so as to improve its screening function.

Since (20) holds, the net output of society is given by (19), and the optimal amount of higher education is obtained by choosing y_o to maximize

$$[\bar{z}/(1 + \bar{z}_n)] - cP(y \geqslant y_o) = F(y_o, c) = H(y_o) - cP(y \geqslant y_o), \tag{21}$$

subject to (20).

The full statement of the derivative conditions implied by this

62

maximization can be easily written down, but they do not appear simple enough for useful interpretation. However, some implications are useful to draw, in particular conditions under which the constraint (20) is binding. When this holds, the filter is working most smoothly, in that every graduate goes into type 2 jobs and every non-graduate into type 1 jobs. In this case, we will say that the filter is *complete*.

First note that the function,

$$G(y_o) = N_g \bar{z}_g + N_g = Z_g + N_g = \int_0^{+\infty} \int_{y_o}^1 y(1 + z)f(y,z) \, dy \, dz,$$

from (3) and (6), is clearly a strictly decreasing function of y_o in any region of positive density. Hence, the equation,

$$G(y_o^*) = 1, \tag{22}$$

has a unique solution, and the inequality (20) can be written, $G(y_o) \leqslant 1$, or

$$y_o \geqslant y_o^*. \tag{23}$$

The variables $\bar{z}_g$ and $\bar{z}_n$ are functions of y_o; their values when $y_o = y_o^*$ will be denoted by $\bar{z}_g^*$ and $\bar{z}_n^*$, respectively. The starred magnitudes characterize the complete filter.

Next we note that the value of y_o which maximizes (21) subject to (20) or, equivalently, (23), must be a monotone increasing function of c. Actually, this conclusion must be stated more precisely, since nothing has been said which implies that the maximum must be unique. Suppose $c_1 < c_2$. Then we show that every maximal value of y_o for $c = c_2$ exceeds every maximal value for $c = c_1$, except that if y_o^* is the unique maximal value of y_o for $c = c_1$, then it can happen that y_o^* is also a maximal value for $c = c_2$.

To see this, let y_o^1 be any maximal value for $c = c_1$ and y_o^2 for $c = c_2$. From (21),

$$F(y_o, c_1) + (c_1 - c_2) P(y \geqslant y_o) = F(y_o, c_2).$$

By definition of a maximum,

$$F(y_o^1, c_1) \geqslant F(y_o^2, c_1).$$

Add,

$$(c_1 - c_2)P(y \geqslant y_o^1) = (c_1 - c_2)P(y \geqslant y_o^2) + (c_1 - c_2)[P(y \geqslant y_o^1) - P(y \geqslant y_o^2)]$$

to this inequality.

$$F(y_o^1, c_2) \geqslant F(y_o^2, c_2) + (c_1 - c_2)[P(y \geqslant y_o^1) - P(y \geqslant y_o^2)]$$
$$\geqslant F(y_o^1, c_2) + (c_1 - c_2)[P(y \geqslant y_o^1) - P(y \geqslant y_o^2)],$$

from the fact that y_o^2 maximizes $F(y_o, c_2)$ in the range (23). Hence,

$$(c_1 - c_2)[P(y \geqslant y_o^1) - P(y \geqslant y_o^2)] \leqslant 0,$$

or, since $c_1 < c_2$,

$$P(y \geqslant y_o^1) \geqslant P(y \geqslant y_o^2),$$

which is possible only if $y_o^2 \geqslant y_o^1$. That is, if the cost of education rises, any optimal cut-off level for entrance must be at least as high as it was before the raise.

But when can the equality, $y_o^1 = y_o^2$, hold? This means that y_o^1 is optimal for $c = c_1$ and for $c = c_2$. Suppose $y_o^1 > y_o^*$. Then the constraint (23) is not effective, so that $\dfrac{\partial F}{\partial y_o} = 0$ at $y = y_o^1$ for both values of c. Let,

$$g(y) = \int_o^{+\infty} f(y, z)\, dz,$$

be the marginal density of y. Then, $dP(y \geqslant y_o)/dy_o = -g(y_o)$, and, from (21),

$$\frac{\partial F}{\partial y_o} = H'(y_o) + cg(y_o),$$

so that if y_o^1 is optimal for two different levels of c and $y_o^1 > y_o^*$, we would have,

$$H'(y_o^1) + c_1 g(y_o^1) = 0,$$
$$H'(y_o^1) + c_2 g(y_o^1) = 0,$$

which is impossible if $g(y_o) > 0$, which we can assume. Hence, the equality $y_o^1 = y_o^2$ can hold only if $y_o^1 = y_o^*$.

To complete the argument, suppose that at $c = c_1$, y_o^* is optimal, but there is also another optimal value, say $y_o = y_o'$. But then, as already shown, $y_o^2 \geqslant y_o' > y_o^*$ for any value of y_o optimal for $c = c_2$. Hence, there can be a common optimal value for $c = c_1$ and $c = c_2$ only if y_o^* is the unique optimal cut-off point for the lower cost.

We can then conclude that the complete filter is optimal, if ever, only for an interval of c-values starting at $c = 0$. If, for any c, y_o^* is not the unique optimal value, then it is not optimal for any larger values of c.

It is, of course, clear that y_o^* cannot be optimal for all c. For consider what happens when y_o is raised to its upper limit, 1; this means approaching the no-filter situation, in which there is no higher education. In that case, $\bar{z}_n \rightarrow \bar{z}$, while $P(y \geqslant y_o)$ approaches zero; hence, the net output tends to $\bar{z}/(1+\bar{z})$, as already seen in (17). On the other hand, if the complete filter were used for all values of c, it can be seen from (21) that the net output would eventually fall below this level (and indeed would eventually become negative and therefore infeasible). Clearly, the complete filter cannot be optimal if it is inferior to no filter. Hence, the c-interval in which the complete filter is optimal, if it exists, is bounded above.

It remains to see if there is any interval of costs of education for which the complete filter is optimal. Actually, this interval can be shown to exist only under an additional, though natural, assumption. Note that $F(y_o, 0) = H(y_o)$. If it is true that $H'(y_o) < 0$ for all y_o, the the only optimal cut-off for free education would clearly be to make y_o as small as possible, i.e., to let $y_o = y_o^*$. What happens for c slightly greater than 0? I shall show that there must be an interval of c-values in which y_o^* is the unique optimum.

For suppose not; then we can find a sequence $\{c^\nu\}$ of c-values, arbitrarily small, such that for $c = c^\nu$, there is an optimal value $y_o = y_o^\nu > y_o^*$. By definition of an optimum,

$$F(y_o^\nu, c^\nu) \geqslant F(y_o^*, c^\nu), \text{ each } \nu.$$

Either the sequence $\{y_o^v\}$ has a limit point $y_o^{**} > y_o^*$ or else $y_o^v \to y_o^*$. In the first case, by continuity, we would have $F(y_o^{**},0) \geqslant F(y_o^*,0)$, in contradiction to the fact that y_o^* is the unique optimum when $c = 0$. Hence,

$$\frac{F(y_o^v, c^v) - F(y_o^*, c^v)}{y_o^u - y_o^*} \geqslant 0, \; y_o^v \to y_o^* \tag{24}$$

From (21),

$$\frac{F(y_o^v, c^v) - F(y_o^*, c^v)}{y_o^v - y_o^*} = \frac{H(y_o^v) - H(y_o^*)}{y_o^v - y_o^*} - c^v \frac{P(y \geqslant y_o^v) - P(y \geqslant y_o^*)}{y_o^v - y_o^*}$$

From the definition of a derivative and other remarks made above, we know that, as v approaches $+\infty$,

$$\frac{H(y_o^v) - H(y_o^*)}{y_o^v - y_o^*} \to H'(y_o^*), \; c^v \to 0,$$

$$\frac{P(y \geqslant y_o^v) - P(y \geqslant y_o^*)}{y_o^v - y_o^*} \to -g(y_o^*);$$

hence,

$$\frac{F(y_o^v, c^v) - F(y_o^*, c^v)}{y_o^v - y_o^*} \to H'(y_o^*),$$

and, from (24), $H'(y_o^*) \geqslant 0$, in contradiction to the assumption that $H'(y_o) < 0$ for all y_o.

Thus, the condition $H'(y_o) < 0$ implies the existence of a cost $c = c_1 > 0$ such that the complete filter is optimal for $0 \leqslant c \leqslant c_1$ and not for higher values of c. It remains only to restate the condition, $H'(y_o) < 0$. Clearly, from (21), this holds if and only if,

$$\frac{d\bar{z}_n}{dy_o} > 0.$$

As already seen in (13), $N_g \bar{z}_g + (1 - N_g)\bar{z}_n = \bar{z}$, and this for all y_o. From (7) and (6),

$$N_g \bar{z}_g = Z_g,$$

and,

$$\frac{dZ_g}{dy_o} = -y_o \int_0^{+\infty} zf(y_o, z)\, dz.$$

If we differentiate (13) with respect to y_o, we find, after some transposition, that,

$$(1 - N_g)\left(\frac{d\bar{z}_n}{dy_o}\right) = \bar{z}_n \left(\frac{dN_g}{dy_o}\right) - \left(\frac{dZ_g}{dy_o}\right)$$

$$= y_o \int_0^{+\infty} zf(y_o, z)\, dz - y_o \bar{z}_n \int_0^{+\infty} f(y_o, z)\, dz$$

$$= y_o \int_0^{+\infty} f(y_o, z)\, dz\, [E(z/y_o) - \bar{z}_n],$$

with the aid of (3). Hence, $H'(y_o) < 0$ if and only if,

$$E(z/y_o) > \bar{z}_n.$$

This asserts that, for any given cut-off admission criterion, the average productivity of those marginally admitted exceeds the average productivity of non-graduates. Notice that this assumption is somewhat strong, for the non-graduates include those with pre-admission records predicting a probability of graduation greater than y_o. Indeed, (25) can hardly hold for $y_o = 0$; for in that case, $\bar{z}_n$ is the average productivity of all those who failed when everyone is permitted to go to college, while $E(z/y_o)$ is the average productivity of the subgroup whose failure was perfectly predictable. By the same token, we would certainly expect (25) to hold when $y_o = 1$. In this case, there is no filter at all, i.e., no higher education, so that $\bar{z}_n = \bar{z}$; we would certainly expect that the expected productivity of those who, on the basis of their pre-college records, would be certain to pass if admitted would be higher than the average in the population.

67

We can therefore assume that (25) holds for y_o sufficiently high; in particular, we assume that it holds for $y_o \geqslant y_o^*$, which is all that is needed.

We can thus conclude as follows: *If (25) holds for cut-off points y_o at least equal to that for the complete filter, then there is a cost, $c_1 > 0$, such that the complete filter is uniquely optimal for education costs $0 \leqslant c \leqslant c_1$ and not for higher cost levels. If (25) does not hold, then the same may be true, or else it may be that the complete filter is never optimal. In any case, for cost levels for which the complete filter is not optimal, the cut-off point increases with educational costs, and the number of graduates is less than the number of type 2 jobs. For sufficiently high costs, the abolition of higher education is optimal.*

As in the one-factor model, it is important to ask to what extent the competitive market achieves an optimal or satisfactory level of education. It remains true that there is a divergence between private and social benefits in filtering, but, as has been shown, it is no longer true that the socially optimal level of college education is zero. The following will now be shown: *If the complete filter is optimal, then it is achieved by the competitive market in which college education is supplied to everyone willing to pay for its cost. The complete filter remains the competitive allocation for higher cost levels, even up to levels such that everyone is worse off than they would be under no filtering. For still higher cost levels, the competitive equilibrium is no longer the complete filter but rather one in which the number of graduates is less than the number of type 2 jobs; it remains true that, under the same informational assumptions made as earlier, everyone is worse off under the equilibrium allocation than they would be under no filtering.*

In the two-factor model, let w_1 be the price per unit of type 1 labour, w_2 the price per efficiency-unit of type 2 labour. Obviously, there will be at least one graduate working at type 2 labour; since the wages per man of graduates must be the same in all uses, a graduate must earn $w_2 \bar{z}_g$ per man. Similarly, a non-graduate must earn w_1 per man. At equilibrium, the expected wage of an entrant, less cost of education, must equal the wage of a non-graduate.

$$\bar{y}_e(w_2 \bar{z}_g) + (1 - \bar{y}_e)w_1 - c = w_1,$$

or, analogously to (14),

$$\bar{y}_e(w_2\bar{z}_g - w_1) = c. \tag{26}$$

Since one unit of type 1 labour and one efficiency-unit of type 2 labour together produce one unit of product, exhaustion of the product implies,

$$w_1 + w_2 = 1. \tag{27}$$

From (26), it follows immediately, that $w_2\bar{z}_g > w_1$. This statement in turn implies that no graduate is working at a type 1 job, for, since all graduates are indifferent in the market place, all can earn $w_2\bar{z}_g$ and therefore none will work for w_1 at a type 1 job. The total supply of type 2 labour by all graduates therefore does not exceed the number of units of type 2 labour used in the economy at equilibrium.

$$N_g\bar{z}_g \leqslant 1 - N_g, \tag{28}$$

a condition which also holds at the optimal allocation, according to (20). If the equality held, then no non-graduate would prefer to work in a type 2 job. Since his income in such a job would be $w_2\bar{z}_n$, we must have, in this case, $w_1 \geqslant w_2\bar{z}_n$. On the other hand, if the inequality holds in (28), some non-graduates are working in type 2 jobs, so that $w_2\bar{z}_n = w_1$. Thus, one of the two following situations must hold at equilibrium:

$$N_1\bar{z}_g = 1 - N_g \text{ and } w_1 \geqslant w_2\bar{z}_n; \tag{29}$$

$$N_1\bar{z}_g < 1 - N_g \text{ and } w_1 = w_2\bar{z}_n. \tag{30}$$

As will now be shown, which of these holds will depend upon the parameters of the problem; in particular, given other parameters, on the education cost c.

As we know from (22–23), when (29) holds, $y_o = y_o^*$. Let $\bar{y}_e^*$ be the corresponding value of $\bar{y}_e$, the probability of graduation conditional on admission. If (29) holds, then, solve for w_1 and w_2 from (26) and (27):

69

$$w_1 = \frac{[\bar{z}_g^* - (c/\bar{y}_e^*)]}{(1 + \bar{z}_g^*)},$$ (31)

$$w_2 = \frac{[1 + (c/\bar{y}_e^*)]}{(1 + \bar{z}_g^*)}.$$ (32)

From (29), these are the equilibrium wages, and the complete filter is the equilibrium allocation, provided that $w_1 \geqslant w_2 \bar{z}_n^*$. From (31)–(32), this condition can be written,

$$c \leqslant \frac{\bar{y}_e^*(\bar{z}_g^* - \bar{z}_n^*)}{(1 + \bar{z}_n^*)} = c_2$$ (33)

Thus, for c in this range, the complete filter is competitive equilibrium.

Recall that, as in the one-factor model, the equilibrium condition for choosing entrance to college implies that the *ex ante* expected income (net of educational costs) is the same for all, and therefore equal to w_1. We can then compare w_1 with the expected output in the absence of a filter, $\bar{z}/(1+\bar{z})$ from (17). Since w_1 is linear in c, from (31), we need make the comparisons only for $c \to 0$ and $c = c_2$, as far as equilibria satisfying (29) are concerned.

First note that from (26) and either (29) or (30),

$$w_2 \bar{z}_g > w_1 \geqslant w_2 \bar{z}_n,$$

so that,

$$\bar{z}_g > \bar{z} > \bar{z}_n,$$ (34)

in any equilibrium. Then, for $c \to 0$,

$$w_1 \to \frac{\bar{z}_n^*}{(1 + \bar{z}_g^*)} > \frac{\bar{z}}{(1 + \bar{z})},$$

as might be expected, when $c = 0$, the competitive equilibrium is better than no filter. On the other hand, when $c = c_2$, we find, on substitution from (33) into (31) and some simplification, that,

$$w_1 = \frac{\bar{z}_n{}^*}{(1 + \bar{z}_n{}^*)} < \frac{\bar{z}}{(1 + \bar{z})}.$$

Therefore, there is a cost level, c_3, $0 < c_3 < c_2$, such that the complete filter is better than no filter for $c < c_3$ and worse for $c_3 < c \leqslant c_2$. *A fortiori*, the complete filter, though a competitive equilibrium, is not optimal for $c \geqslant c_3$. Hence, if there is any range of costs for which the complete filter is optimal, the upper limit of that range, c_1, must be less than c_3.

Now consider equilibria which are not complete filters, those for which (30) holds. The argument here is simple: from (27) and the condition in (30) that $w_1 = w_2 \bar{z}_n$, it follows immediately that,

$$w_1 = \frac{\bar{z}_n}{(1 + \bar{z}_n)} < \frac{\bar{z}}{(1 + \bar{z})} \qquad (35)$$

from (34), so that again the equilibrium filter is worse for everyone than the absence of college education.

(One technical remark is needed here. If $c > c_2$, the only possible competitive equilibrium must satisfy (30). However, it is possible that for some values of $c \leqslant c_2$ there may be more than one equilibrium; one will be the complete filter, but there are others which satisfy (30). Note that if we substitute (35) and the corresponding value of w_2, $1/(1 + \bar{z}_n)$, into (26), we have,

$$c = \frac{\bar{y}_e(\bar{z}_g - \bar{z}_n)}{(1 + \bar{z}_n)} = A(y_o),$$

say, and therefore there is an equilibrium satisfying (30) for any c in the range of $A(y_o)$, with $y_o \geqslant y_o^*$. From (33), $A(y_o^*) = c_2$; hence, if $A(y_o)$ were an increasing function of y_o, there could not be any equilibria satisfying (30) for c-values for which the complete filter is also an equilibrium. I have not studied whether this monotonicity condition is reasonable; if not, then it is possible that the minimum value of $A(y_o)$ for $y_o \geqslant y_o^*$, say $\underline{c}$, may be less than c_2. In that case, for any c, $\underline{c} < c < c_2$, the equation $A(y_o) = c$ may have one or more solutions, so that there will be several competitive equilibria, one a complete filter and the others not.)

There are perhaps two final remarks that should be made, though I

71

must be cursory in both. One is the comparison between this model and a human capital model. It has long been clear that measures of return to human capital may well be biased upwards because ability differences are confounded with differences in the inputs of schooling. Attempts have been made to correct the measures of return to schooling (see e.g., Griliches and Mason, 1972 and Hause, 1972) by introducing a variable designed to measure ability. But unfortunately these ability measures are wrong in principle. Typically, they are measures of intelligence; but "ability" in the relevant sense means the ability to produce goods, and there is simply no empirical reason to expect more than a mild correlation between productive ability and intelligence as measured on tests. Intelligence tests are designed to predict scholastic success, and this is a function they perform well. But there is considerable evidence in direct studies of productivity (e.g., by the U.S. Navy) that ability to pass tests is weakly related to ability to perform specific productive tasks. It is only the latter ability that is relevant here.

Unfortunately, this argument raises another difficulty; the model of this paper depends upon an unmeasured and unmeasurable variable, "ability". There may be no way of ever achieving a direct measurement; after all, a premise of the model is that employers cannot measure ability directly, and there is no reason to suppose that the economist is going to do better. It remains to be seen if the theory can be made to yield interesting and testable implications in the absence of direct measurements of ability.

Indeed, if we revert to the one-factor model, the filter model has some implications for macroeconomic observations. It says that an increase in the resources devoted to college education will have no positive effect on output in the non-educational sector, if all other variables are controlled for. This is indeed a strong inference, but its usefulness in making intertemporal or international comparisons is limited by the need to hold the statistical distribution of ability constant. If "ability" is influenced by cultural factors, then it will certainly vary internationally and may also be thought to vary over time.

There is also one particularly needed elaboration of the model (which is not to say that it doesn't cry out for elaboration in many other directions). This is the relation between college filtering and on-the-job filtering. Once an employee has been hired, the employer can gradually draw on more directly obtained information to determine his productivity. However, this filtering may be costly. To the extent that the employer does filter and does so accurately, the value of the college filter is reduced. The employer pays the average product of a group with given educational achievement only during the period before his own filter has become effective. Conversely, however, an increase in the college population will mean (and has meant) a depreciation in the quality of non-college students (this is *not* necessarily the same as a decrease in the quality of college students). It may be that, with the increased supply of college-filtered students and with a decrease in the quality of non-college students, the alternative filters become less worthwhile and eventually cease to be profitable. This means that the improvement in the equality of income due to increased college education may therefore be offset by the decrease in alternative filters leading to qualification for type 2 jobs. In particular, it means that the criteria used to select for type 2 jobs become narrower in scope, and it can easily be true that both efficiency and equity suffer.

Notes added in proof

*It is easy to see that both (9) and (10) hold if we make the following,

Positive Screening Assumption: $E(z/y)$ is an increasing function of y.

Under this assumption, it is obviously true that,

$E(z/y \geqslant y_o) > E(z/y_o) > E(z/y < y_o)$, so that from (11), (9) holds.

Also, under any condition on the range of y, the covariance of y and z is the same as that between y and $E(y/z)$, by the definitions. But the covariance between any random variable, over any range, and an increasing function of it is certainly positive, so that, from (12), (10) is certainly true.

**To see that an increase in y_o will increase $\bar{z}_g$, first differentiate the definition (7) logarithmically with respect to y_o.

73

$$\frac{1}{\bar{z}_g} \frac{d\bar{z}_g}{dy_o} = \frac{1}{Z_g} \frac{dZ_g}{dy_o} - \frac{1}{N_g} \frac{dN_g}{dy_o} = \frac{-y_o E(z/y_o)g(y_o)}{Z_g} + \frac{y_o g(y_o)}{N_g}$$

(from (3) and (6)) $= [y_o g(y_o)/Z_g][\bar{z}_g - [E(z/y_o)]$

which is positive if $\bar{z}_g > E(z/y_o)$; but since every graduate has a record at least equal to y_o, the last inequality follows from the Positive Screening Assumption.

Part III

The University as a Productive Unit

4. The University as a Multi-Product Firm

by Donald V.T. Bear

Introduction

In this chapter we adopt the position that there is some merit in viewing an institution of higher education in the context of the traditional theory of the firm, whereby the university is hypothesized to maximize net social product subject to a set of production relations. The hypothesis of profit maximization is, of course, patently false, but the purpose of this exercise is not the prediction of university behaviour. Rather, we seek to begin the development of a normative model within the context of which prescriptive proposals can be deduced for improving the allocation of resources within the higher education industry and, consequently, society's allocation of resources between higher education and competing uses.

Several other attributes characterize the analysis in this chapter; it is worthwhile to mention these traits at the outset, for many of them represent, in fact, disclaimers. In the first place, it should be noted immediately that this paper does not report on completed research; rather, it sketches a framework within which fruitful research on higher education might take place.

Second, a predominant theme here is that the output of a university is multi-dimensional and that many of the individual components of the output vector are subject to joint production or external effects. Thus, implicit in much of the argument that follows is that the university might not easily decompose into sub-firms or "divisions" for which decentralized optimization is appropriate. This is not to say that no fruitful decomposition is possible, but rather that only a careful examination of underlying production relations can delineate them. That might well be one of the tasks to be performed within the research framework proposed here. Third, we assume that the individual university is a price-taker in both product and factor markets — or more precisely, that it will act as though it were a perfect competitor in these markets in order to maximize net social product. Fourth, except in those instances where they are given explicit treatment, it is assumed throughout that the prices of outputs and inputs are reliable guides to social marginal opportunity costs; that is, the kinds of issues raised by second-best and externalities between higher education and the rest of the economy are supposed not to exist. Fifth, the educational firm is viewed here as maximizing social profits within a single period within which all factors are variable. This framework thus ignores the problems associated with the costs of capital formation in the form of buildings, laboratories and other such facilities as a function of the investment rate. Sixth, for simplicity we assume the absence of "corner" solutions to the university's maximization problem, so that first-order conditions will necessarily be in the form of equalities. Seventh, the analysis is nonstochastic; uncertainties regarding the values of outputs and inputs and stochastic elements in the production relations are ignored.

Finally, this chapter does not pretend to present a new model specifically tailored to higher education. Rather, we use an existing, well-worn model to organize some of the issues that must be resolved before meaningful policies can be designed for the higher education industry. The problems posed here for resolution are primarily empirical in nature. Some suggestions are made along these lines, but this paper does not contain the required empirical results themselves. In their stead there are some tentative hypotheses regarding functional forms and operational measures of inputs and outputs.

The remainder of this paper is organized as follows. In the next section we suggest how the university might be cast into the framework of the traditional theory of the multi-product firm. Then we discuss the measurement and valuation of educational output, followed by a discussion of production technology. We conclude with a summary.

Specification of the university's maximization problem

To facilitate our treatment of this subject, we assume that the outputs and inputs of a university are well-defined in advance — in the sense that an output under one set of circumstances cannot be an input under any other set of circumstances. This is of course not generally true[1]; but the assumption does lend concreteness to the following discussion, and it is trivial, technically speaking, to do away with it. We denote by y the non-negative vector with components giving the quantities of educational outputs – e.g., the number of BAs (MAs, PhDs) in each of the various disciplines per period and the quantity of research in each of those disciplines per period[2]. Let x denote the non-negative vector of input quantities – e.g. hours per period of faculty time in various disciplines, hours per period of non-faculty labour, hours of utilization per period of laboratory equipment, hours of students' time and ordinary materials inputs. We denote the prices of the outputs by the components of the vector p and the prices of the inputs by w. The dimension of y and p is $N \geqslant 2$, while x and w have dimension $M \geqslant 2$.

The value of net social product of the educational firm is, then,

$$V \equiv p' y - w' x \tag{1}$$

It is this that the university should maximize with respect to (y, x), subject to the production or technological relation linking outputs and inputs,

$$f(y, x) = 0. \tag{2}$$

For the present, (2) is simply a convenient summary device; it might or might not decompose into a number of independent sub-functions that delineate how subsets of the components of y are technologically related to subsets of the components of x.

The university maximizes net social product (1) subject to its production relation (2) only if the vectors of outputs and inputs that it chooses satisfy

---

[1] For example, a university that switches its emphasis from a primarily undergraduate to graduate institution has BAs as net outputs in the first circumstance and as net inputs in the second.

[2] We ignore for the moment the units in which research will be reckoned. This is a matter to which we return below.

$$f_1/f_n = p_1/p_n \qquad n = 2, 3, \ldots, N$$

$$f_{N+1}/f_{n+m} = w_1/w_m \quad m = 2, 3, \ldots, M$$

$$-p_1 \, (f_{n+1}/f_1) = w_1 \qquad\qquad\qquad (3)$$

$$f(\underset{\sim}{y}, \underset{\sim}{x}) = 0.$$

That is, when the university's net social product is at a maximum, the rate at which any pair of its outputs can be transformed into each other, given the optimal inputs, must equal the relative value of the two outputs; further, the rate at which any pair of inputs can be substituted for each other without altering outputs must equal the relative price of the two inputs; finally, the marginal value product of any input on any output must equal the price of the input.

These, then, are the rules that economists should urge upon universities. Unfortunately, it is trivial to deduce them relative to giving them operational content. The crucial problems consist of measurement of the outputs and inputs, the valuation of them, the specification of tractable production relations, and the delineation of the extent to which decentralized units within the university can be assigned their own decision rules. These are the difficult matters that concern us in the remainder of the chapter.

The measurement and valuation of university output — human capital, private returns

In broad terms, there are three general categories of output produced by the higher educational firm. They are:

(i) increments in human capital, having both a yield appropriable by the individual in whom the capital inheres and a stream of benefits to "society" as a whole;

(ii) entertainment services consumed currently and privately by students; and

(iii) increments in the stock of knowledge.

We discuss the measurement and valuation of each of these types of output in turn. This section covers the measurement of the output of human capital and the valuation of the stream of private returns that flow from it, while in the next section there is a discussion of its public returns.

Although the data are not available for supporting the assertion, casual observation suggests that the largest share of value-added by higher education is in the form of producing human capital. Unfortunately, there are not any obvious natural or physical units, such as bushels or tons, in which to measure the human capital that a university produces. In seeking some acceptable metric, it is important to recognize that there are many different kinds of human capital, just as physical capital is composed of numerous distinct items like lathes, materials handling equipment, structures, and so on. In the case of human capital, the most natural corresponding disaggregation for that produced by higher education appears to be by the conventional academic and professional disciplines – physics, philosophy, economics, medicine etc. Thus, we must speak of human capital in physics, human capital in philosophy, and so on. Such a disaggregation is tedious, to be sure, but it appears to be necessary if any operational normative rules are to be deduced for the university administrator to follow.

Given a willingness to deal with a fairly fine subdivision of human capital along disciplinary lines, there still remains the problem of measuring the amount of, say, human capital in physics that a university produces. A direct measure of the quantity of human capital appears impossible, however; the best that can be done seems to be the measurement of some indirect reflection of it. Human capital in physics is an unobservable attribute, and its measurement must therefore hinge on some other attribute that is (a) measurable and (b) attributable to human capital. In short, human capital is a "black box" and the measurement of the contents of the box can be only in terms of one or more "outputs" that flow from it.

Granted that this is the case, two closely related reflections of human capital that might serve as surrogate measures come to mind. The first is the test score that a student of physics achieves on a standardized comprehensive "achievement" examination; the second is the student's grade-point average in his BA (or MA or PhD) degree programme in physics. Both of these surrogates share the property that they need not be – and undoubtedly are not – proportional to the quantity of human capital in physics inhering in the student. More important, it is probably not even true that equal differences in the surrogate reflect equal differences in the underlying quantities of human capital. For example, it is highly unlikely that as much more human capital will inhere in a student having a test score of 85 percent than one with a 75 percent score, as a student with a 95 percent score relative to the 85 percent student. In fact, these interval differences can be insured by altering the structure of the examination producing the scores. Similar remarks hold in the case of the degree-cum-grade-point measure of human capital in physics. All we can really determine with these reflections of human capital is an ordering of the underlying quantities; in short, they are ordinal measures of the "amount" of human capital residing in the black box.

In spite of this shortcoming, we propose the degree with an associated grade-point average as the appropriate quantity measure of the outputs of human capital produced by the university. We select it in preference to the approach through a comprehensive examination only on the grounds that the compilation of grade-point averages is a more routine piece of data collection than the setting of comprehensive examinations. But, regardless of which measure is used, their ordinal character must be corrected for. One means for achieving this is further disaggregation, treating each interval in the grade-point average as a distinct type of human capital[3]. The length of the intervals can be selected according to some sort of homogeneity criterion[4]; the intervals need not be of equal length.

If this suggestion is accepted, it means that the output vector $\underset{\sim}{y}$ consists of a hierarchy of partitions into subvectors. There is, first, the human capital subvector, as distinguished from the subvectors defined by (ii) and (iii) above. The human capital subvector, in turn, can be partitioned into subvectors associated with the various academic and professional disciplines. Next, each of these is subdivided into vectors corresponding to the degree programmes – PhD, MA, etc. And finally, each of these subvectors has components with

---

[3] For purposes of convenience only, we no longer distinguish between the "true" quantity of human capital and its reflected size in the surrogate measure. Hereafter, we talk of them as though they were the same thing.

[4] For example, a fixed number of intervals might be selected so as to equalize the variances in the prices of the types of human capital defined by the intervals.

the number of students achieving the degree with a grade-point average falling within the interval identified by the component. Thus, in this context, the normative rules emerging from the first equation in (3) above have the form: with the optimal set of inputs, produce the quantities of history BAs with grade-point averages in the interval 2.5 − 2.8 and physic PhDs in the grade-point interval 3.2 − 3.7 such that the rate at which one can be transformed into the other is equal to the relative price of the two products.[5]

Such a prescription, in order to be operationally complete, must identify the relevant relative price, which raises the broad issue of assigning values to the human capital components of the the vector $\underset{\sim}{p}$. It seems only natural to set these prices equal to the present value of the stream of returns flowing from the various types of human capital. Unfortunately, there are several ambiguities associated with this kind of calculation. In the first place, some of the returns are not explicitly traded on markets, and thus an imputation of such non-pecuniary returns is required. Moreover, some of the returns are alleged to redound to the public at large rather than to the "owner" of the human capital, which makes it impossible to infer a value for such returns from the owner's behaviour. Finally, it is not entirely clear which rate(s) of discount should be used to calculate the present values of the various kinds of returns, particularly in view of the differential uncertainties associated with them. We confine ourselves here to the problems associated with the private returns; the public returns to human capital are the subject of the next section.

The private returns to human capital acquired through higher education have both pecuniary and non-pecuniary components. The precuniary component consists of the additional wage and salary income that the owner of the capital earns over his lifetime as compared with what he would have earned had he not acquired the higher educational human capital. An enhanced ability to enjoy leisure − e.g., to read and understand a wider variety of books, or to

---

[5] To spare the reader the further tedium of still another level of disaggregation, we only record here the possibility that, since degree programmes typically require more than one year of a student's input and since many students do not finish such multi-year programmes, we might wish to make the basic unit of output the number of years of a given degree programme completed with a given range of grade-point averages.

appreciate more fully various cultural activities — constitute the non-pecuniary portion of the stream of private benefits. Given a willingness to undertake the necessary collection of data, values can be assigned to these benefits.

In essence, each university should undertake to construct from cross-section life-time labour income profiles of its graduates, one for each discipline, by degree and by grade-point average. Simultaneously, the same income profiles for non-students with characteristics (e.g., IQ, secondary school preparation, demographic attributes) similar to those students in the particular degree programme should be compiled for the post-university years. Discounting the differences in these two profiles from the present by some measure of the cost of capital in the private sector of the economy would then constitute a price for the private pecuniary returns flowing from the human capital produced by the university.

This price is not entirely adequate for the purpose at hand, for to the extent that market prices in the future will alter the income streams of the various types of human capital, the price so constructed will be out of date as soon as it is calculated. Nevertheless, until adequate models are developed for making long-term forecasts of prices for the services of diverse kinds of human capital, probably the best that can be done is to recalculate the profiles from cross-section data on a periodic basis and to use their discounted differences as the price to be attached to these pecuniary returns.

There is no reason why an individual university should confine itself to these calculations regarding its own students. Given the task of maximizing its net social product, it might well be the case that a Harvard or Yale should become a San Diego State or a Stanford, or vice versa, if it is determined to be socially optimal to do so. This, of course, would involve changes in the bundle of inputs (e.g., enrollees of different quality, changes in the size and quality of faculty), so the decision cannot be based on the comparative price calculations alone. However, it is nevertheless true that a knowledge of the prices of other universities' human capital is an essential ingredient to the decision by a single university to upgrade or downgrade the quality of the human capital it produces in one or all of the disciplines.

The income profiles that are compiled for the valuation of the private pecuniary returns can also be used for the construction of the price to be attached to the non-pecuniary benefits that accrue in the

84

post-university years to the proprietor of the human capital acquired in higher education. For if we assume that the individual optimally allocates his time between work and leisure, an hour of the latter can be valued at the price paid for the former. Because the university-acquired human capital alters both the work and leisure opportunities of the owner, there is no reason to expect that the work-leisure composition of the owner's time will be the same as for a comparable non-student − or, for that matter, that the composition will be the same for an MD with a 2.5 average as for a physics PhD with a 3.5 grade-point average. However, it is unnecessary to collect data on this composition, since a knowledge of the hourly rate of return to work, multiplied by the number of hours in a year, will give the pecuniary-cum-non-pecuniary income of both the student and non-student[6].

This approach to the measurement of the non-pecuniary component of the returns from human capital depends, of course, on the ability of the individual to alter the work-leisure composition of his time in the post-university years. More important, it requires that there be no differential non-pecuniary component to the work experience. For otherwise the types of university-acquired human capital with relatively high work-related non-pecuniary benefits will be undervalued in *both* the work and leisure components.

This raises the broader issue of rationalizing any difference in the private present value of two types of university-produced human capital as measured in the manner suggested above. To take a specific example, consider two students that are equal in every respect (i.e., are subject to identical opportunity sets). Suppose one obtains a BA

---

[6] Both Arrow and Brainard have pointed out that this approach is deficient in that it fails to capture gains in leisure-related utility attributable to the acquisition of human capital. For consider the case in which additional human capital adds nothing to pecuniary opportunities and improves only the "quality" of leisure. The budget constraint in the goods-leisure plane is then unchanged, and hence the valuation method suggested above yields the same pecuniary-cum-non-pecuniary income estimate before and after the acquisition of the human capital. Arrow suggested that inclusion of human capital as a shift parameter in the utility function would − conceptually, at least − allow for the improvement in the quality of leisure; but this approach does not appear to lend itself to empirical valuation. It seems, therefore, that to salvage the argument in the text, it is necessary to assume that human capital improves earning opportunities and the value of leisure in the same proportion.

in history with a specified grade-point average, while the other earns a BA in physics with its associated GPA. In all likelihood, the values calculated by discounting future earnings for these two types of human capital by the method proposed above will differ. How can this difference be explained in the presence of optimizing behaviour and equality of rates of return on all forms of human capital?

That is, given that the two students' opportunity sets are identical, we ought to attach the same values to the two sets. Yet the assignment of different values to the chosen forms of human capital accumulated by them appears to cause differences in the valuations placed on those two sets. Some of the explanations listed below are consistent with the proposed valuation method; others are not.

(a) The assumption that the two opportunity sets are identical might, in fact, be false. The two students might have different amounts of the special skills particularly suited to history and physics.

(b) The students might not optimize, contrary to assumption. This is not a comfortable "out" at all, especially in view of the optimization assumed above for the valuation of leisure.

(c) Information regarding the future income streams, both pecuniary and non-pecuniary, might be imperfect. This is undoubtedly likely to be the case, but in a certain sense it is simply another facet of the possible falsity of the assumption that the opportunity sets are identical.

(d) The two students' preferences with respect to the mix of pecuniary and non-pecuniary rewards of post-university work experience might differ. This has already been mentioned, and it constitutes a deficiency of the suggested valuation method.

(e) In the presence of imperfect capital markets, whereby borrowing against future income earned by the services of human capital is impossible, differences in the students' preferences between near-term and long-term earnings, taken in conjunction with different time-shapes of the income streams from the two types of human capital, might result in the distinct choices.

(f) If the students' preferences with respect to current versus future goods differ, and if one of the two degree programmes during the university years has a higher consumption component (either in the form of greater entertainment services or less effort required for the degree programme), their career choices might differ.

86

(g) The variance in one set of future benefits might differ from that for the returns from the other degree, and thus mean rates of return on the two kinds of human capital differ. This suggests that different discount rates should be used in the calculation of present values for the two degrees, and in this respect the suggested valuation method is deficient.

All of the remarks just given apply to the explanation of the portfolio choices of a student acquiring human capital through a university programme and an individual who chooses not to attend college. If the latter chooses, say, to become an automobile mechanic because he likes to tinker with engines, the foregoing valuation scheme undervalues the present value of his lifetime allocation.

The upshot of this discussion is that the proposed method of pricing the private return to human capital acquired in a university requires at least one of the following assumptions: students and non-students do not optimize in making career choices; potential students choosing different lifetime allocations (in the sense of choosing careers) do not face identical opportunity sets; potential students' information regarding the future is highly imperfect; or capital markets are imperfect. In addition to one of these, we must also assume proportionate equality of non-pecuniary returns in all types of work experience and no substantial differential variances in the alternative income profiles.

In spite of the restrictive nature of these assumptions, it nevertheless appears reasonable to calculate the present values of the pecuniary and non-pecuniary benefits of the various types of university-related human capital as proposed above. Such a list would at least provide insight into the magnitudes of the work-related non-pecuniary benefits that would be required to justify the conclusion that all types of human capital produced by the higher educational firm have the same value. Alternatively, it would delineate the differences in opportunity sets enjoyed by potential students. And if we really believe in the equality of work-related non-pecuniary benefits, such a list would give the university administrator the appropriate set of prices at which to value a major component of his firm's output. It is on this basis that we propose to proceed.

The measurement and valuation of university output — human capital, public returns

Among university educators it is virtually axiomatic that the human capital acquired by college students yields a flow of services that is enjoyed by the entire society or by large subsets therein. It is alleged, for example, that college-educated citizens are "better" citizens than those who are not so educated. Presumably, they make "better" decisions when they cast their votes in public elections, or they contribute to "better" causes and candidates for public office, or they lead to a more stable society. Thus, so the story goes, some additional value should be placed on the human capital acquired in universities to reflect the public benefits that it confers to society at large.

The position adopted here is that such an argument is, at best, non-operational and, at worst, aristocratic elitism. It is interesting to note that this kind of argument is made almost exclusively by university-educated advocates. The argument, in an extreme form, presumes that some choices are better than others and that only the college graduates can know which those are. If this is the case, then why vote on the issues at all! Or, as a compromise, limit the electorate to those with college degrees. Or, if McGovern represented a "better" cause and was a "better" candidate than Wallace, why allow contributions to and votes for the Wallace campaign? On the other hand if one views elections as allowing the populace to express its preferences between efficient alternatives, there is no reason to believe that the preferences of degree-holders are to be preferred to those of the rest of the electorate. Finally, it is not clear what is meant by a "stable" society; and, however the term is defined, it is not obvious that such a society is "good" or "better" than an unstable one.

The argument for a public goods type of component to university-acquired human capital seems to be a natural extension of a similar line of reasoning used to justify education generally. But, it is argued here that there is, in fact, a definite difference between the public goods generated by primary and secondary education, on the one hand, and higher education, on the other. The principal public benefit of the former is that it enhances the ease of communication in society — that the ability to read, write and perform elementary arithmetic calculations, taken together with the inculcation of a common cultural heritage, permits any member of society to communicate with others and that such ease of communication is a benefit that cannot be withheld from some subsets of society and granted to others. But once these abilities are reached — and surely that occurs prior to higher education — it is questionable that the ease of communication is enhanced by further education. For this reason there appears to be no inconsistency between the view that lower education does produce a public good, while the production of human capital by higher education does not result in a comparable public benefit.[7, 8]

But even if this view is incorrect and there is a public-good dimension to the human capital produced by universities, there appears to be no operational definition of it. How would the benefits be measured quantitatively? Such measurement would require the quantification of the "goodness" of voters' decisions, the extent to which it is "better" to have supported McGovern over Wallace, etc. And something like a production function linking the quantities of human capital inputs with the output of "good" decisions would also be required to determine the productivities of the various types of human capital. An alternative would be to hold elections on various tax-supported budget levels for instruction (as distinct from research) in higher educational institutions, and to let the chosen instructional subsidy measure the overall public benefit.[9] But then we might ask — somewhat rhetorically, to be sure — whether the members of society without college degrees ought to be allowed to participate in that election.

---

[7] This does not argue that no output of higher education has the characteristics of a public good — research output is an example. But we do claim that the human capital accumulated by university students has no public dimension.

[8] Arrow and Attiyeh have noted that there is a genuine indirect externality associated with higher education deriving from the external benefits of lower education: the children of college-educated parents are less costly to educate through elementary and high school. If this is the case, this cost reduction could be used in the calculation of the difference between the social and private value of attending a university.

[9] This, presumably, is the manner in which we value the production of national security.

Finally, it should be noted that the establishment of the existence of a public dimension to the services of university-acquired human capital is insufficient grounds for recommending a particular subsidy level for instruction (in our context, a particular additional value to be placed on each type of degree). To establish qualitatively the presence of an externality does nothing more than say the subsidy should be somewhere in the open interval $0, \infty$). As we noted earlier, the whole notion of the benefit of higher education-related human capital is perilously close to being non-operational. For these reasons, we propose that no value be assigned to the various kinds of human capital produced by a university over and above the present values of their private returns.

The measurement and valuation of university output — entertainment services

In the process of acquiring human capital, a university student presumably enjoys a current benefit in the form of the entertainment provided by his curriculum and other facets of college life; such consumption output should be included in the university's output vector $\underset{\sim}{y}$.[10] The aggregate value of this portion of higher educational output is probably not large in relation to the whole, although the apparent absence of empirical confirmation makes this tentative assertion speculative at best. Those who share this impressionistic belief will probably not quarrel with the short, suggestive treatment that we give the problem here.

There is, first, the question of the units in which we should measure the quantities of entertainment services. But this will be dictated, it seems, by whatever unit we are able to value. For the possibilities for valuation of the consumption component are so difficult to isolate that we will have to end up by letting the available

---

[10] Alternatively, if an annual value can be placed on these services on a *per capita* basis, then this value can be subtracted from the opportunity value of the student's time, viewed as an input, to obtain a net factor price. Or, if we relate the consumption value to the various types of degrees, these values can simply be added to the values of the human capital of the degrees, in which case no additional dimensions of $\underset{\sim}{y}$ are dictated.

value per unit determine the units. Thus, our search begins by looking for a means by which to value the service.

Basically, what we seek is a comparable kind of educational entertainment that has little or no human capital component. Unfortunately, anything that is "educational" almost always has a capital dimension to it, frequently in the form of non-pecuniary services that it yields in the future. And thus, all we can hope to do is to pick a form of "education" in which the human capital component is minimal and use its value as an upper bound for the value of education's entertainment services. A number of candidates, apparently with this characteristic, merit discussion.

It has been suggested that an old-style women's college might serve as a bench-mark in this regard.[11] The caricature of such institutions — particularly those in the northeastern US — is that the only career for which the students are prepared is marriage. Thus, so the argument goes, the tuition fees paid for attendance in such a programme might serve as the price of consumption services afforded by undergraduate programmes generally. Even if it is true that the students pursuing such programmes have no intention of pursuing a career with pecuniary returns, it is still likely that they acquire substantial human capital yielding non-pecuniary returns beyond graduation. To this extent, tuition at these colleges is an overly generous price to place on the entertainment services of higher education. However, if we choose to categorize university output along slightly different lines than proposed above — into, say, pecuniary output, non-pecuniary output (except research), and research — then tuition in such institutions might well measure the present value of present and future non-pecuniary services rendered by the university programme. But if this approach is adopted, it still seems unlikely that there exist colleges with the essential characteristic — i.e., the value of human capital with pecuniary potential is nil to the enrollees — especially in view of the widespread influence of Women's Lib.

A second candidate for gaining insight into this valuation problem is suggested by educational TV, for some of the programmes have both an academic flavour and an entertainment dimension. More-

---

[11] This suggestion appeared in a set of preliminary, informal notes by G.C. Archibald. It is not clear that the following discussion does justice to his position.

over, the typical TV "course" does not carry credit toward a degree, indicating some presumption that the viewer's primary purpose in watching it is not to acquire human capital. To the extent that these assertions are valid, we could then take the viewer's opportunity cost of following the course as its entertainment value. This would involve sampling viewers to determine their hourly wage and the total number of hours devoted to the course. Multiplying these two items and averaging over the sample would yield an estimate of the per-student entertainment value of a comparable block of material covered in a university programme. If a related course in a higher educational institution covered more (or less) material, then the ratio of the "quantities" of material covered in the two courses (university to educational TV) would serve as the factor by which to adjust the value of the TV course per student to apply to the university course. This approach would dictate that the number of students taking a course be the unit in which entertainment services are measured; and to the extent that different courses are assigned different per student and/or have different enrollment values, this scheme would include a component in the vector y for each course.[12]

Although this approach appears to deserve further consideration, certain questions need to be raised. Do any of the courses on educational TV really have the same academic flavour as corresponding university courses? Some probably do — a test would be the similarity of textbooks — but it is likely that there are many university courses having no counterpart in the offerings of educational TV. Is it clear that the human capital element is absent in the viewer's decision to follow a TV course? As far as pecuniary returns are concerned, we are probably safe; but there very well might be an element of expected future non-pecuniary returns — e.g., a course in "music appreciation", by its very title, conveys the impression of acquiring human capital for the improvement of future leisure. Finally, is it clear that the price paid by watchers of educational TV courses in terms of their opportunity costs is relevant to the full-time student? In the first place, to the extent that the relative value (in

---

[12] Alternatively, the curriculum of the typical degree recipient (in each of the fields specified by the human capital components of y) could be calculated, with an entertainment value attached to the typical curriculum. This could be added to the value of the human capital of the degree, thereby adding no components to y.

consumption) of academic courses declines with the number of courses, the suggested scheme would over-value entertainment services in universities – on the grounds that viewers of educational TV follow only one or two courses at a time. Second, it is not entirely clear that the preferences of the generally older TV audience are the same as of the university population. The answer to these questions will determine the suitability of valuing the current entertainment services of university programmes through the medium of educational TV.

Another possibility for valuation of this component of educational output is offered by attendance at university extension courses and adult education classes. These share most, if not all, of the characteristics of educational TV, and the construction of values for courses would follow the same lines. To the extent that fees are charged for these courses, however, they would have to be added to the cost of foregone earnings or leisure to obtain the total value of the course per student. To the extent that the shortcomings of the valuation method through educational TV are acceptable, data based on extension and adult education courses are equally acceptable. One advantage of the latter, however, is that the data would be easier to compile.

A final approach to this valuation of entertainment services might well be achieved by calculating the opportunity cost paid by elderly persons who "go back" to college to obtain degrees. The advantage of calculating the price of a degree programme (or course) to the elderly is that their time horizon is, presumably, short, and thus we would be assured that the human capital aspect of university attendance would be held to a minimum. An offsetting feature of this method, however, is the possibility that the preferences of the elderly might well be a poor surrogate for the preferences of the typical university student. In particular, the rates of substitution in consumption between the university's entertainment services and all other goods might differ for the two generations – for example, it is difficult to suppose that a student in his 60s would value the delights of dormitory life and the social functions that attend universities in quite the same way as a student 20 years old.[13] Nevertheless, the

---

[13] The absence of social aspects from educational TV and, to a lesser extent, from extension and adult courses suggests that valuation methods based on them will undervalue entertainment services even more in this regard than the present method.

short time horizon appears to be a useful feature of this scheme.

Each of the methods proposed here for the valuation of the current consumption component of university output have certain features that make them attractive; but each has at least one serious drawback. It is unfortunate that there seems to be no obvious way to extract the attractive features of each in the construction of some sort of composite measure. Therefore, it appears that the value of a university's entertainment services will be one of the shaky aspects of the research design in this paper. But it still seems better to include them with an estimated value, however crude, than to ignore such services altogether.

The measurement and valuation of university output — research

Perhaps the most nebulous subset of outputs produced by the educational firm is that consisting of the additions to the stock of knowledge. This is especially unfortunate since most of us intuitively believe that the value added by the university in the form of research (especially our own?) is of considerable magnitude. Yet the absence of conventional units in which to measure research and of conventional market or non-market prices by which to value it speaks to the intuitive, non-operational character of that belief. In this section we propose a crude remedy for the current vague state of affairs which research, viewed as an output, occupies.

There are at least two aspects of research that need to be distinguished at the outset. The first is the discovery or creation of "new" knowledge by one person (or perhaps a few persons). The second is the dissemination of that knowledge to society. Assuming, for the moment, that we could measure knowledge, it would be possible to record output at either the discovery stage or the dissemination stage. But the two measures would not necessarily agree, for it is likely that much knowledge is discovered, yet never disseminated. On the grounds that the major benefits of the knowledge are realized only when it relatively widely shared, we opt for measuring research output — conceptually, at least — at the dissemination stage. Thus, research will be, for us, the discovery *and* dissemination of new knowledge.[14]

94

But this only highlights the need to devise a metric that would record quantities of disseminated new knowledge; yet no natural unit or "bit" of knowledge is readily at hand. If it were, we could form the product of the number of "bits" of knowledge and number of people acquiring it, obtaining thereby a measure of the quantity of disseminated knowledge. A highly imperfect approximation to this sort of metric that we propose here is the following: let the published page (or alternatively 1,000 words of published material) be the unit by which the quantity of disseminated knowledge is measured. Several remarks — some supportive, but mostly critical — are in order at this point.

First, we require that the new knowledge be published only because it is a means by which to include the requirement that the knowledge be disseminated. Unfortunately, the publication of knowledge is neither a necessary nor sufficient condition for its dissemination; many published papers are read or cited far less frequently than some "unpublished" papers. This raises the ambiguity of the notion of publication as a surrogate for dissemination. Is a departmental "discussion paper" considered to be a published piece of research? An informal departmental seminar might entail the dissemination of new knowledge, yet the paper might never be published. And what about papers delivered at meetings or conferences that do not reach the publication stage? Finally, is classified research disseminated? Clearly, some exceedingly arbitrary rules-of-thumb would have to be adopted in order to give answers to these questions and to make the concept of published research operational.

Second, it is quite clear that some prior disaggregation of knowledge into its various types is required in order to reduce the crudity of the proposed metric. As a starter, we would want to distinguish published pages by the academic disciplines to which they are directed — i.e., the number of published pages in physics would be a different component of the output vector $\underset{\sim}{y}$ than the number of published pages in history — on the grounds that they are different

---

[14] Viewed in this manner, research is not unlike the accumulation of human capital by students in a university, only the "students" in this case are typically professionals in the particular discipline; however, this is not a line of thought that we pursue here.

goods. It would be possible to disaggregate within each discipline, as well, according to special fields in much the same fashion as the American Economic Association. If, further, the need to distinguish research of differing quality is necessary, this could be done by additional subdivision of fields in a given discipline according to the medium in which the published page appeared — e.g., by the journal in which it is published. This level of disaggregation could presumably capture both the quality of the new knowledge (some journals have higher standards than others) and the extent of its dissemination (different journals have different circulations).

But surely the notion that the quantity of research can be calculated simply by the counting of published pages must be the hardest of all to accept. Even after controlling for discipline, special field and journal, it remains difficult to accept that, by this measure, one paper twice as long as another represents twice as much disseminated research. The shorter paper might be of much higher quality and read by many more people, and it might have a much greater eventual impact on society, which is, in some sense, the ultimate measure of the quantity of research. Nevertheless, it appears that some sort of counting procedure like this is required if any headway is to be made in the measurement of research. And besides, there is a very strong element of page-counting in the decision-making of appointments committees, especially when faculty peers from other disciplines constitute a majority.[15] This does not justify the procedure, but it does speak to the absence of operational alternatives.

Assuming the acceptability of this measure of the quantity of research, we are still faced with the need to set a price on each page. Although certain journals and certain publishers of research monographs do pay authors according to the number of pages, such a value per page is unacceptable for measuring the benefits society receives from the dissemination of the knowledge the pages contain. In the first place, it is difficult to imagine that the publishers that engage in this sort of remuneration do so on the basis of consideration of society's benefits. Second, it is even more difficult to accept the notion that, because the *Bell Journal* pays its authors while *Econometrica* does not, the research disseminated through the *Bell Journal*

---

[15] Presumably this is an affliction not only of the University of California, San Diego.

has positive value per page while that appearing in *Econometrica* does not. Clearly, these price mechanisms do not reflect the societal benefits of research.

But certain institutions do pay for research and, more importantly, they do so with some notion of public well-being in mind. We refer here to organizations like the NSF, NASA, NIH and various private foundations, the very existence of which is testimony to the public goods character of disseminated research, the absence of markets based on private property and private decision-making for the allocation of resources to it, and the possibility of making judgments – implicitly at least – regarding the benefits which society receives from it. These considerations suggest that the prices they pay for research in various disciplines and fields therein might be useful for constructing prices per page of all such disseminated knowledge. Specifically, we propose that, however pages of research are disaggregated into disciplines, fields, etc., the total dollar value of grants of such institutions to a particular type of research to be performed in universities in a given year, divided by the number of pages published under such grants, serve as the price per page for all research of that type.

There are several deficiencies associated with this pricing scheme. In the first place, the granting agencies do not specify the number of pages to be published under the grants; the price per page results only *ex post* and with considerable uncertainty attached to it. Second, it might be argued that grants are given on average to the better researchers in the field, so that the resulting price per page overstates the value of all research in that field. Finally, given the form of the budgets that accompany the research proposals, it might be argued that the value of the research is being imputed by the cost of the inputs and not by the societal benefits that emerge from it. However, since the granting institutions face the problem of allocating fixed budgets, the relative benefits of competing proposals must enter their decisions if they are made in a reasonable manner at all. Moreover, the overhead component of these budgets certainly has the strong suggestion of a subsidy element.

If the foregoing measurement and valuation schemes are adopted, the normative rules implied by the analysis in the second section to be followed by the university administrator with respect to research would be: produce the numbers of published pages of physics research and history research such that the rate at which one can be transformed into the other, given the optimal set of inputs, is equal to the relative price per page that research-subsidizing institutions have paid for such pages in the recent past. Admittedly, both the quantities and prices entering this statement are only rough approximations' to the true variables we would like to see there; yet, if nothing else, the approximations to those variables move us in the direction of making the normative rules operational with regard to research.

Inputs and the specification of educational technology

To complete this survey of the requirements for an operational treatment of the university as a social profit-maximizing firm, we must complement the foregoing discussion of the measurement and valuation of outputs with an enumeration of the university's inputs and associated implicit factor prices and a set of remarks on the production relationships that transform those inputs into outputs. This section treats the input-related issues first; a general discussion of some of the issues that confront the construction of possible technologies follows. The following cursory treatment represents a mere introduction to them.

Regarding inputs, the two most important in aggregate are undoubtedly student time and faculty time, although in certain experimental disciplines the rental cost of capital equipment might well exceed either of these. In the case of student time it would be necessary to collect data indicating how much time students with a particular IQ range and secondary preparation in various programmes devote to their education, for the quantity of this input presumably varies with the student's IQ, preparation, discipline and the level of the degree. The input price or wage rate to be attached to this time should be the market wage rate (for full-time employment) that the student foregoes. This, of course, would vary with the amount and type of human capital that the student has already acquired in higher education. Thus, for example, a third-year student in physics would have a higher implicit wage rate associated with each hour of his time that a freshman history major. Such differentiation of various kinds of student time means that the partition of the input vector x

relating to student time would have several components, one for each year of study with a given grade-point average in each discipline or profession. And, clearly, the factor price vector w would be similarly partitioned in the student-time components. The data for these components of w would already be available from the calculation of output values (the private returns to human capital) proposed above, where the hourly wage rates of a student completing a certain stage of a particular degree programme with a particular GPA was the principal ingredient. Thus, as far as the students' input is concerned, the only new empirical requirement is the survey indicating the quantity of time students devote to acquiring human capital.

The measurement and valuation of total faculty time is moderately straightforward. After a disaggregation of faculty by disciplines, the amount of time that faculty personnel in each discipline devote to university duties, including summer activities, could be obtained by a survey or sample. A very detailed survey of this type was recently completed by the University of California, for example. The price per unit of such time would be determined by dividing the appropriate salary by the total number of hours worked.

A couple of knotty issues do arise here, however. In the first place, should the total number of input hours be divided by a nine-month salary or the eleven- or twelve-month equivalent? For consider two faculty members of equal qualifications in the same discipline. Assume that both work the same number of hours during a year, but that one receives a summer salary from an outside agency supporting his research, while the other does not. Should we use the nine- or eleven-month salary to value an hour of the two individuals, who have equal qualifications (their hours are perfect substitutes) by assumption? We opt here for using the lower figure − on the very casual empirical grounds that most faculty would pursue research endeavours during the summer whether or not they received financial support. True, summer salaries might influence the direction of those endeavours, but it is asserted here that the total effort is relatively insensitive to summer "bonuses". This assertion is subject to empirical test, of course; and should it be wrong − i.e., should summer research support call forth more hours of work − then a formulation involving overtime pay would be required. But assuming it is correct, it is not in conflict with the requirement that faculty be paid for their normal nine months of work, for the mix of activities when school is in session is quite different than during the summer. However, this position – i.e., using the nine-month salary – is not a wholly comfortable one, for it involves viewing the summer salary as an accident that is incidental to the supply of faculty labour, and no economist should be at ease when information contained in a price is discarded. Fortunately, the assertion is testable and can be corrected if found to be in conflict with reality.[16]

A second issue involved in the pricing of faculty time by the use of academic salaries is the explication of salary differentials. Perhaps more than in any other occupation academic salaries reflect cumulative past accomplishments more than current contributions to output, and it is not entirely justifiable to assert implicitly (by the use of current salaries) that the current social opportunity cost of a faculty member's time is directly related to his cumulative accomplishments. True, there is an element of human capital accumulation through "on-the-job training", but we are all aware of the counteraction to this that takes place through the obsolescence of that same intellectual capital as a discipline advances through the acquisition of new techniques and empirical laws. Yet, having admitted all of this, we are probably forced to use current salary information anyhow in the construction of the social cost of faculty labour.

Finally, we must address the problem of the allocation of faculty time, given the total, over the various activities in which the faculty member engages – e.g., teaching, research, and general university or departmental "chores". The data for this allocation, hopefully, would be contained in the survey proposed earlier.[17] The categories that should be used, however, depend critically on the specification

---

[16] An alternative hypothesis leading to the use of both the nine- and eleven-month salaries would be to assert that, although the *total* summer effort is uninfluenced by the summer salary, its distribution over alternative research projects is affected. The differential can then be viewed as compensation for the loss in non-pecuniary benefits that the researcher suffers as a result of working on a less preferred topic.

[17] Such data were gathered in the University of California survey mentioned earlier. In fact, a very detailed list of activities was enumerated, including in- and out-of-class time for lower division, upper division and graduate teaching, general advising of students, dissertation guidance, research, general departmental duties and university-wide responsibilities.

of the underlying production function(s). For example, if teaching and research outputs are truly joint products — as is frequently alleged — then there is nothing to be gained by disaggregating faculty time into the portions devoted to each. Yet, the initial testing of such joint-output hypotheses will nevertheless require information on the allocation of time. It is to these questions of production technology that we now turn.

There are a few preliminary issues regarding production that deserve brief mention. In the first place, given the classification of outputs and inputs delineated above, we must be sure that the production relations have the same arguments. That is, the number of history BAs with GPAs in a given range, for example, must be one of the dimensions (one of the outputs) of the production surface. This is an obvious point, but it emphasizes the fact that choice and degree of disaggregation of outputs and inputs does place constraints on the production relations by specifying which variables must appear in them.[18]

A second preliminary relates to the problem of specifying the unit of time to be used in the analysis. We casually assumed in the introduction a single-period framework so that differences between desired and actual capital stocks could be ignored. This requires, in turn, some investigation of speeds of adjustment in order that the selection of the time unit will approximately justify that assumption. But another consideration must enter this selection; it arises from the fact that a degree programme might well be longer than the capital adjustment period and that the market value of the last year to the student of a programme typically exceeds the value of prior years, while the social marginal costs of those years are more or less the same (or at least not as different as the social values). Thus, if a one-year period were selected, profit maximization would undoubtedly imply the production of a very large number of degree recipients and very few, if any, first, second and third-year students. One means of correcting for this would be to inflate the prices associated

---

[18] The converse is also true; the choice of arguments of the production surface specifies the arguments of the criterion function. As a matter of practical research strategy, neither will precede the other and the choice of outputs and inputs will be influenced both by the extent to which prices can be attached to them and by their appeal as arguments in a production function.

with the pre-degree years to reflect the probability that a student completing each of them will go on to reap the "rent" associated with completion of the last year. An alternative would be to make the time unit of the analysis as long as the longest degree programme so that the intermediate products (completion of pre-degree years) would be netted out, except for those students failing to finish.

A third obvious point hinges on the decomposability of the production relation, equation (2) above. If it can be resolved into N separate production functions, one for each of the N separate outputs, then the general university maximization problem contained in (1) and (2) decomposes into the form;

For $n = 1, 2, \ldots, N$, maximize (with respect to $y_n, x_1{}^n, x_2{}^n, \ldots, x_M{}^n$)

$$V_n \equiv p_n y_n - \sum_m^M w_m \, x_m{}^n, \tag{1'}$$

Subject to

$$y_n = f^n(x_1{}^n, x_2{}^n, \ldots, x_M{}^n) \tag{2'}$$

In this formulation, $x_m{}^n$ is the quantity of the mth input allocated to the nth activity, so that, with the definition that $x_m = \sum_n x_m{}^n$, (1') and (2') are equivalent to (1) and (2) under the decomposition of the production relation. This highly tractable, but unrealistic formulation results in treating the university as N separate firms or "divisions", each with its own maximization problem, thereby permitting complete decentralization of decision-making. This is the case in which the university is not a multi-product firm in any genuine sense.

However, there is a multitude of reasons for expecting that (2) does not decompose into (2'). Given the rather fine disaggregation of degree types within an individual discipline, it is totally unrealistic to expect that the output, of, say, history BAs with a GPA of 2.4 − 3.0 would be uninfluenced by the resources devoted to the production of history BAs with a GPA of 3.0 − 3.5, for both are taught in the same classes. (The same sort of argument could be made for MAs and PhDs in the same discipline, for both types of candidates share certain courses; but the case is not as strong here as for the same degree with different GPAs, for PhDs require courses and advisory and capital inputs in addition to those required by MAs). Thus, at a mini-

102

mum, these considerations regarding the production of human capital within a single discipline argue for aggregating certain production activities into "teaching institutes" which comprise the usual instructional duties of conventional departments.

At this level of aggregation, by ignoring other interdependent aspects we might conceptualize the production relations underlying the production of BAs in a given discipline by letting the output of each GPA interval within the BA type be a function of all the inputs devoted to the entire BA programme. Let there be J GPA intervals (defined to include dropouts) in the degree programme under consideration, so that y_{n_j} is the number of BAs in the jth GPA interval in the discipline, while $\sum_{j}^{J}=1 \; x_m^{n_j}$ is the total quantity of the mth input allocated to that entire degree programme. Then we could write

$$y_{n_j} = f^n j \left(\sum_j x_1^{n_j}, \sum_j x_2^{n_j}, \dots, \sum_j x_M^{n_j} \right) \tag{2a}$$

for $j = 1, 2, \dots, J$. We still have individual production functions as in (2'), but the inputs are joint here, unlike (2'). A further condition on the f^n_j would be required in (2a) — namely, the number of BAs (inclusive of dropouts) produced would have to be equal to the number of students entering the programme. That is, where $x_{m_i}^{n_j}$ is the number of entering students with the ith set of characteristics (IQ, preparation, etc.) receiving BAs in the jth GPA interval, the relations in (2a) must satisfy

$$\sum_{j=1}^{J} y_{n_j} \equiv \sum_{i=1}^{J} \sum_{j=1}^{J} x_{m_i}^{n_j}{}^{19}$$

The production functions in (2a) exemplify the "mutton-wool" phenomenon (Frisch, 1965, pp. 270–271), whereby no change in output proportions is possible for a given vector of inputs. However,

---

19 It is also true, of course, that y_{n_j} must be equal to $\sum_i x_{m_i}^{n_j}$ for each j. But, given the form of the arguments of the f^n_j, this fact is of little help — except to imply the identity in the text which, when taken together, the set of f^n_j must satisfy.

changes in the input vector can lead to changes in output proportions. If the f^{nj} are assumed to be homogeneous of the same degree, then a knowledge of factor proportions implies a knowledge of output proportions. But this formulation, even though it does not imply rigidly fixed output proportions for all input vectors, is too restrictive to capture a phenomenon that might well be significant in higher education — namely, gearing a degree programme to a certain class of students. In particular, it seems possible that, without altering input levels at all, instructors in a programme could direct their lectures to the better students, thereby increasing the number of high GPA degrees (and, probably, dropouts), while reducing the number of medium or low GPA degrees. Equation (2a) does not allow for these kinds of substitution possibilities for given inputs.

If this kind of substitution is considered important, then a formulation more general than (2a) would be needed. We might postulate the single relation,

$$g\,(y_{n_1}, y_{n_2}, \ldots, y_{n_j}) = f^n\,(\sum_j x_1^{nj}, \sum_j x_2^{nj}, \ldots, \sum_j x_M^{nj}). \qquad (2b)$$

Here, as in (2a), the condition that the number of entering and leaving students be equal would have to be satisfied. For fixed total input quantities, (2b) defines a smooth production possibility function among different GPA intervals for the same degree, while (2a) implies a rectangular production possibility set.[20] If both g and f^n are homogeneous, then the production frontiers defined by (2b) for given factor proportions are radial projections of each other. And these frontiers will display increasing (decreasing) returns to scale whenever the degree of homogeneity of f^n exceeds (is less than) that of g.

These are but a few of the technological considerations that seem pertinent to the production of various GPA intervals within a given discipline's individual degree programme. Next, we comment briefly on the relationships that might exist among different degree programmes within the same discipline. Like the foregoing paragraphs,

---

[20] However, only if $y_{n_j} = \lambda_j\,y_{n_1}$ for $j = 2, 3, \ldots, J$, will (2a) define, for alternative input vectors, production sets with vertices lying on a ray through the origin.

we confine ourselves to the production of human capital – i.e., teaching – and ignore the interactions with research activities and other disciplines. The production ties that link graduate and undergraduate programmes are probably substantially weaker than the relationships among various GPA outputs within, say, a BA programme. Expressions of the same general form as (2a) or (2b) are too strong for this purpose, for it is unlikely that additional faculty resources devoted to a graduate programme will have the same impact on the output of BAs as those same resources allocated directly to the BA programme. Yet it is nevertheless likely that the preparation of a graduate course does reduce the amount of faculty time required to prepare an undergraduate course in the same field, and conversely. This suggests inserting some of the inputs of one programme as separate arguments into the production function(s) of the other programme. Let there be K GPA intervals in the graduate programme, while there remain J intervals in the BA programme. Then, corresponding to (2b) there would be two relations, one undergraduate and the other graduate:[21]

$$g\left(y_{n_1}, y_{n_2}, \ldots, y_{n_J}\right) = f^n \left(\sum_j x_1^{nj}, \ldots, \sum_j x_m^{nj}; \sum_k x_1^{n'k}, \ldots, \sum_k x_M^{n'k}\right)$$

$$h\left(y_{n'_1}, y_{n'_2}, \ldots, y_{n'_K}\right) = f^{n'} \left(\sum_k x_1^{n'k}, \ldots, \sum_k x_M^{n'k}; \sum_j x_1^{nj}, \ldots, \sum_j x_M^{nj}\right).$$

One short-cut to capturing the externalities between the two programmes would be to insert only one additional argument into f^n and $f^{n'}$ – namely, the total number of degrees (inclusive of dropouts) in the other programme. This would yield the alternative specification,

$$g\left(y_{n_1}, \ldots, y_{n_J}\right) = f^n \left(\sum_j x_1^{nj}, \ldots, \sum_j x_M^{nj}; \sum_k y_{n'_k}\right)$$

$$h\left(y_{n'_1}, \ldots, y_{n'_k}\right) = f^{n'} \left(\sum_k x_1^{n'k}, \ldots, \sum_k x_M^{n'k}; \sum_j y_{nj}\right). \tag{2d}$$

---

[21] Since only some of the resources devoted to one programme would influence the outputs of the other, the partial derivatives of f^n and $f^{n'}$ with respect to the remaining variables in the second set of arguments would be identically zero.

105

There is mis-specification present in (2d) insofar as only some inputs of one programme influence outputs of the other and insofar as there are substitution possibilities among inputs in one programme that do and do not influence the output of the other. Empirically, however, something like (2d) is probably the most that can be expected.[22]

So far our arguments have justified aggregating a university's decision units up to the level of autonomous undergraduate-graduate teaching departments in the conventional disciplinary sense. If the externalities cited in the foregoing discussion were the only ones present, we might well expect to observe only teaching institutes and research institutes, a pair for each discipline, instead of full-blown universities, which combine the research as well as teaching functions of a number of disciplines. The next step is to argue along familiar lines that the production of human capital and the discovery of new knowledge are sufficiently technologically complementary to merge the teaching and research institutes into single departments. One obvious consideration here is that the PhD is a research-oriented degree; in the process of producing a PhD, new knowledge drops out as a by-product. Presumably a faculty member cannot teach a student how to do research unless he does research himself. But the relationship does not have to be that strong to justify the externality between teaching and research; it need only be the case that it is easier to teach the PhD to do research if the faculty member is similarly engaged. A similar — but probably weaker — relationship exists between the production of research and the production of undergraduate human capital. A converse link is also operative: the issues raised in the classroom often suggest research topics and give clues to their solution. Here it is not clear that the link is weaker from undergraduate than graduate teaching.

It is unlikely that the connection between teaching and research is sufficiently strong to warrant a formulation like (2a) — i.e., the total resources devoted to both (with no specification of their distribution between the two types of activities) is insufficient to specify a production frontier between human capital and research outputs — for

---

[22] It is obvious that the general form of the right-hand sides of (2c) and (2d) can be used to modify (2a) to allow for the externalities between graduate and undergraduate programmes for the case where no output substitutions are possible with given inputs.

106

we are all aware of the possibility of augmenting research output by cheating on instructional preparation. Rather, a formulation like (2c) or (2d) appears to be more appropriate for capturing the externalities connecting teaching and research; in fact, the particular mix of inputs into the research activity intuitively seems far less important to teaching than the research output itself, which argues in favour of an analogue to (2d). Since the notation is becoming burdensome, for purposes of illustration we assume only one kind of BA, PhD and research output within the particular discipline, with quantities denoted by y_b, y_p and y_r. Our argument can then be summarized by

$$y_b = f^b \left(x_1^b, \ldots, x_M^b ; y_p, y_r \right)$$

$$y_p = f^p \left(x_1^p, \ldots, x_M^p ; y_b, y_r \right) \qquad (2e)$$

$$y_r = f^r \left(x_1^r, \ldots, x_M^r ; y_b, y_p \right).$$

Of course, if it were felt that input proportions in teaching, rather than teaching output alone (number of degrees), influences the other outputs, then y_b and y_p could be replaced by their respective input vectors on the right-hand side of the first two (or all three) relations in (2e), for all that we have argued above is that y_r, not research inputs, should appear as an argument in the first two functions.

One phenomenon that we should allow for in specifying explicit functional forms for (2e) is the possibility that the production frontier between teaching and research outputs, with given total resources, need not have a negative slope everywhere. Imagine a situation where all resources are allocated to, say, the production of BAs, so that $y_p = y_r = 0$.[23] Then, reallocating some of those resources to research might lead to an increase in *both* y_b and y_r, the argument being that the indirect effect on BA output of research activity outweights the direct effect of reducing resources to it, while research output benefits from both the direct effect of additional resources and any indirect effect of higher BA output that might be present.[24]

---

[23] Presumably, the three functions in (2e) should have the property that, when the first M arguments are zero, the function values are zero.

[24] "Higher" BA output in this case has to be on the quality dimension, which the reduction to one kind of BA output is not capable of rendering.

This kind of reasoning thus supports the view that appropriate decision-making units in higher education should consist of a physics institute, a history institute, etc., that combine the production of degrees and new knowledge. But what kind of technological externalities argues for grouping these institutes together in the conventional multi-disciplined university? Why should there not simply be "university parks", much like industrial parks that consist of separate firms ("institutes") that take advantage of locational proximity? Frankly, it appears difficult to justify on technological grounds a conventional university over a university park. We consider here only a few of the reasons — all unjustified, in our view — for believing that a university is the more efficient organizational form.

There is, first, the assertion that the liberal arts tradition in American higher education, whereby students do not completely specialize in one discipline (especially in the early years of their work), generates the need for housing several instructional departments within a single administrative unit. Thus, a BA in history, for example, takes more than one-half of his courses outside the history department. Even in a more specialized setting, extra-departmental courses would be required — e.g., mathematics for physics, engineering and economics majors. Thus it is possible to construct an input-output table, showing the number of student-class-hours majors in one discipline are given by other disciplines and how many student-class-hours one discipline gives to other disciplines' majors. It is highly unlikely, given "general education" requirements in most undergraduate institutions, that such a matrix is capable of block-diagonalization or triangularization. Thus, it is impossible to isolate autarkic departments or groups of departments, and — according to this argument — it is necessary to put them all under one roof. But surely this position — at least as stated here — cannot be correct, for it would argue that any indecomposable system, like most national interindustry relations and international trading systems, should be one organizational unit for decision purposes. Mere interdependence in the form of the purchases of inputs and sales of outputs, does not by itself rationalize the "vertical integration" that is the norm in higher education. It is important not to confuse interdependence, in the form of one department's using a *part* of another's output as a direct "purchased" input, and a genuine externality, which arises from one department's output being influenced by *total* activity levels in another. The former *is* present in higher education (and in the economy as a whole), while it remains to establish the presence of the latter.

A second, somewhat related argument hinges on the notion of a "community of scholars", whereby students and faculty benefit from interaction with the personnel of other disciplines. Although there is some reason to believe that the importance of this phenomenon is exaggerated, it is an example of a genuine external benefit (or cost, in the eyes of some). Nevertheless, it is not at all clear that it cannot be captured outside the organizational framework of a conventional university. There is no reason why the same externalities would not exist in a university park kind of setup, whereby faculty and/or students from diverse disciplines would meet in the independently operated cafeteria, faculty club, and dormitories. Finally, it appears that the external benefits of the community-of-scholars type are much stronger within departments rather than among them anyhow.

Third, and last, there is the huge administrative component of a university's operation — e.g., record-keeping, legal and library services. It might well be argued that some of these activities, which are inputs into departmental production functions, are subject to scale economies in production beyond the size that an individual department would warrant. But this implies only that the production of administrative services be put under one roof, not that all the purchasers of these services be merged into the producer. The very existence elsewhere in the economy of accounting firms and computer-based bookkeeping, private legal practices and libraries speaks to the possibility of divorcing administrative and academic activities.

To this point we have spoken against a conventional university form of organization on the grounds that no genuine technological externalities exist that argue for it. There is at least one very strong reason favouring a university park of disciplinary institutes; think of the great saving in faculty time that the elimination of university-wide faculty and committee meetings would make possible!

Conclusions

This chapter has been addressed to the following questions; suppose a university were to set itself the task of maximizing net social output; then (i) What kinds of information would it require to fulfil this task? (ii) How centralized should the decision-making be in the light of the technological considerations that make the university a multi-product entity?

Our conclusions regarding both issues can be summarized by recourse to a set of Q maximization problems, where Q is the number of distinct academic disciplines and professional schools. A teaching-research institute for the qth discipline is assumed to be established in a university park, in which additional firms to produce administrative, dormitory and ancilliary services are supposed to exist. Letting superscripts b, p, r and a denote undergraduate, graduate, research and administrative, the qth institute is assigned the problem;

$$\text{maximize } (\underset{\sim}{p}^b, \underset{\sim}{p}^p, \underset{\sim}{p}^r)'_q (\underset{\sim}{y}^b, \underset{\sim}{y}^p, \underset{\sim}{y}^r)_q - (\underset{\sim}{w}^b, \underset{\sim}{w}^p, \underset{\sim}{w}^r, \underset{\sim}{w}^a)'_q$$

$$(\underset{\sim}{x}^b, \underset{\sim}{x}^p, \underset{\sim}{x}^r, \underset{\sim}{x}^a)_q \tag{4}$$

$$\text{subject to } g^b (\underset{\sim}{y}^b_q) = f^b (\underset{\sim}{x}^b_q; \underset{\sim}{x}^a_q; \underset{\sim}{x}^p_q; \underset{\sim}{y}^r_q)$$

$$g^p (\underset{\sim}{y}^p_q) = f^p (\underset{\sim}{x}^p_q; \underset{\sim}{x}^a_q; \underset{\sim}{x}^b_q; \underset{\sim}{y}^r_q)$$

$$g^r (\underset{\sim}{y}^r_q) = f^r (\underset{\sim}{x}^r_q; \underset{\sim}{x}^a_q; \underset{\sim}{x}^b_q; \underset{\sim}{x}^p_q)$$

The central fiscal agency (the "university") assists each institute by supplying information on certain ps and ws. In particular, as the result of discounted lifetime earnings calculations, together with values for consumption services obtained from opportunity cost calculations for the elderly that return to college, it establishes the prices contained in $\underset{\sim}{p}^b_q$ and $\underset{\sim}{p}^p_q$. From the same present value calculations, the components of $\underset{\sim}{w}^b_q$ and w^p_q relating to student time are also established. The components of $\underset{\sim}{p}^r_q$ are set by the "prices" per page of published research that institutions like the NSF have been observed to pay in the recent past. The remaining inputs each institute buys or rents on the open market at competitive prices.

Each institute is charged with the task of finding the solution to

(4). Assuming it knows the three production relations specified there, the externalities that exist among outputs within each of the three general output categories (as expressed by including as arguments the sums of inputs assigned to that activity), as well as the externalities among the three types of output (as expressed by including as arguments the inputs and/or outputs of other output types) are comprehended in the solutions. Having solved (4), each institute requests of the central fiscal agency the funds necessary for out-of-pocket expenses — i.e., expenditures on inputs purchased on open markets. Summing these solutions over q yields the maximum net social product for the university park.

The foregoing analysis sidesteps many issues. Many of these appear in the introduction. But there are at least three more that deserve mention here. First, nothing has been said about the explicit functional forms or econometric techniques required to give operational content to each institute's production relations. Second, without the appropriate tuition charges, there is no mechanism to ensure that the excess demand for human capital by students would be zero — a rationing scheme by which an institute accepts students into its programme is absent from the analysis. Finally, no system of incentives is present by which inputs — especially faculty — will be encouraged to allocate their time optimally to the production of the various types of output; in this analysis, they must simply be assigned their duties. These are some of the issues that further research must address.

5. On the Measurement of Inputs and Outputs in Higher Education

by G.C. Archibald

Introduction

In the present state of knowledge, it is tempting to experiment with a variety of "positive" models of university behaviour. Here I shall, however, attempt to stick to my brief, which is to explore some of the conceptual problems of measuring inputs and outputs, and their relation to the study of efficiency.

In any production function study, a critical choice is that of the appropriate level of aggregation. "Choice" is forced upon us by the difficulties of measurement of non-homogeneous inputs and outputs. Production studies have, of course, proceeded at all levels from the micro-engineering to the most highly aggregative, or national. In the case of universities, the problem is aggravated by the fact that we can aggregate (or disaggregate) by disciplines, institutions, courses, states, and so on. One of the objects of these notes is to discuss some aggregation problems peculiar to the study of universities.

It is convenient to distinguish now between a "university" and a "system of higher education". We may define a system of higher education as the set of all post-secondary institutions in an area (country), together with all the rules of hierarchy, entry, transfer, subsidization, and so on. The system has attributes and functions which are not the immediate concern of the individual university: it generates more or less occupational and social mobility, income redistribution, and so on; it acts as a store of knowledge, and it more or less sets the standards of intellectual activity and social criticism. In what follows, I shall usually disaggregate at least this far: I shall be concerned with the individual university (partial equilibrium) rather than with the system, and shall therefore not be concerned with such outputs of the system as social mobility.

We may note here that, if universities do not in fact cost-minimize (and how, in the present state of knowledge, could they be minimizing the cost of what?) then attempts to discover cost or production functions by cross-section study (e.g. regression across universities) are more than normally hazardous.

It turns out that specification of the appropriate unit of *time* is critical to measurement of outputs and particularly inputs, and, *a fortiori*, to the specification of production functions, or the discussion of efficiency. Some aspects of the problem are identified here, but it is by no means solved.

By analogy with the firm, a university is an area "within which the market is superseded". No more than in the case of any other planning institution is it obvious what the optimal size of unit or extent of decentralisation may be. Furthermore, markets for some of the outputs, whether of the individual university or of the "system", do not exist. When we consider efficiency we shall have to consider not merely the optimal level of aggregation for study but that for decision-taking.

Universities differ (at least internationally) in their decision-making procedures, internal structure, and relation to the "system" (information and extent of decentralisation). It would be foolish not to exploit the extension of the sample offered by this circumstance. We shall return to it in the last section.

Some aspects of student unrest in recent years have been concerned with issues which an economist can easily classify as "the extent of Consumers' Sovereignty". "Consumers' Sovereignty versus Paternalism in Universities" is clearly on the agenda. Even where this is not so, an economist concerned with efficiency in higher education would naturally be tempted to model the university as a firm and consider the efficiency with which it catered to its customers. He might go further, hoping to establish a system of atomistic market competition which would, by familiar analogy, render our researches, and possible interference, redundant. He should remember that this model requires that all payoffs are appropriately internalized, and that information is perfect. Consideration of such models is beyond the scope of this chapter but the discussion of the nature of the university's output is relevant to the Consumers' Sovereignty issue and the consideration of efficiency.

114

The teaching output

There are many ways in which we might consider the university's teaching output. We might proceed course by course, looking at the students' attainments partly as an end in themselves, partly as an input into subsequent courses. For the time being, let us arbitrarily aggregate, and consider the unit of teaching output as "a degree", whether in engineering or economics. We may in turn look upon a degree as a vector of attributes. The attributes of education, or of a specific programme, which we are calling "a degree", may be classified as follows:

(1) investment in a consumer durable
(2) investment in a source of future externalities
(3) a current consumption activity
(4) investment in a producer good (human capital).

Each degree programme offers some weighted combination of these four elements (attributes). A university produces all four, with different weights in different programmes, and, in addition, produces (5), research. I am going to argue that the fact that different programmes produce these four attributes with different weights is of central importance to our measurement problems.

It is probably fair to say that, from the time of classical Greece to the Industrial Revolution, only the first two rewards to education were much considered. About a century ago, technological change fairly suddenly gave importance to attribute (4) (consider the dates of foundation of the Land Grant schools in the US and the major civic universities in the UK). Economists have largely been concerned with quantification of attribute (4), and have been resisted by humanists who emphasized the importance of the other, traditional, attributes. It seems incumbent upon us to consider the problem: must we, and if so how might we, measure the first three attributes of the output?

I cannot provide any answer (some comments on externalities are offered below), but, at the risk of digression, I am going to suggest that a good deal of contemporary difficulty in universities is due to confusion over the relative importance of attributes (1) and (4).

We may notice that attribute (1) (with, certainly, some of (2) and

115

(3) in the package) has traditionally been "bought" (at Oxbridge and the Ivy League) by members of a rentier class who were not concerned to buy (4) (and, of course, by a few poor but able men seeking an entry to "public life"). "Liberal Arts" programmes, in which attribute (4) may have a very low weight, are now offered cheaply to thousands of students who cannot themselves afford a heavy indulgence in the other attributes.

This is not all. It may be conjectured that recent technical change (the phonograph, radio, and finally TV) has drastically reduced the importance of the printed word and of do-it-yourself entertainment. We may regret this; but we should also note that it has been roughly coincident with a huge expansion in the number of non-rentier students enrolled in programmes traditionally weighted towards attribute (1).

A Liberal Arts degree does, in fact, have a market value. It is not, of course, vocational, and there is increasing evidence that employers are indifferent to the syllabus but look upon it as a useful pre-screening device: its possession is evidence of some minimum of ability and industry.[1] If this is the case, and the conjecture in the last paragraph is correct, then students can perceive little or no cost to themselves in syllabus changes designed to increase the weight given to attribute (3). This seems to be consistent with the evidence: we have seen considerable erosion of arts requirements in recent decades (abolition of latin requirements, of Anglo-Saxon in English programmes, etc.).

The force of all this in the present context (apart from its possible relevance to student unrest) may be briefly summarized:

(i) in measuring output, it is likely to pay to disaggregate considerably, since the importance of the four attributes varies substantially by field (e.g. engineering, economics, English literature);

(ii) it is not necessarily at all safe to assume that the market value

---

[1] An empirical test of the screening hypothesis may be found in Taubman and Wales (1973). They did not disaggregate by subject or type of degree, i.e. they did not distinguish between individuals such as chemists and engineers, whose degrees are heavily weighted towards attribute (4), and "others". Thus their study, which in fact lends some support to the screening hypothesis, must be biassed against it.

of a degree reflects the investment in productive human capital: it may be a screening device the social and private costs of which are poorly related;[2]

(iii) in considering efficiency (and the Consumers' Sovereignty issue) it is again likely to pay to disaggregate since, in the nature of things, students (customers) are well informed about attribute (3), and badly informed about the other attributes of a degree programme.[3]

Let us now briefly consider a rival to the screening hypothesis. This is that non-vocational degrees, with apparently a low weighting on attribute (4), do in fact contribute significantly to the productive capital stock, but in a round-about way. This is the hypothesis that the university's output is an input into subsequent training: a man with a degree in, say, history, will be a cheaper on-the-job trainee than one without, other personal attributes held constant. We may call this the "versatility hypothesis". It is, at least in principle, testable.[4]

Closely related to the versatility hypothesis is what we may call the "communications hypothesis". This is that a degree in, say, history, gives a man skills in comprehension and exposition that constitute valuable human capital. Operationally, it may be impossible

---

[2] Note that, if we take the screening hypothesis seriously, we have to disaggregate not merely by subject but by school. The screening offered by Harvard or Oxbridge is very different from that offered by Boondocks State University or Boondocks Polytechnic.

[3] We shall return to the Consumers' Sovereignty issue in the final section. We should, however, note here that a degree, at least a "vocational" one heavily weighted to attribute (4), carries with it some "public certification": we expect a man with a degree in civil engineering to know something about bridges, and even one with a degree in economics to know something about taxation and unemployment. Aggregation once again: do we consider the "degree" or the elements thereof?

[4] And it is even possible that the necessary data samples exist in military records. One would ask the question: in "crash" programmes for officer training in World War II, did students with liberal arts degrees, other attributes held constant, do any better than those without?

to distinguish between the versatility and communications hypotheses. They are, however, certainly distinct from the screening hypothesis. Measurement of output, assessment of efficiency, and policy implications would all hinge on which we accepted. The design of an experiment to discriminate between "screening" and "versatility", at least, would be a major contribution.[5]

It is now clear that measurement of the teaching output is an extremely complex task. Disaggregation is required; but more than that. At least for the less obviously vocational degrees, there is even doubt as to what the output is. Up to date, economists have concentrated on the measurement of attribute (4), via calculation of rates of return. If we could accept these measurements, it would be easy to calculate the university's value added (contribution to human capital). It appears that this procedure may be proper for chemists and engineers for example, but is, at least, premature for liberal arts graduates.

Let us now consider some of the other attributes of a degree. Valuation of the investment in consumer durables is clearly most intractable. If, however, the argument given above is correct, this attribute is of dwindling importance, even in non-vocational fields of study. I incline to think that degrees in which this attribute is heavily weighted should be "sold"; but they should be clearly advertised. At present it is clear that, in many programmes, students are very badly informed as to what combination of attributes they may expect. I see no way of making progress.

As for externalities, they are, as usual, hard to quantify. The importance of "an educated electorate" may, indeed, be inestimable (although some people suspect sharply diminishing social returns to the supply of educated citizens).

It may, however, be possible to make some progress with one particular externality, the intergenerational effect. Many studies have reported on the effects on students' success, *ceteris paribus*, of parental education and occupation. It might now be possible to consider attaching price tags to the parents' education, regarding it as an intermediate good. (This suggestion itself illustrates the difficulty we

---

[5] See the last footnote. One wonders if the principles of recruitment of the British civil service are based on tacit acceptance of the "screening", "versatility", or "communications" hypothesis, or some mixture of all three.

118

may have in distinguishing inputs from outputs, unless at least the unit of time has been specified.)

Existing work on education has used a wide variety of measures of output at levels of aggregation lower than "a degree." Besides market values, research workers have used "understanding of the subject" (as measured by some test scores), degree class or grade-point results, proportion of the entry that graduates, number of credit hours, etc. Leaving aside the consumption and externalities components, why would one use any measure other than the market? Besides data availability, the answer must be "ambiguity as to what the output is" and/or "market failure." Externalities and inefficiencies account in turn for much market failure. As an example, bad teaching may lead to "good" degrees and poor "understanding", and the market may be imperfectly informed. Thus it is clear that the level of understanding of economics by economists in the public service may convey important externalities on the entire public. It follows that a measure of their understanding may be a much better measure of the universities'. teaching output than their market prices. On a well-informed (perfect) market, we should expect the two measures to be closely correlated. But consider the situation in Britain. The government exercises tremendous influence on the price of economists, via civil service recruiting and its control of academic salaries. It follows that an independent measure of output is highly desirable.[6]

These considerations may suggest a rather familiar moral: the better informed and more perfect the market for attribute (4), the more readily should one accept market valuation, and vice versa; and similarly, the less important the externalities consequent upon "understanding", the more readily should one accept market valuation. When, however, independent measures of understanding are used, it remains to consider their relation to market values. Discrepancies suggest inefficiencies or distortions in the system, and are important *explicanda*.

The main suggestions of this section may be summarized as follows:

---

[6] If this is correct, it follows that the approach taken in the Economics Education Project, while dictated by the requirements of a micro-engineering production function study, can be further justified and should be more widely applied.

(i) Since different programmes weight our four attributes very differently, it is important to disaggregate by field when measuring the "return" to university education (or the university's value added).

(ii) In liberal arts programmes particularly, it is unclear what the output is: some experiment to discriminate between at least the screening and versatility hypotheses is called for.

(iii) In some fields at least, market failures or inefficiencies may be important, in which case it may be useful to try to measure "attainment" separately from market price, and to enquire into the reasons for discrepancy.

(iv) In sum, there is no single simple measure of the "teaching output", whether provided by market price or otherwise.

Research

It may be quickly conceded that there is no way of valuing the stock of knowledge, or of increments to it. We can, however, suggest a crude method of estimating what universities are presently paying for research. It is not implied that output can or should be valued by inputs (as, of course, it is in the GNP treatment of education) but that an estimate of implicit prices may be of interest.

We neglect the markets for industrial research and patents (and also the behaviour of research foundations, which may be important) and consider only what universities themselves may be paying for research.

In most countries, we can recognize a hierarchy of institutions by status (universities and polytechnics in the UK, universities, colleges, junior colleges, etc. in the US). Casual observation suggests that, across institutions of different status or rank (inter-rank), salaries and teaching loads are negatively correlated (I assume, which needs checking, that inter-rank differences are more important and systematic than intra-rank differences). We may display the "stylized" situation as in Fig. 5.1, where teaching loads are measured on the x-axis and salaries on the vertical. For simplicity, we assume that teaching loads vary discontinuously; there are four typical, or standard, loads increasing as the rank of the institution diminishes. The vertical lines correspond to some scatter of salaries (intra-rank, and by personal rank). There may be overlap, as illustrated, or not.

120

Figure 5:1

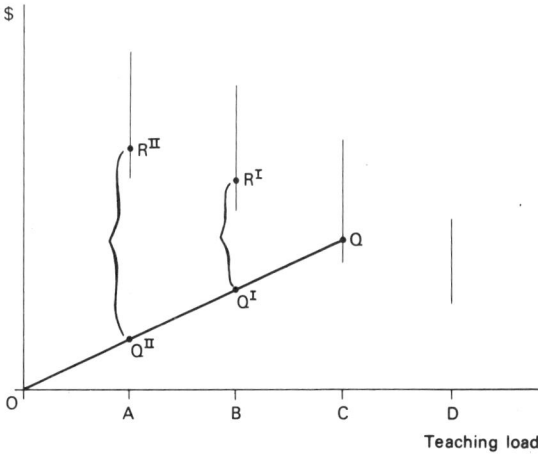

Now, as we move down by rank, we find some variation in the qualifications required of staff as a minimum for first appointment. Let us assume that the PhD is required in all ranks except D. Then we consider the PhD as the qualification to teach in all ranks, A, B, and C (this may apply fairly straight-forwardly in the US; the situation in the UK is confused). Now consider a "typical" individual of rank R in a C-class institution. He is located at Q, teaches OC hours for CQ. The slope of the line OQ gives the supply price of teaching inputs (by a minimum qualified man) to all institutions of higher education. Thus an individual of rank R in a B-class institution, located at R^I, is implicitly being paid R^IQ^I for his non-teaching contributions and the individual of rank R in an A-class institution is implicitly priced at $R^{II}Q^{II}$ for his non-classroom hours contributions.

This seems conceptually very simple, although doubtless troublesome to quantify. There is, however, a qualification. Not all the non-classroom hours contributions are research: universities also value an ill-defined attribute called "excellence", and colleagues value the externalities provided by their colleagues. The payments $R^{II}Q^{II}$ are for a package rather than a single product. In our ignorance, please let us call it research ("From Omsk to Tomsk the news did run").

Two more qualifications are obviously called for. It is well known

121

that a distinguished institution may pay a distinguished scholar no more, or even less, than a less distinguished institution (in the same rank) pays a less distinguished scholar in the same discipline. Any labour economist can tell us that this is to be attributed to the non-pecuniary advantages of the job (quality of colleagues and of students, etc.). It is not peculiar to the study of institutions of higher education that we do not really know what to do about this. Furthermore, the most casual observation suggests that there are pockets of rent all over the academic market place. The same remarks apply, *mutatis mutandis*.

The second qualification is that "jointness" in production, a problem not yet considered, may well be serious. We return to this problem in the next section.

All in all, however, it seems that the method of computing the price of research illustrated in Fig. 5.1 is about as respectable as any we generally use to obtain an implicit price. It may approximate, subject to the usual qualifications, what society, acting through the universities as its market agents, is actually paying.[7]

The measurement of inputs

In considering the measurement of costs, we have the usual aggregation problems discussed above, the possibility that market prices do not properly reflect opportunity costs, the problem of time, and the allocation problem (identification of the output to which the cost is to be attributed). I shall discuss briefly the relationship between faculty salaries and opportunity cost, the choice of the time unit and the measurement of capital costs, and the allocation or attribution problem.

I submit that we hardly know what is fixed and what variable, or what is long-run and what short-run in university affairs. If we take an extremely short-run view, using market prices to compute opportunity costs, most faculty (outside vocational schools such as

---

[7] We may note here an analogy to the screening hypothesis. Universities probably use past research performance to predict future performance, from which it does not follow that they get what they pay for. Further analysis of the market place and individual careers might be of considerable interest.

medicine or law) enjoy substantial rents. It is well known, however, that for most individuals, and most occupations, occupational specificity increases with age. Thus when a man chooses to be an academic he usually makes — must make — a lifetime commitment (cf. concert musicians, ballet dancers, and football players). It is therefore the expected value of the lifetime income that matters. The rents to the individual are quasi-rents to the system: we can take them away in the short-run, but the capital will not be replaced (flow supply of committed individuals will diminish) if we do. This is doubtless the economic reason for existing institutional arrangements of an otherwise curious nature, such as tenure and irreversible promotions, which we also see in the armed and civil services (which is not to imply that they might not be improved upon; but these long-run considerations are important to the assessment of schemes for "payment by results" or by "piece-work"). Thus we may look on an academic as a quasi-fixed factor with a substantial capital component.

Given that the market place for academics is competitive, as it is in the US, I see little reason to suppose that salaries do not broadly reflect opportunity cost in the long-run sense. An attempt by any individual university to appropriate its faculty's personal rents will lead to a loss of quality. Competition for quality by the system as a whole will ensure, in a broad sense, the continued supply of individuals with appropriate talents and training. (Only, of course, in a "broad" sense: the market may be oscillatory; and imperfect knowledge may lead to "error" in the treatment of many individuals.)

Academic salary scales are determined in the UK by monopsonistic (or, at least, by somewhat one-sided) bilateral bargaining. I see no reason to suppose that they measure opportunity cost except that, if they provide lifetime income profiles that differ from the life-time opportunity cost profiles of individuals currently committed, the adjustment will, in the long-run, be made up by quality rather than quantity change. If government policy changed infrequently relative to the length of the academic life-time, opportunity cost (for the quality) would equalize itself with salaries; but this is not the case.

The UK structure leads to a second problem: its uniform, non-competitive, non-discriminatory nature means that there are indeed rents, according to discipline and institution, while the rents of ability are largely expropriated (as is possible if the employer is a monopsonist). It does not seem to be worth pursuing these matters here. I conclude that I see little reason why academic salaries in the US should not be assumed to measure opportunity cost (in the long-run, life-time income, sense), and no reason why academic salaries in the UK should be assumed to measure anything but what it is found politically convenient to pay in the short-run to quasi-fixed factors.[8]

If it is granted that the academic is a quasi-fixed factor with a substantial capital component, and, further, that he produces a mix of teaching, research, externalities, administration, and "outside" or "consulting" activities, some of which, at least, are inter-related, it is obvious that the allocation of his inputs to his outputs is a difficult task. How do we compute the shadow price of an "academic hour"? If we cannot do this, how do we compare the efficiency of alternative teaching methods that use academic inputs of different sorts in different combinations?

The problem of allocating faculty time between teaching, research, administration, and consulting has received considerable attention in the UK, much less in the US. (One wonders if this does not reflect the relative importance of the bureaucrats and the market place in the two academic systems. People who administer non-equilibrium prices are liable to end up wondering how quantities and qualities are actually behaving.)

In the UK the Committee of Vice-Chancellors and Principals (CVCP) has been using resources, chiefly other peoples', to attempt to discover how faculty time is allocated. For this purpose, it has caused a sample of academics to keep most detailed diaries. The effort, however misguided, is so earnest that comment is called for.

The obstacle to proceeding in this manner is a familiar one: jointness. Thus suppose that a man spends h hours reading a paper in a learned journal that (a) stimulates or otherwise pleases him, (b) will contribute to his teaching, and (c) will contribute to his own research. In this common case, to what category should he allocate his h hours? We know that the question is unanswerable, but it has been asked — and even answered. An analogy may be apposite. How do we

---

[8] It might be rewarding to analyse the determination of doctors' salaries under the National Health Service, and compare it with the determination of academic salaries, and consider consequences.

allocate the grass eaten by a sheep between wool production and mutton production? We know certain methods of procedure (comparison of inputs between sheep yielding different wool-meat mixes, etc.) but one thing is certain: if sheep could talk, economists, if not farmers, would have more sense than to ask silly questions about the allocation of the grass. Since the unfortunate academic sheep can talk, it is asked, and, from a sense of public duty endeavours to answer, equally silly questions.

This is not the only flaw in the proceedings of the CVCP. Behind such an allocation-questionnaire there is, we may suspect, an implicit appeal to the labour theory of value (already too common in consideration of academic affairs). Thus time spent in teaching, *including preparation*, will be "good", time spent in the bar (or in the john) "bad", or "wasted". Yet clearly a man who can make up a competent lecture as he walks to his classroom is more efficient than the man who takes all day and half the night to do it; the bar is a place where externalities are exchanged between colleagues; and many a man has claimed to get his best ideas in the john (or, at least, while appearing to be devoting his time to some utterly irrelevant or trivial activity).

Since, however, the allocation problem is both difficult and critical to the study of efficiency, let us ask if the CVCP's laboriously collected data could be put to any good use. There is at least a chance. Harry Johnson has remarked of the British system that, while the government may determine the annual salary, the market still determines the price per hour. By this is meant that the supply of time to "outside earnings" (consulting, book reviewing, work for the media, etc.) is positively associated with the (market determined) consulting price, and negatively associated with the official salary. If we assumed that teaching hours were fixed (which is actually inappropriate in the British system) and that the individual supplied a constant number of hours of effort, irrespective of price (generally false) we could draw Fig. 5.2. In equilibrium, OB consulting hours are supplied at price BQ, and BT hours are kept back for research. Thus BQ measures the reserve demand price for research time at the margin. (Note that the integral under the supply curve − demand curve for research time − to the right of BQ may not be finite. "Researchers' surplus" is this integral minus BQ.BT.) The information we need is how the supply curve in Fig. 5.2 moves in response to salary. If the CVCP's enquiry were to be regularly repeated, we might eventually have the information on which to base an estimate. We might, in other words, learn something from the behaviour of sheep pastured on grass of differing qualities, and able to reach another source of food at some cost to themselves.

Figure 5:2

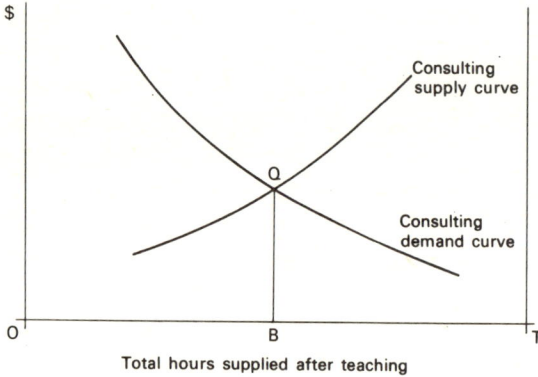

Total hours supplied after teaching

Measurement of current inputs (non-faculty) to a university appears to present no particular problems. There remains the other capital item: buildings. It is hard for any non-profit-making institution to have a rational capital account unless its fixed capital is entirely non-specific. Further, different teaching methods will, in general, require different inputs (classroom usage, etc.), and judgment of efficiency requires that these be priced.

I can offer no suggestion for progress with this problem, but instead only a disturbing conjecture about the specificity of university plant. This is that most university buildings currently constructed, not to mention the old stock, are far too specific. I do not mean that they are too education-specific, but too specific within education. Thus I regard it as preposterous to embody in steel and concrete, at vast expense, our current notions of optimum classroom size, optimum mix of classrooms and seminar rooms, and optimal mix of teaching space and office space. What we should do with all this enduring concrete in a world that made heavy use of TV teaching or computerized programmed learning, I cannot think. It

126

may well be that university architecture is a subject requiring some economic analysis.[9]

Some notes on efficiency

We argued earlier that, outside the heavily vocational programmes, we do not presently know enough about the nature of the university's teaching output to measure it. This, in conjunction with our difficulty in allocating and pricing academic inputs, appears to preclude any discussion of efficiency. We may, however, be able to make some progress if we distinguish between "what" and "how": syllabus, or subject matter content, and pedagogic method. If "what" can be held constant, we may be able to consider efficiency in method.

This was essentially the procedure of the Economics Education Project, an engineering or micro-production function study referred to earlier. "Understanding of Economics 1", as measured by a common test, was agreed as the (non-market) measure of output. The inputs fall into two classes, those that are "used up" such as lecture or tutorial hours, and those that are not, such as the individual's IQ and the IQ of his classmates. The regression coefficients measure the productivity of these inputs in units of test score. It would seem natural to proceed by now attaching price tags. In fact, however, this appears extremely difficult. Not only have we no market price for "Understanding of Economics 1", we do not even know if it is a final or an intermediate output (it may be an intermediate input to Economics 2; worse, it may be an input into "versatility"). And we argued in the last section that estimation of unit prices for academic inputs is far from easy.

---

[9] A gloomy conjecture may be added here. This is that the public, or body politic, tends to drive universities (chiefly by the level of financial support) through the rear-vision mirror (a method well-known to be prone to oscillation). (It may be supposed that the lavish building programmes of the 1960s, which the administrators told us had zero opportunity cost, will be paid for out of our salaries in the 1970s.) Presumably a more centralized system should be better able to look forward and depend less on the rear-vision mirror than a less centralized one. Comparison of actual performance in the UK and US in this context might be rewarding.

Let us grant, then, that we cannot attach market prices to the variables of the EEP. If, however, we hold the measurement of output constant, we may at least be able to compare the effectiveness of different input combinations (broadly, pedagogic techniques). We should ask questions of the sort: could a given institution (identified by a given salary bill or staff student ratio) adopt a mix of teaching methods (classes, lectures, tutorials, etc.) that increased its teaching effectiveness (weighted sum of regression coefficients)? If we were to proceed in this fashion, the greater the diversity of institutions in our sample the better. Indeed, we might start to think of systematic international comparison.

One of the most striking differences between North American and British universities is the prevalence of the "sole proprietorship" system in the former and its absence in the latter. In the former, "courses" are designed, taught, and examined by a sole proprietor;[10] in the latter, a variety of teaching inputs and individuals prepare the student for common or "comprehensive" final examinations. It appears that the techniques of the EEP might well be adapted to compare the two systems. We might then ask if, under the overall budget or staff student ratio constraint, either system might beneficially be altered.[11]

We may for a moment consider a university as an adaptive system, acquiring and processing information, and altering its behaviour. It is interesting to note that the sole proprietorship system does not of itself provide feedback about the teaching effectiveness of individual faculty members. Indeed, many North American universities use resources to obtain information (student evaluations) of unknown quality, and then yet more resources to assess the information. The

---

[10] We might reflect on the common practice of treating Economics n as an intermediate good, by making it a prerequisite to Economics $n + 1$, but appealing to "academic freedom" to justify leaving the *content* of Economics n at the discretion of the sole proprietor.

[11] We may note another international comparison. The UK system is structured in the sense that students majoring in the same subject have virtually identical timetables: they are kept together as a group. In contrast, the student in a North American university is wheeling a trolley around a super-market, in only casual contact with his fellow shoppers. In so far as the quality of the peer group is an important un-used-up input, the UK system would appear to be adapted to make more efficient use of it.

128

common examination system generates much of this information as a free by-product. On the other hand, it is probably much less quickly responsive, at least to student preferences. If we are seriously concerned with Consumers' Sovereignty, this is a defect (what should we infer from the institution of graduate comprehensives in North America?).

A further difference between the UK and the US is, of course, in the degree of centralization. In the former, an attempt is made at the national level to forecast demands and adapt by giving signals (and funds) to individual universities. In the latter, forecasts may be made, but there is no "central planning". Let us consider this further.

Assume that we have a good national forecast that, whether for demographic reasons or otherwise, in t years, say, there will be a sharp increase in the demand for "places" to study subject(s) S in high school, followed by a similar increase in demand at the university level in $t + 4$ years. To meet this demand, we must start to increase the undergraduate programmes (to supply school teachers) and the graduate programmes (to supply their teachers) at some earlier dates.[12] Presumably if information was perfect and all markets worked, the incentive to individual universities to expand in S at the right time would be increased demand prices. In the absence of these perfections, it is not obvious how any individual university may capture the social return on this behaviour.

This argument suggests that the greater degree of centralization of the UK system might be more efficient (since information is imperfect, and it is hard to internalize the gains to prescient adaptation). Whether it has *in fact* been more efficient is another matter, and one that might repay study.[13]

---

[12] Note the inconvenient way in which outputs (short-run) become inputs (long-run).

[13] Universities in the UK, responding to the central authority, have recently been heavily overendowed with places in chemistry, in the sense that a student could obtain a place to study chemistry with a far worse high school record than was required to obtain a place in arts subjects. It is not clear if this has been "wrong" in terms of market prices. If so, it is still not clear whether the error has been due to bad forecasting by the central authorities, or indifference to market prices, or both. It would be interesting to know which system, the US or the UK, has in fact been doing a better job of adapting to changing demands for particular skills.

We may conclude with a comment on the Consumers' Sovereignty issue.[14] As far as content or syllabus is concerned, it appears that the extent of consumers' sovereignty might well depend on the weighting of the attributes in a degree programme. Matters are, however, more complicated (the consumers' information regarding most attributes of education is necessarily defective). If the screening hypothesis were accepted, at least for some programmes, there would appear to be no reason why consumers' sovereignty should not be absolute. On the other hand, if the versatility hypothesis were accepted, consumers' sovereignty might properly be limited even over choice of teaching methods (where it might at first be thought that it should obviously be absolute) since learning to use the library (instead of being provided with reference numbers) or even, however, painfully, to digest a disorganized course (instead of "learning" faster from a well programmed one) may be part of the training process that produces versatility. We may conjecture that at least some tentative choice between these hypotheses is a prerequisite to further measurement and research into efficiency.

---

[14] Familiar and intractable problems arise if we assume that university education changes consumers' tastes. Definition of the utility function over some vector of characteristics may afford a means of avoiding some of these problems; but many humanists, at least, believe that the consumer durable component of education and change of tastes are closely connected, whence they may justify much paternalism.

6. Educational Production and Human Capital Formation

by Richard Attiyeh and Keith G. Lumsden

Introduction

Because higher education lacks many of the characteristics associated with traditional industries composed of profit-maximizing firms operating through competitive markets, it also lacks many of the forces which serve in other industries to promote the efficient utilization of resources. It is possible to imagine institutions of higher education operating in pursuit of profit by producing and selling educational services to consumers (students or the parents, private foundations and governments who pay for the education of students). If, in addition, competition were to prevail among universities, externalities were absent (or all externalities were internalized by a tax-subsidy scheme), consumers were rational and both producers and consumers were to have good information, then it would be reasonable to expect market forces to bring about efficient practices. Under such an arrangement there would be strong incentives to adopt cost-reducing or quality-improving techniques, to employ least-cost combinations of inputs and to produce output at a level where marginal social cost and benefit are equal.

Historically, higher education has developed within a very different form of economic organization. Output is produced by private and public non-profit institutions, services are sold at prices that are well below social marginal cost, and average costs are covered when necessary through government subsidy and private charity. It would be possible to rationalize this development as arising out of the difficulties involved in trying to establish the ideal conditions under which the market-type scheme would operate efficiently. And, it is conceptually possible that non-market decision-making procedures in higher education could allocate resources approximately as would

131

the market-type system under ideal conditions. Casual observation of actual decision rules and the resulting allocations, however, suggests that existing procedures are far from efficient.

Unfortunately, one result of the present structure of the higher education industry is that there is a lack of the kind of information, such as directly observable prices of educational outputs and profits of educational institutions, that would provide a basis for rational decision-making. In an attempt to provide the information required to adopt more efficient practices in economics education, we have undertaken a long-term project, preliminary results of which have been reported elsewhere (Attiyeh and Lumsden, 1971, 1972 and forthcoming). While the scope of the project is limited to economics teaching at the university undergraduate level, it is hoped that the methods employed in the project will have general applicability and that some of the results will be directly useful in other fields of study and at other educational levels. In this chapter we discuss some conceptual problems involved in deciding what information is required and some econometric problems that arise in trying to obtain that information.

The concept of efficient teaching

In order to provide a framework for defining the information requirements for rational decision-making in higher education, we set up in this section a formal maximization problem. While oversimplified in many ways, the problem in its present form is too complex to be solvable in any practical situation. Nevertheless, it does put into sharp focus some of the issues involved in trying to use educational resources efficiently and it does make clear what information gaps confront educators.

Before meaningful conclusions can be drawn from available data about how to increase efficiency, it is necessary to model the teaching department in a way that identifies the efficiency problem that the department faces. Such a model of the department should not be conceived of as describing the way departments actually behave, but rather as describing the objectives and constraints under which a department operates and as a conceptual basis for recommending how a department should behave if it is to operate efficiently. The approach adopted here focusses on the course as the basic educational process and the department as the basic decision-making body. In this model the department enrols students in a course at the beginning of the academic year and adds to their knowledge of economics during the year. Gross output for each student is the knowledge he has at the end of the year, which is determined by his knowledge at the beginning of the year, his other characteristics and the inputs contributed by the student and department during the year. A student's knowledge of economics is assumed to be one-dimensional in nature and to be produced independently of other educational services (e.g., faculty research output). The objective of the department is assumed to be the maximization of social profit, given student enrolment. Social profit is defined to be equal to the value of students' knowledge at the end of the year, less the value of their knowledge at the beginning of the year less the cost of university and student inputs.

Formally, consider a course in which each student enrols in one of K sections. Let the knowledge of the ith student at the beginning and the end of a course be represented by Q_i^0 and Q_i^1, respectively. Let the quantities for the ith student of the J kinds of student characteristics other than this initial knowledge be denoted by the J dimensional vector

$$X_i = \{x_{i,1}, \ldots, x_{i,J}\}, i=1, \ldots, I$$

Also, let the quantities for the kth section of the M kinds of departmental inputs be denoted by the M dimensional vector

$$Y_k = \{y_{k,1}, \ldots, y_{k,M}\}, k = 1, \ldots, K$$

Finally, let T_i be the time spent on the course by the ith student and let L_k be the number of students enrolled in the kth section. The production function for knowledge of the ith student at the end of his course is given by

$$Q_i^1 = F(Q_i^0, X_i, T_i, Y_{k_i}, L_{k_i}), i=1, \ldots, I, \tag{1}$$

where k_i is the section assignment of the ith student. How much an individual student knows at the end of the course depends on his initial knowledge, his other characteristics, the time he spends on the course, the department's inputs and the enrolment in the section. The same function is meant to apply to all sections, any differences among sections are interpreted as being due to differences in the quantities of department and student inputs. The value of knowledge of the ith student at the beginning and end of the course is represented by H^1_i and H^0_i, respectively, where H^t_i is determined by the valuation function

$$H^t_i = G(Q^t_i, X_i), \quad i = 1, \ldots, I, \quad t = 0, 1. \tag{2}$$

Given an enrolment of I students, who have initial quantities of knowledge (Q^0_i) and who will contribute given quantities of inputs (X_i), the department must decide on the number of sections (K), the department inputs for each section (Y_k), and the assignments of students to each section (k_i). If the department is to maximize social profit, defined as the aggregate increase in the value of its students' knowledge less the cost of university and student inputs, it must solve the following programming problem:

$$\underset{K, \ Y_k, \ k_i}{Max} \quad \sum_{i=1}^{I} H^1_i - H^0_i - wH^0_i T_i - \sum_{k=1}^{K} S'Y_k$$

$$s.t. \qquad Q^1_i = F(Q^0_i, X_i, T_i, Y_{k_i}, L_{k_i}) \tag{3}$$

$$H^t_i = G(Q^t_i, X_i), \quad t = 0, 1$$

where w is the rental rate on human capital and S is a vector of M prices corresponding to the M departmental inputs and where the course assignments k_i of the I students determine the individual course enrolments, L_k.

It should be noted that the given objective function provides only one among several reasonable definitions of social profit. This definition treats dollars of knowledge equally, regardless of whose knowledge it is or how students' initial endowments of knowledge happen to be distributed. An alternative procedure would be to replace H^t_i with $U(H^t_i)$. If society leaned toward an egalitarian educational policy then the appropriate form of U might be such that $(\delta U/\delta H) > 0$ and $(\delta^2 U/\delta H^2) < 0$. This specification was rejected in favour of that shown in (3) on the assumptions that any equalization of wealth or income would presumably want to be based on differences in

134

individuals' total wealth or income not just those due to differences in the value of knowledge, and that any social redistribution policy could be achieved equally well outside the educational system through a tax-subsidy scheme of the kind that already exists in our fiscal system. If the goal of such distribution policy is to reduce inequality of income, it may be that a policy that tries to equalize educational attainment through the choice of the functional form of U will be inefficient in two respects. First, it may reduce the efficiency with which the educational system can produce human capital (H). If $\delta^2 G/\delta G^2 > 0$, then it may be possible, given the department's resources, to make a greater addition to total wealth by educating persons with high initial human capital and achieving equity through redistribution of income or non-human wealth. Second, it may discourage educational investment in persons with low total wealth but high human capital and encourage such investment in persons with high total wealth but low human capital contrary to the assumed policy objective. Weighing against these arguments is the possibility that the market distortions created by using the tax-transfer mechanism to redistribute income, may be greater than the distortions created by using the educational system to reduce inequality in endowments of human capital.

A further point on the distributional aspects of the efficiency problem defined in (3) is that the efficient solution could imply either an egalitarian or an elitist educational system depending on the parameters of the functions F and G. If F is such that it is increasingly expensive to add a unit of knowledge to a student the higher his initial endowment and if G is such that the increment to human capital resulting from an increment in knowledge decreases as the level of knowledge increases, then an efficient system would definitely be egalitarian; that is, it would be optimal to invest more in the education of students with low initial endowments. If the reverse were true about both F and G, then the optimal educational policy would be elitist; that is, efficiency would require greater investment in the education of students with high initial endowments. Otherwise, whether the system were elitist or egalitarian would depend on which of two countervailing effects dominated.

As the efficiency problem has been posed, the number and characteristics of enrolled students is given. The department is viewed as assigning inputs and students to different sections, so as to make the best use of society's resources in educating these students. The problem could be modified to permit consideration of optimal enrolment by modelling the department as a seller of educational services and students as buyers. If the department is required to admit all students who want to enrol in the course and to charge each the marginal cost of educating him (exclusive of his opportunity cost), then optimal enrolment hinges on finding the marginal cost and on the rationality of student decision-making. The department cost associated with optimally educating $I+1$ instead of I students has two components: the cost of additional university inputs required and the cost of reduced learning by the other I students. If each student is charged this amount then rational students will enrol when the value of the learning they will obtain exceeds the marginal cost of university inputs, the "crowding" cost they impose on other students and the opportunity cost of their time.

The marginal cost of educating a student will depend on the characteristics of the individual student and of the other students. For example, if all students enrolled in a department have a given level of initial understanding and an additional student is considering enrolling, the cost may be higher (as is plausible), in terms of either or both components, the more the additional student's level of initial understanding diverges from the existing students' level. What this suggests is that from an efficiency point of view a department should establish a scholarship scheme whereby a student's tuition fee will depend on the marginal cost of his education which in turn will depend on his characteristics. While this would require considerably more information than is presently available, consideration of such a scheme suggests that it is by no means clear that every department should charge a lower fee (i.e., give a larger scholarship) to the brighter or more able student.

Assuming that the optimal enrolment in any single department constitutes only a fraction of the total student population, the foregoing argument implies that there may be significant gains from departments specializing in educating particular types of students. Which department should specialize in educating what type is indeterminate if we imagine all departments starting from the beginning with no endowments of either university inputs or enrolled students or if all educational inputs were perfectly mobile. The problem is similar to that of determining the location of each firm in an

136

industry. In actuality, a department will start with particular quantities of department inputs which cannot relocate at zero cost and which have a comparative advantage in educating students with a particular bias in their characteristics. Given these quasi-fixed factors of production, a department setting an optimal tuition fee schedule will attract students which can make the best use of these resources and thereby develop a specialized educational programme.

As indicated above, it is practically impossible for any department to find the precise solution to the maximization problem given by (3). In order to do so the department would require data on the variables S (although there are difficult problems in assigning joint costs to individual students), X_i and Q_i^0, knowledge of the parameters of F and G, and an algorithm for solving the programming problem. Each department would ordinarily have data on S, X_i and Q_i^0, but it would not ordinarily know the parameters of F and G. An alternative to having each department solving its own efficiency problem would be to have a centralized research centre, with an efficient algorithm for solving the programming problem and with estimates F and G consistent with readily available data on Q_i^0, that could provide any department with an optimal solution appropriate to its particular circumstances. A less refined, but more practicable, alternative would be for optimal solutions for different typical sets of circumstances to be worked out from which a department could select an appropriate prototype in designing its educational programme.

Critical for making any of these or other alternatives feasible is the estimation of the production function of F and the valuation function G. The following sections discuss the research problems that arise in trying to specify and estimate these key relationships.

Estimating the educational production function

The first task in obtaining an estimate of F is defining and measuring the variables involved, particularly educational output (Q). With respect to defining and measuring Q, the procedure that has been proposed and followed in both the US and the UK by researchers concerned with improving economics education, is to construct national examinations following these three steps (EEP, 1969,

1970, 1971 and Joint Council on Economic Education, 1967). First, establish a consensus on what concepts and methods are to be tested (Lumsden and Attiyeh, 1971 and Committee for Economic Development, 1961). Second, assemble a set of questions designed to test this material which are constructed, reviewed and revised by both economists and psychometricians. Third, revise the test questions based on a trial with a sample of students with varying amounts of economics education and further review by the test committee. The goal of this procedure is to design a test for which there would be near unanimous agreement that a higher score was a reflection of greater understanding of basic economics concepts and methods. The use of the total test score as a measure of output does not, however, allow for the possibility that economics knowledge has several dimensions that are not perfect substitutes and which might relate in different ways to the inputs. Nor does the total test score necessarily measure general aptitudes which might be developed in the process of studying economics and improvements in which might properly be regarded as components of educational output. Both of these limitations of the tests as measurement instruments could in principle be overcome — by the use of factor analysis of the test items in the first instance and by administering a battery of tests at the beginning and end of the course in the second. We ignore these problems in this chapter. It should be noted, however, that the ability of educators to measure knowledge in any field remains at a very primitive level.

The other student characteristics that need to be measured (X_i) include such variables as general intelligence, age, sex, previous educational experience and attainment and attitudes toward the teacher, course and subject. In principle, observations on these variables can be obtained through examinations and questionnaires, but as with the measurement of subject knowledge, our ability to measure some of the affective characteristics, which apparently have profound influences on learning, falls far short of what is required to explain a substantial portion of the variance in observed learning.

The department inputs (Y_k) can be divided into several categories: faculty characteristics, course materials and capital goods. Each category may vary with respect to quantity and quality. Instructors, for example, may be employed in courses for different quantities of time, but they may also have different characteristics, e.g., age and professional training, which may influence student learning. To take another example, written course materials may vary with respect to number of pages (quantity), but also may vary with respect to content or method of presentation (quality). Much of this information can be easily collected from the instructor, but as with other categories of variables serious measurement problems exist. How, for example, are we to measure all of the characteristics that determine the teaching ability of the instructor?

Even if it were possible to obtain meaningful measures of all of the variables involved, serious problems in specifying the statistical model remain. First, a large number of inputs obviously interact in complicated ways. While there is no well developed theory of educational production that governs the specification of a statistical model, there seems little question that students with different characteristics respond differently to given department inputs. For example, students with mathematics training might be expected to learn more economics from a course with a mathematical presentation than would students without mathematics training. To allow for all possible interaction effects substantially increases the number of parameters to be estimated and, consequently, the data requirements. For almost any conceivable data set, it will be necessary to use theory to exclude many of the potential interaction effects.

Second, even the existence of a very large number of observations does not necessarily rule out serious information gaps. In principle an experiment could be designed which would provide an optimal selection of observations. If, however, students and/or teachers are allowed to optimize in choosing "treatments" then it may be impossible to obtain data which would provide information on certain parameters. Suppose, for example, that there were only one student characteristic and one university input, each of which could take on a value of zero or one. (x might be mathematics training and y might be mathematical presentation.) Then, ignoring L and T, as well as interactions of x and y with Q^0, the statistical model might be:

$$Q_i^1 = \alpha_0 + \alpha_1 x_i + \alpha_2 y_{k_i} + \alpha_3 x_i y_{R_i} + \alpha_4 Q_i^0 + \epsilon_i$$

If the optimal arrangement is for students for whom $x=1$ to choose sections for which $y=1$, then x, y and xy would all be perfectly correlated and it would only be possible to obtain estimates of α_0

and the sum of α_0, α_1, α_2 and α_3. It would be impossible to assess what the effect of x and y not being equal might be.

If x and y were continuous variables or if the optimization were incomplete, the result would tend to be less extreme, but qualitatively similar. The greater the degree of optimizing self-selection, the less information there would be about certain parameters and the higher would be the standard errors of the parameter estimates. In the absence of control by the experimenter over the allocation of inputs in university economics courses, it may prove difficult to decide whether estimates of parameters for certain variables are statistically insignificant because the variables do not in fact have a substantial effect or because there is not much information about the effect of the variables. To assist the reader of the statistics, the pertinent characteristics of the sample should also be reported.

A third problem is that many of the variables involved are ordinal or qualitative in nature. The scales of such variables are necessarily arbitrary and the question arises as to how they should be handled in specifying the statistical model to be estimated. If a variable (e.g., sex) can assume only one of two values, then what scale is chosen is entirely irrelevant, at least for the standard regression model, since alternative scales will generate compensating alternative parameter estimates. When a variable (e.g., rank of instructor) can assume more than two values, then, given the form of the function relating the dependent variable to the independent variable in question, it is no longer irrelevant how the independent variable is scaled. In order to prevent the arbitrary choice of scale from influencing the results, it is desirable to allow as much flexibility as possible in deciding on the functional form of the relationship to be estimated. When an independent variable, z (e.g., textbook used), can take on N values, which correspond to the possible qualitative states (e.g., Samuelson, Lipsey, etc.), the natural procedure is to replace z with dummy variables, D_n, $n=1, \ldots, N$, which correspond to the possible states of z. When z takes on its nth possible value, then $D_n=1$ and, for $m \neq n$, $D_m=0$. The coefficient on any D_n would indicate the effect on the dependent variable of z taking on its nth possible state. This procedure can also be applied when z (e.g., student rating of instructor) is an ordinal measure that takes on discrete values. In this case each dummy variable would correspond to a different possible value on the ordinal scale and would equal one when z took on its corre-

140

sponding value and would equal zero otherwise. This serves to avoid the scaling problem altogether.

When the dependent variable is an ordinal measure the problem is a little more complicated. In the context of our model, total test score (Q) is the dependent variable. Since it is impossible to say how much knowledge a given difference between two scores represents, either in some absolute sense or relative to the difference between any other two scores, this measure is neither a ratio nor an interval scale. The most one could hope to be able to say would be that a higher score reflected a greater knowledge of economics. Thus, in the best of circumstances, total test score would be an ordinal measure. It would be possible to mitigate the necessarily arbitrary choice of the scale of Q from influencing the results by allowing sufficient flexibility in the form of F. But, if non-linear estimation techniques are excluded on pragmatic grounds, then there is limited scope for attaining the desired flexibility in this way. An alternative solution to the problem is the use of dummy variables to infer the "correct" scale for the dependent variable. (For a detailed discussion and application of this idea in a different context see Rubinfeld, 1972.)

Suppose that there are N possible scores on a test. Let D_n, $n=1, \ldots N$, be a set of dummy variables, where D_1 corresponds to the lowest possible score, D_2 to the next higher possible score, $\ldots$, and D_N to the highest possible score. When a student gets the nth lowest possible score, D_n takes on a value of one and all other D's take on a value of zero. The statistical model for estimating the parameters for F could be represented by

$$\alpha_1 D_1 + \ldots + \alpha_N D_N = F(\cdot) + \epsilon \tag{4}$$

If each α_n is assumed to be equal to the nth lowest possible score, then (4) would be equivalent to using actual total score as the dependent variable. Suppose instead, it is assumed that $\alpha_1 = 0$ and $\alpha_N = 1$. Equation (1) can then be rewritten as

$$D_1 + \alpha_2 D_2 + \ldots + \alpha_{N-1} = F(\cdot) + \epsilon \tag{5}$$

which can be transformed into

$$D_1 = F(\cdot) - \alpha_2 D_2 - \ldots - \alpha_{N-1} D_{N-1} + \epsilon \tag{6}$$

which can be estimated by standard regression techniques. The estimated α_n, $n=2, \ldots, N-1$, will determine a new scale for Q^1. If it could be assumed that F had the "correct" form for the production function for knowledge, then the new measure for Q^1 could be interpreted as an interval scale, whereby differences in Q^1 could be ranked. Unfortunately, it is impossible to know what is the true form of the function relating inputs to knowledge and equally impossible to identify the extent to which the new scale of Q^1 incorporates adjustments to compensate for any misspecification of F. For example, if the form of F incorporated the assumption of constant returns to scale and in fact there were decreasing returns to scale, then the estimated α_n would be lower for each n than if in fact there were constant returns. Consequently, the estimated α_n cannot be interpreted as implying a cardinal measure of knowledge.

In order to avoid serious computational problems, we propose to proceed in our estimation of a production function for economics teaching under the constraint that the statistical model be linear in parameters. While this ensures that the model can be economically estimated, the issue remains how it should be specified to capture the essential features of the actual production process. To facilitate the discussion let the initial knowledge and the J characteristics and time spent of the ith student and the M departmental inputs and the course enrolment in the k_ith course be represented by the N dimensional vector

$$Z_i = \{z_{i,1}, \ldots, z_{i,N}\} = \{Q^0_i, X_i, T_i, Y_{k_i}, L_{k_i}\}, i = 1, \ldots, I$$

where $N = J + M + 3$. Then the production function may be rewritten as

$$Q^1_i = F(Z_i), \quad i = 1, \ldots, I. \tag{7}$$

Two specifications of (7), which are linear in the variables, have been fitted to data on first-year economics students in the UK (see Attiyeh and Lumsden, forthcoming). These are

$$Q^1_i = \sum_{n=1}^{N} \alpha_n z_{i,n} + \sum_{n=1}^{N} \sum_{m=1}^{N} \beta_{n,m} z_{i,n} z_{i,m} + \epsilon_i \tag{8}$$

and

142

$$\ln Q^1_i = \sum_{n=1}^{N} \alpha_n \ln z_{i,n} + \sum_{n=1}^{N} \sum_{m=1}^{N} \beta_{n,m} \ln z_{i,n} \ln z_{i,m} + \epsilon_i. \quad (9)$$

Equation (8) is familiar as a standard second order analysis of covariance model. Equation (9), which is simply the analysis of covariance model in terms of logs, has been termed the transcendental logarithmic production function by Jorgenson *et al.* (1970). This model has the desirable feature that its very simple form is a generalization of a wide range of functions, including the CES function, and can attain any arbitrary set of elasticities of substitution for given levels of output and input.

Estimating the valuation function

As with the production function, estimating the relationship between the value of human capital and individual characteristics including Q encompasses numerous data, sampling and specification problems. Since the data problems here are even more severe than for the production function estimation, the actual empirical work is further into the future and, consequently, our remarks here will be less detailed.

By human capital we mean the present value of all labour income. As indicated above, an individual's stock of human capital is determined by his various characteristics, including his knowledge of subject matter. Our presumption is that it is by influencing a person's knowledge of a subject that the educational process produces human capital. (In actuality education may affect an individual's human capital through other characteristics as well, but this multidimensional problem will be ignored here.)

While a substantial amount of research has been undertaken in an attempt to identify the relationship between education and human capital, most of that work does not yield the detailed results that are required by educational decision-makers on a microeconomic level. These studies have been primarily concerned with levels of educational attainment (in terms of years of schooling completed) and income for the average person to have attained each level. Because these studies concentrate on the reduced form relationship between average educational inputs and human capital, they fail to identify the relationship between educational output and human capital. Knowledge of the latter relationship is essential if educators are to evaluate the economic impact of adopting alternative educational production techniques.

Most of the difficulties involved in measuring human capital arise from the fact that there is no market for the stock of human capital. All that we are able to observe in any one time period is the sale of services from that stock during the period. What would be needed to calculate the stock for any individual would be the anticipated time path of income over his remaining life and an appropriate discount rate. Since neither of these is directly observable, the best that can be expected would be an approximation based on observations of income for one or more periods, past income profiles for individuals with similar characteristics and the assumption that past and future income profiles are similar.

The problems involved in measuring the arguments of the valuation function G have already been discussed in the preceding section. What that discussion does not make clear is that although it may be possible to obtain observations on the relevant characteristics of individuals, data do not now exist which contain observations on both these characteristics and human capital for the same individuals. To fill this void, the Economics Education Project has begun two data collection efforts. One is to follow the students who were included in the sample drawn for the Project's production function study beyond graduation into employment. The other is to interview past graduates for whom human capital estimates can be made and also from whom it will be possible to obtain measures of relevant characteristics including knowledge of the subject.

Conclusion

In this chapter we have discussed a number of issues that have arisen in developing a general framework for analyzing efficiency in higher education. Obviously, other issues remain to be resolved, our general framework needs refinement, and many of our proposals will need to be modified in the process of carrying them out. Nevertheless, we feel that as long as institutions of higher learning operate outside a competitive profit-making framework, this type of analysis will be required if significant gains in economic efficiency are to be made. Without quantitative research results that relate the variables that administrators control to additions to the value of human capital, which is what they should be trying to affect, resource allocation decisions in higher education cannot adequately take advantage of opportunities to add to social profit.

Part IV

New Techniques in Universities

7. The Cost-Effectiveness of the New Media in Higher Education[1]

by Richard Layard

If industries are ranked by rate of technical progress, communications comes high and higher education low. This may seem surprising, since much of higher education is communication. The new media of television, videotape, film, and computers can clearly be used for teaching purposes and, like books, can carry a given material far beyond the range of the live human voice. Yet higher education continues to use much the same mixture of books and live instruction that has prevailed for many centuries, and even the possibilities of programmed texts to replace some live exposition are little exploited. Why is this?

There seem to be two main reasons. First, there are genuine doubts about what the advantages of the media are, if any. Even the educational technologists are divided on this matter. One group considers that the new media are bound to cost more per student-hour; the gain lies in the still higher increment to the value of output. The Congressional (McManus) Commission on Instructional Technology (1970, p.23) took this view, as have a number of other experts.[2] By contrast others believe that the real strength of the media is their ability to reduce costs per student-hour, while holding outputs con-

[1] I am extremely grateful for help and advice on this chapter to Michael Oatey. It draws on a number of ideas in Oatey (1972). I am also grateful to the Nuffield Foundation for a Small Grant that enabled me to visit the USA in Summer 1971.

[2] See for example Committee for Economic Development (1968) and Bright (1970). Bright believes that the main advantage of the new media is that they could make possible a reduction in the length of course, but he goes on to say that the public is unlikely to accept such a reduction. However, if the media are as cost-effective as he suggests, a reduction in the period of study would probably mean foregoing a profitable investment in further learning.

149

stant. (Office of Educational Communications, State University of New York, 1970). According to this view, educational technology so far has been mostly, though not always, used as an "add-on" to existing inputs, whereas its chief use should be as a substitute for existing inputs, especially teachers.[3]

The first two parts of this chapter are an attempt to resolve this issue. The conclusion is that *so far* there is no clear evidence of widespread gains in performance per student-hour using the new media, but equally no evidence of loss. If this is so, the media should be judged on the basis of cost, where we find that they are cheaper, provided the same materials are used on a large enough scale. This scale often exceeds the pitifully small scale on which they are typically used at present.

This brings us to the second reason why innovation has been so slow — namely the problem of incentive. Unless universities have incentives to be cost-effective, they will not exploit the new possibilities open to them. This issue is discussed in the last part of the paper and some suggestions made for improvement.

I. Benefits

Let us begin by restating the problem. The question is not whether we can have a completely mechanized university. The universities produce research as well as teaching, and teaching consists not only of imparting cognitive skills but also of promoting attitude change, self-knowledge and so on, which may depend heavily on human contact between teacher and taught. The issue is simply whether *some* of the task of exposition, testing students' understanding and answering their questions, which is now done by live teachers, can be done better by capital. To answer yes, we must show that, in making the change, the value of the benefits per student-hour rises by more than the costs, or falls by less.

We begin with the benefits. Some say performance per student-hour would be improved, others that it would be impaired. The arguments for expecting higher outputs depend of course on the medium in question, but there are some common elements.

---

[3] This substitution is presumably easiest in higher education, where teachers are not needed to keep order in class.

150

(a) *Individualized instruction*

Most of the media in principle permit the student to study more at his own pace than is possible under live instruction. Some of them (though not all) can also provide the student with more immediate awareness of whether he understands what has been presented to him. Moreover, if different students learn best in different ways, a multi-media system could allow each to work where his comparative advantage lay.

Against these theoretical advantages, Oettinger (1969) has forcibly pointed out the administrative difficulties of permitting greater individualization of timetables and work schedules. He quotes with relish the instructions in the Watertown Language Laboratory Procedures, 1966: "No one is an individual in the laboratory. Do nothing and touch nothing until instructions are given by the teacher." These difficulties may be less in higher education than at the school level, but they still exist. Then there are the motivational problems of individualized learning. The optimal level of external pacing is clearly not zero, though it may be lower than the amount we now provide. Finally one should not overlook the versatility of all media of instruction (Gagné, 1970, p.364). A live lecturer can pause in a lecture and ask each student to write out their answer to a question, before revealing his own. However, programmed texts and computer-assisted instruction may be more intrinsically suited to this method of proceeding; and even televised lectures, which are the least flexible of the new media, can be repeated for the benefit of one student, which live lectures cannot.

(b) *Better-prepared materials*

The second alleged advantage of the new media derives from their ability to carry the same material to many more students than can be reached by one live instructor. This means that the potential returns from additional work in preparing the material are that much higher. If as a result more preparation is done, output per student-hour will be higher.

Educational technologists regularly urge that up to 100 hours of teacher time should be devoted to preparing material which will take one hour to present to the students using it (Bright, 1970). This

151

excludes time spent by the teacher mastering the subject matter and refers only to the time he spends in designing the content of what is presented. For television, teachers often allow less than 100 hours, but still a great deal more than one would consider justified in the case of a live lecture, even if it was going to be repeated for some years. Textbook writers may well, of course, spend 100 hours preparing one hour's worth of reading, for books reap the economies of scale. But the new media may be able to replace some of the functions of the live instructor better than the textbook can.

(c) *Fuller use of outstanding talent*

They also offer the possibility of replacing bad instructors by good ones. Teaching talent is, after all, in quite limited supply, and it is wasteful and inegalitarian to exclude from access to the finest teachers those who cannot get into the institutions where they happen to teach. Textbooks have hitherto been the students' main protection against bad teaching and have disseminated the works of the masters. But television in particular offers further possibilities.

(d) *Reducing the optimum size of institution*

There are of course internal economies of scale within individual institutions using live instruction.[4] These arise mainly from the low marginal costs of expanding lecture audiences, though the savings are often obscured by the tendency of large institutions to offer more options and thus a higher quality of output. If the purely instructional economies of scale were fully exploited, they would probably require very large institutions — say, 20,000 students in a university teaching all the main branches of knowledge. But, with the new media the costs per student-hour may be less dependent on the size of institutions. If large institutions are felt to involve psychic loss, one advantage of the new media may be in making more economical the smaller institution.

---

[4] These will be documented for the UK in the forthcoming results of a study of university costs at the Higher Education Research Unit, London School of Economics. See also Bottomley *et al.* (1972) and Carnegie Commission on Higher Education (1972A).

Against all these advantages are the alleged *disadvantages* of loss of human contact between teacher and student, which some consider the central element in higher education. If this is significantly reduced, some believe that the mental development of students and their motivation to learn will be seriously impaired. It is therefore time to turn from *a priori* theorizing to evidence.

Evidence on student attainment

There have been two major surveys of the effects of television, compared with live instruction, on student attainment as measured by normal final examination results.[5] Chu and Schramm (1967) surveyed 202 comparisons in higher education and concluded that though television on balance performed as well as live instruction, the case for this was not as clear in higher education as in schools. However, Dubin and Hedley (1969), applying more sophisticated statistical tests to 42 studies involving 193 independent comparisons, showed that, as far as standard one-way television was concerned, there was no significant difference in performance. This was so for all the major subject groups. In the majority of cases there was no significant difference between the two media, and the cases of significant difference were evenly balanced between the two (p.19). Paradoxically two-way television, with talkback, performed less well, presumably because the technology and use of the medium is less well developed.

The cumulative evidence of many studies is more relevant than the quoting of particular instances. However, the finding of indifference between the media is confirmed by more recent experiments in teaching elementary economics at the Universities of Nebraska and Illinois (Urbana) and the State University of New York (Oneonta) (McConnell, 1968; Paden and Moyer, 1969; Gordon, 1969).

For programmed learning the balance of the survey evidence is the same — results are, if anything, better than those for live instruction plus textbook (Schramm 1964). In economics the results obtained by students who read Lumsden, Attiyeh and Bach's microeconomics text for an average of 12 hours, were as good as those of students

---

[5] Some of the experiments reported in this section may be fouled up by Hawthorn effects and self-selection among the students. But most of them are not.

taught live for 21 hours who also used a textbook (Attiyeh, Bach and Lumsden, 1969). This evaluation study differed from most in collecting data on study time, which is unfortunately treated as a free good in most of the psychological literature. Its results imply of course a higher output per student-hour (including private study) than under predominantly live instruction, but strong conclusions should not be drawn from a single study.

At this point one should perhaps sound a note of caution. For it appears that live instruction can be effectively replaced not only by TV and programmed learning but by unaided self-instruction from the textbook alone. This has been shown in a number of studies surveyed by McKeachie (1963) and Dubin and Taveggia (1968), and in economics by an experiment of McConnell and Lamphear (1969). The surveys also show that for live teaching large lectures are as effective as small tutorial groups. These findings are of course deeply disturbing, for they seem to suggest that all our teaching institutions could be disbanded without loss of teaching output. But this conclusion is misplaced. For many of the studies are open to methodological objections (MacKenzie *et al.*, 1970, Ch. X) and students may have made unrecorded adjustments in work effort in order to ensure what they consider their appropriate grades. More important, the experiments surveyed normally represent a small part of the total experience of the students concerned. In this sense they show the effects of a marginal adjustment, against the background of a campus life involving regular meetings of staff and students. However, from a policy point of view it is marginal adjustments that interest us, and if the marginal benefits of the new media are similar to those of the old, it is clearly essential to compare their costs to see if fruitful adjustments are possible. It may also be well worth considering a simple reduction in the amount of organized teaching combined with an increase in reading.

Evidence on attitudes

However, what changes are desirable, and even feasible, depends not only on their effects ôn students' attainments but also on their attitudes. Here the evidence on television is that students prefer it to large lectures but rate it lower than live teaching in small groups (Dubin and Hedley, 1969). However, students who have actually experienced television have more favourable attitudes to it than

154

those who have not, and the same is true of teachers. People like what they know. In general students attach more importance to the quality of teaching than to the medium, and the great majority of students say they would prefer an "excellent teacher" on television to the probability distribution of live instructors which they would alternatively face. They also believe that they will do as well in their examinations if taught by TV as live — a correct view, as we have seen, although teachers tend to expect them to perform worse and exaggerate the degree of student opposition to TV.

When individual experiments are examined, there are of course stories of success and failure. At the State University of New York at Oneonta elementary economics has been taught mainly by two periods a week of televised instruction plus one period of discussion with a graduate student. However, a live course was also offered, taught in 1968 by one of the most popular instructors. The latter only attracted 23 out of over 300 students, and elementary economics as a whole in the meantime attracted a growing proportion of all social science students on the campus (Gordon, 1969). By contrast, Paden and Moyer (1969) suspect that economics on TV discouraged some students who would otherwise have gone on to major in the subject. Their experience was not unique, and the amount of teaching by TV fell sharply during the later 1960s at Urbana and some other campuses due to student aversion to it, especially when it was inappropriately shown in large lecture theatres. In computer-aided instruction success stories are reported from Stanford, where the computer-assisted course in Russian in its first year kept 73 per cent of its students throughout the course, as against 32 per cent for the live course (Suppes and Morningstar, 1969). The computer-assisted students also performed better in the final examination, and the course has since steadily attracted a growing proportion of students. The fact that the media fail to provide human contact between staff and students evidently does not rule them out as expository and testing devices, provided contact occurs in other (more suitable?) ways.

II. Costs

We can therefore concentrate our attention on cost differences between the media, provided we confine ourselves to cases where there is no good reason for expecting different outputs.[6] Even so the problems are formidable. The only correct procedure is of course to cost separately all the alternatives which could be considered in any particular situation. Since each situation is different it is not easy to generalize, and on top of this the relative costs of new media are always changing — in a downwards direction. Nevertheless, from a public policy point of view, it is important to get some idea of the orders of magnitude of long-run costs involved, and in particular to see at what scale of operation the new media show signs of becoming competitive.

Sources of scale economies

The costs of any medium can usefully be looked at in three parts:

(a) The preparation of a master copy of the material (master costs), involving content design as well as production;

(b) The making available of the material to presentation points, either by duplicate copies or other forms of transmission (duplication costs);

(c) The presentation of the material at the presentation points (presentation costs).

The lines of division are often rather arbitrary but Table 7.1 shows the broad idea.

This table shows at once the fundamental difference between most of the media and the live instructor. Most of the other media have high master costs and fixed presentation costs, while for the live lecturer it is the variable presentation cost which is crucial. We shall explore the implications of this, first in general terms and then specifically for videotape and computer-assisted instruction.

Suppose we are considering replacing live lectures by some other form of group-teaching based on the media (such as communally-viewed videotape, TV, slide-tape or film). The "presentation-hour" is the natural unit of output with which to begin the cost comparison. For live instruction the long-run cost may be crudely regarded as constant (say $£v$) per "presentation-hour". We want to compare this with the average cost per "presentation-hour" of say a videotaped

---

[6] For example, if pictorial motion is necessary for achieving some particular objective, it is meaningless to compare the costs of slides and videotape.

TABLE 7.1

The main costs of different media

	Master	Duplication	Presentation	
			Fixed	Variable per presentation
Live lecturer	-	-	-	Lecturer's time
Videotape	Recording and photography	Duplicate copies	VTR + TV set	Equipment and duplicate wear
Film	"	"	Projector + screen	"
Slide-tape	"	"	Projector, screen + tape-recorder	"
Broadcast TV	"	Transmission	TV set	"
Computer-assisted instruction	Programme production	Computer	Terminal + cable	"
Books/programmed texts	Compositing	Printing	-	-

Note: All master costs also include the costs of designing the content of the material.
                   All variable presentation costs also include the cost of student time and space used.

lecture. This is not given, but depends on the master costs of the material being used (say £m per year) and the fixed presentation costs at each presentation point (say £p per year) and also on the annual number of presentations over which each of these is spread. In the simplest case the numbers of presentations of a given set of course-material, such as a videotape lecture, is equal to the number of institutions (I) in which the course material is being used. Nothing general can be said about the number of presentations per year at each presentation point (P) except that it reflects the degree to which institutions are using the medium in question. The new medium is cost-effective if

$$v < \frac{m}{I} + \frac{p}{P}$$

or, in other words, if enough institutions use the same material and these institutions use their plant with sufficient intensity. There are thus both external and internal economies of scale that have to be reaped.

Of course this approach is irrelevant to marginal decisions where materials may already exist and the issue is whether they should be used in more institutions, or where equipment already exists and the issue is whether to put more courses onto it. But in the present context we are concentrating on long-run changes from scratch. We shall also in due course have to bring in student-hours rather than presentations as the unit of output, but this is best done in terms of specific cases.

Videotape versus the live lecture

If we try applying the approach to the comparison of live lectures and videotape teaching, we run into two main problems. First, what is the cost of a live lecture? One approach is to adopt a conventional estimate, while the other is to specify clearly the pattern of substitution which one has in mind. For the moment we shall adopt a conventional estimate and revert to the second approach later. We assume that lectures and videotape programmes are rewritten every seven years (perhaps it should be more often) and that their once-for-all content design takes 10 hours. This, together with an allowance for variable presentation costs, makes a cost of £10 per live lecture.[7]

The second problem is in deciding what quality of videotape can do the same job as a live lecture. If a professional producer is let in on the act he will insist on "exploiting the potentialities of the medium". This can make for very expensive productions costing up to £15,000 per hour of material, as in the case of Sesame Street. However there is good reason to think that quite cheap productions can be effective in higher education. They have for example been used with success in science and engineering courses recorded in Colorado State University and used widely in neighbouring firms and colleges (Baldwin, Davis and Maxwell, 1972). From the organizational point of view, discussed in the last part of the paper, there

---

[7] For details of the cost, see Annex A. Throughout the comparison we omit the cost of student time and space, assumed the same for each medium.

may of course be arguments for more elaborate productions, if they raise the number of institutions using the material more than proportionately to the extra master cost. But for the moment we shall assume something near to the bare minimum. A simple recording of an unrehearsed lecture has a master cost of about £40. Instead we shall assume about £60, which allows for 10 hours' extra work by the teacher specifically linked to the videotape recording.[8] As for duplication costs, these are mainly the costs of tape and we shall assume that with effective planning our tape can be shared between three institutions. Presentation costs at each presentation point consist mainly of the cost of the videotape-recorder and TV set and their maintenance. The resulting costs per presentation are summarized in Table 7.2. Figure 7.1 shows the combinations of institutions (I) and

TABLE 7.2

Costs per presentation-hour of videotape and live lecturer (£)

	Master	Duplicate	Presentation	
			Fixed	Variable
Live lecturer	2.5	-	-	7.5
Videotape	$\dfrac{13.5}{I}$	0.8	$\dfrac{138}{P}$	0.2

Source: See Annex A.

presentation hours per presentation point (P) at which videotape is as economic as live teaching. Whatever the number of institutions, videotape can never justify its fixed presentation costs unless the equipment is used for at least 15 hours a year, as can be seen by writing the break-even equation in the form:

---

[8] Dubin and Hedley (1969) p.52 quote the findings of Macomber and Seigel at Miami University that open circuit TV lectures take a median of 9.6 hours compared with 1.7 hours for live lectures. Presumably the material was already partially designed. Bartlett (1970) also reports 10 hours spent on each mathematics lecture prepared for closed circuit TV; his lectures had already been delivered live.

$$P = \frac{138I}{9I - 13.5}$$

Similarly, whatever the number of hours usage, it can never justify its master costs unless each course-hour is used by at least two institutions, as can be seen by writing the equation in the form:

$$I = \frac{13.5P}{9P - 138}$$

However, even with only two institutions the equipment only has to be used for about 60 hours a year — say for 15 hours a year on each of four courses. This is of course for a very simple production. If the master costs of the production are doubled the number of institutions needed is doubled too.

Figure 7:1

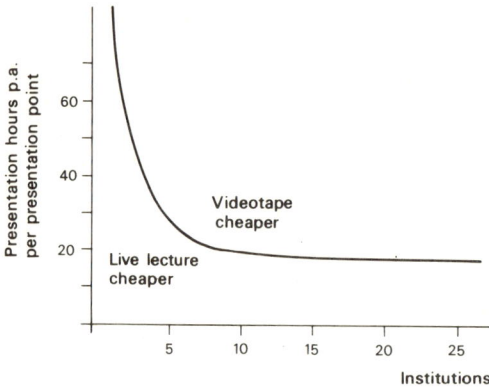

So much for the cost per presentation. But if we are choosing between the media, can we assume that the number of presentations needed to present a given body of subject matter to a given set of students is the same for both media? Clearly not. For videotape, the maximum number of students who can watch a 23-inch TV set is about 20. Suppose every institution has 30 students taking each of the courses we are concerned with. Unless its equipment is being used to less than half of its full capacity of, say, 1,000 hours a year, the university can simply double the number of presentations of all the material. The additional cost of these repeat presentations is

160

negligible. If the equipment is approaching full capacity use, the university can instead link up more than one TV set to each videotape-recorder; at these levels of utilization the additional cost of this per presentation is again negligible. So our previous comparison in Figure 7.1 remains roughly valid, provided we reinterpret the vertical axis to refer to course-hours of material shown per presentation point (or videotape recorder.)

To be precise, if each videotape recorder is showing less than 100 hours of videotape programmes a year, the cheapest way of presenting each programme to two groups of students is to repeat the presentation.[9] As can be seen from Table 7.2 this simply raises costs per programme shown by £0.2, which compares with the cost of £10 per live "programme". If more than 100 programmes are being shown a year it is cheaper to buy an extra TV set and the additional cost is less than £0.2 per programme shown.

So the number of students attending a course shown on videotape at any one institution has little effect on the cost of the course. The cost per student-hour thus falls more or less in inverse proportion to the number of students per course. But is the same true of live instruction? Only if additional students simply attend the already existing classes. But if each additional group of, say, 20 students is organized into a separate section, then videotape becomes more favourable relative to live teaching the more students there are per course. In this way it can easily happen that videotape is economic even if used in one institution only.

These points are illustrated in Table 7.3 which shows the costs per student-hour, assuming that for up to 20 students the two media cost the same. An example of videotapes that proved economic when used in one institution only comes from Oneonta, where the cost per student credit-hour in economics taught by videotape to 476 students was, in 1967, $5.40 per student credit-hour compared with $22.30 per student credit-hour in "equivalent courses at other Colleges of Arts and Science" in the State University of New York (Office of Educational Communications, 1970). These figures are equivalent to about £0.14 and £0.65 respectively per student-

---

[9] The fixed presentation cost is unchanged and the variable presentation cost of £0.2 per presentation comes (for less than 100 presentations per year) to less than £20, which is about the annual cost of an extra TV set.

hour.[10] The cost-accounting conventions used are not explained, but the reason is clearly that the live lecturing is more expensive than it would be if all the students were taught in one group.

TABLE   7.3

Cost per student-hour where videotape and live lectures cost
the same for less than 20 students per institution per course (£)

Students per institution per course	Videotape	Live	
		One Section	Sections less than 21
1	10	10	10
.	.	.	.
19	0.525	0.525	0.525
20	0.500	0.500	0.500
21	0.485	0.475	0.952
.	.	.	.
40	0.255	0.250	0.500

Source: See text.

Computer-assisted instruction

If the total costs of communally viewed videotape vary little with student numbers per location, the opposite is true of computer-assisted instruction, since this is a completely individualized method of instruction. Its costs depend very heavily on the number of terminals, and thus, assuming full utilization of terminals, on the number of student-hours. The technology of CAI is probably changing faster than that of any other medium and cost-estimates are

---

[10] A student credit-hour normally involves one hour a week of teaching for 15 weeks.

162

correspondingly more tendentious. The most flexible system so far developed is the PLATO system at the University of Illinois, Urbana. The plans for the new PLATO IV system envisage 4,000 terminals spread over a wide area, and its projected annual costs (with amortization over five years) are shown in Table 7.4. If each console is used 44 hours a week for 45 weeks a year the cost per student-hour is $0.34–0.68 or £0.13–0.27. Of this, between a half and three-quarters is directly dependent on the number of student hours. Though one should point out that the PLATO IV project is not yet in operation and the costs of most existing systems are a good deal higher,[11] it is interesting to compare these costs with those of around £0.5 per student-hour in live lectures in Britain.

TABLE 7.4

Projected costs of PLATO IV CAI system ($m. per annum)

Central management services	0.2
Computer systems software	0.1
Central computer facility	0.9
Communication channels to console (at $18 - 50 per console p. a.)	0.1 - 0.2
Student consoles (at $360 - 1000 per console p. a.)	1.5 - 4.1
Total	2.8 - 5.5

Source: British Computer Society (1971) p. 122. (This presents a survey of 17 leading CAI projects.)

---

[11] Jamison, Suppes and Butler (1970) report that the cost of the New York City system of compensatory CAI in schools costs about $3.5 per student-hour, or ten times more than the PLATO IV system, partly because its utilization rate is only one-third of that assumed in the PLATO calculations. However, they also describe a mini-computer system, suited to school drill and practise and tutorial work in foreign languages, which will operate at half the cost of the New York system.

Live instruction

This figure is got by dividing our notional cost of £10 a lecture by the average lecture attendance in 1961/2 of around 20 students (see Table 7.3). However, it is time to define rather more closely what we mean by the cost of live instruction. The universities are joint product enterprises and the question we are asking is "Can their existing outputs be produced at less cost? " To find the marginal cost of a lecture under the existing system we therefore ask how much money we could save if we produced our existing outputs minus, say, x lectures; the cost per lecture is this saving divided by x. Now if x were at all significant, the number of teachers would fall and each remaining teacher would do more research and less teaching. We should save not just the short-run cost of the lectures but the long-run cost involved in apprenticing the extra teachers and improving their knowledge of the subject over their working lives.

There is, of course, no fully defensible way of estimating the marginal cost implied in this approach. However, suppose that every teacher needed to spend a certain amount of time on private study and other activities, but that over the range of change with which we are concerned, his research output could be considered proportional to the time he spent on research and his teaching output proportional to the time he spent on teaching. If the teaching output of live teachers is reduced, the cost saving per unit of teaching output is then the annual cost of a teacher *times* the proportion of his total annual time spent on teaching and research which it takes to produce one unit of teaching output.[12] Becoming specific, the cost of a lecture is the annual cost of a teacher *times* the proportion of his annual time on teaching and research spent on teaching *times* the proportion of this attributable to one lecture. According to a recent survey (Committee of Vice-Chancellors, 1972) British teachers

---

[12] If the annual time per teacher spent on teaching is t and on research $k^° - t$, the number of teachers is n, and the total annual teaching output (T) and research output (R) are measured in units such that each requires one hour of a teacher's time, then

$$T = tn$$
$$R^° = (k^° - t)n$$
$$\therefore T = kn - R^°$$
$$\therefore \frac{dn}{dT} = \frac{1}{k}$$

164

attribute about 60 per cent of their allocable working time at the university to teaching. (The actual proportions were: work for under-graduates 37 per cent, for graduate course-work students 5 per cent, for graduate research students 5 per cent, personal research 24 per cent, unallocable university work 18 per cent and outside work 11 per cent.) As regards the distribution of teaching time, Table 7.5, column (1) shows the latest available data. If one assumed that a lecture-hour requires twice as much preparation as any other teaching event and that teaching proceeds for 25 weeks a year, then each lecture represents 0.75 per cent of a teacher's annual teaching effort.[13] As for the university costs attributable to one teacher, these are clearly less than the total cost of the institution divided by the number of teachers, since costs of maintenance and so on are more dependent on the number of students than of teachers. If we include only the teacher and his share of secretaries and technicians, this might be about £4,000 p.a. of which £2,400 p.a. goes to teaching and £18 to each lecture. This is a little higher than our earlier estimate which may have been unduly biassed against the new media. The new estimate implies an average cost per student-hour in lectures of around £0.8 and in all forms of teaching of nearly £1.[14]

The Open University

So far we have been concerned with marginal changes in campus universities. However, higher education is possible without campus universities, as the Open University is already showing. Here the relevant cost comparison is of a different character, and as it is not the central theme of the paper, only a brief discussion is included.[15] The Open University's teaching system depends on correspondence material, TV and radio broadcasts, and some class tuition at local study centres and summer schools. Most students have hitherto taken

---

[13] Lectures represent $2(2.3)/(8.2 + 2.3)$ of his annual teaching load and he gives 25×2.3 lectures a year. So each lecture is $2/(8.2 + 2.3)25$ of his annual teaching.

[14] £2,400 ÷ (students per teacher x student hours per student per week x weeks per year) = £2,400/8(12.5)25.

[15] For a full account of the University, see Perry (1972) and on costs, Wagner (1972) and Laidlaw and Layard (1973).

TABLE 7.5

Teaching arrangements in universities

GB 1961/2

	Average hours a week given per teacher			Average hours a week received per student	Student/Staff ratio	Average size of class (students per teacher)
	Given by teachers	Given by postgraduates	Total			
	(1)	(2)	(3)	(4)	(5)	(6)
Lectures	2.3	0.2	2.5	7.1	8.0	23.0
Discussion periods	3.2	0.3	3.5	1.5	8.0	3.6
Practicals	2.4	0.9	3.2	3.4	8.0	8.4
Written exercise classes	0.4	0.1	0.5	0.4	8.0	7.3
All teaching	8.2	1.4	9.7	12.5	8.0	10.4

Source: Committee on Higher Education, (Robbins Report) (1963) p. 351.

Note: Col(6) = Col(5) x Col(4) ÷ Col(3).

one course per year requiring in principle 10 hours work a week from January to November, including on average one half-hour TV programme and a half-hour radio programme. These hours compare with an average for full-time students in campus universities of 38 hours a week (Committee on Higher Education, 1963, p.277) during the six term-time months of the year. On these grounds each student could be considered to be about half a full-time student. The university regulations imply a similar approach in that six courses are normally required for a pass degree and eight for an honours degree. Working on this assumption we can now compare in terms of cost these two totally different learning systems.

TABLE 7.6

Open University's budgetary estimates for 1973 (£000 (1971 prices))

Fixed (independent of student members)	
BBC	1,647
Academic staff and library	1,588
Administration	
Central	1,093
Regional	1,244
Other (e.g. media production, ed. tech. etc.)	1,373
	6,945
Variable with student numbers	2,232
Total	9,177

Source: Wagner (1972)

The projected Open University budget for 1973 is reported by Wagner (1972) as £6.9m fixed costs (independent of student numbers) and £2.2m variable costs (see Table 7.6). The student numbers associated with the budget were 36,500. Though the ultimate size of the university is still unsettled, the only basis for provisional analysis is to assume a steady state. The University intends to revise its materials continuously and thus its fixed outlays are likely to be maintained at a roughly constant rate: though many of them are intrinsically for capital formation they can for the present purposes be crudely treated as if they represented an annual flow of services. Thus the University's cost function is (in £, 1971 prices)

$$C = 6,945,000 + 61\ S$$

167

where S is student numbers. For the planned number of students, which substantially fails to reap the full economies of scale, the average cost is £250 p.a. or £500 per full-time equivalent. In campus universities the total institutional expenditure divided by the number of full-time equivalent students (unadjusted for faculty mix and the like, but omitting expenditure financed by research grants and including notional rent) is about £1,300 (again in 1971 prices). How much of each of the two figures should be attributed to research is clearly debatable, but any adjustment would reduce the Open University's relative advantage. On the other hand, adding in the resource cost of students' time (however one valued leisure) would enormously improve the relative efficiency of the Open University. Until these adjustments are made and more evidence collected on the outputs of the two systems, no sensible judgement can be made. Nor, from a policy point of view, is there any need for an all-or-nothing judgement, since a major aim of the Open University is in any case to provide for people such as housewives and workers for whom attendance at a campus university is not really practicable.

However, from the point of view of campus universities, the Open University may have much to contribute both in terms of actual teaching materials and in lessons about the cost-effectiveness of different media. This is being actively studied in the University's Institute of Educational Technology.[16] At present television absorbs the main part of the University's BBC budget. Supposing it absorbs £1,500,000 and that the 36,500 students watch on average 25 half-hour programmes (an overestimate) a year, the cost per student-hour is around £3 whereas for radio it is about one-tenth of this. The reason lies in the complexity of the TV programmes,[17] which, if 300 are made per year, cost on average around £10,000 per programme hour. Clearly this is a quite different type of operation from the low quality videotape programme discussed earlier. While the latter may be adequate for substituting a portion of live teaching in a campus rich with social and cultural life, the TV programmes of the Open University may provide the main sense of institutional belonging and also act as important recruiting agencies for the Open University and

---

[16] See Bates (1973).

[17] Transmission costs are only about 5 per cent of total BBC costs.

the life of the intellect generally. These are questions on which work is proceeding. But perhaps the greatest single achievement of the Open University is that it has broken through the organizational obstacles which seem everywhere else to have inhibited a really large-scale substitution of one system of learning for another.

III. Organization and incentive

If the new media have so much to offer, the problem is how to bring about their introduction. What are the obstacles? These have been discussed at some length elsewhere (Layard and Jackman, 1972) and a few basic points will suffice here. There are difficulties on both the demand and the supply sides of the market. However, textbooks are fairly efficiently supplied by commercial publishers, who could equally well do the same for the new media. So it seems that the real problems lie on the side of demand.

The people who decide whether to demand the new media are the teachers, and the main things that teachers value are probably their income, the way they spend their time and the university's outputs of teaching and research. These provide us with a framework for analyzing the factors influencing demand.

The financial incentives to introduce new teaching methods are clearly extremely limited. There is no mechanism by which the members of a department can appropriate a share of its increased social profitability. Given the lack of financial competition between institutions, it may be as well that teachers are not as free as workers in the classic labour-managed corporation to set their own wages. However, it is highly unsatisfactory that, owing to the stress on research as the criterion for pay, individual teachers have no incentive to devote time to organizing the introduction of new teaching methods, especially when, as with the new media, this involves a considerable investment of time. In fact, there may in some cases be positive disincentives in that an individual teacher who mechanizes his course may not be considered to be pulling his weight in teaching. Unless positive recognition is given to the management of innovation, the prospects for change are bleak. It is also said that teachers fear technological unemployment. If this is used to explain the absence of labour-saving innovation, this implies a degree of collusive cooperation between teachers for which there is little evidence. However, innovation is obviously easiest in a period of expansion, when the capital/labour ratio can be raised without a reduction in the absolute number of teachers. For this reason the prospects for innovation in the 1970s may be brighter in the UK than the US. If expansion is accompanied by a reduction in university income per student, this might add to the pressures for labour-saving innovation.

Turning to the way teachers value their use of time, they may in general prefer exposition to other forms of staff/student contact, either because it best advances their own thinking or because they like holding forth. Yet this is the task most readily substituted by the media, none of which unfortunately can read a student's essay. Teachers are naturally unwilling to reduce the ratio of exposition to other teaching, as the majority of them would have to. The problem would be sharpened if the new order were organized on a hierarchical basis — with a group of superstars producing the media and a race of helots handling students' problems. Yet the new media are bound to add to the kind of division of labour which already occurs when many of us use one man's textbook. There are simply limits to the number of teachers who can efficiently be involved in supplying new media — or textbooks. But, subject to this, it is important from the demand point of view that as many teachers should be involved as possible.

Even so there is still a puzzle. For, as we have seen, if university outputs were held constant, each remaining teacher could do more research. Moreover, if the departmental or university budget remained unchanged during the period of innovation, it could offer its teachers many additional non-pecuniary perks — more secretarial assistance, equipment and so on. Yet innovation lags. A major reason seems to be the fear that if the department or university shows that it can save money it will lose the money it has saved. This is of course what happens ultimately in a perfectly competitive economy, but those who innovate have a period during which they experience quasi-rents before their profits are again eroded. The climate for innovation in universities would be much improved if the financing agencies would guarantee not to remove the non-pecuniary profits of innovation for a certain limited period of years. Otherwise there is a real danger that our semi-decentralized arrangement will turn out to be less efficient than either decentralized firms or the centralized armed forces, both of which use the new media a lot more than the universities.

This brings us to the teachers' concern for the teaching and research output of their institution. Many teachers fear that if they showed that teaching could be done more efficiently, research output would not in fact be held constant but would fall. If research has been financed covertly out of money that the donors thought was going on teaching, this is certainly a possibility. Whether or not the world would be poorer if it lost some of the research done in the weaker institutions is debatable, but if the teachers feel it would then this helps to explain their resistance.

Teachers are also legitimately concerned about the quality of teaching offered to their students. Most of the videotape programmes currently available are used only in the institution where they were produced, simply because other institutions do not consider them suitable or good enough. If the market for materials is to become large enough for their production to be economic, one approach is for consortia of institutions to produce them. This involves at the minimum joint sponsorship and at the maximum sharing of the actual work, in such a way that a number of institutions stand morally committed to using the resulting materials. The seven regional "cooperative learning-technology centres" proposed for the U.S. by the Carnegie Commission on Higher Education (1972B) are an example of this approach.

Turning to the supply side, there are two main issues: first, whether firms or universities should be the entrepreneurs and, second, how to provide incentives to attract really good people into the field. Clearly there will be all kinds of entrepreneurs: publishing and information-processing firms, individual universities, consortia of universities, professional associations and governments. Given the past weakness on the side of demand, as well as copyright problems, one cannot expect firms to rush in yet, and heavy subsidies will be needed. Hitherto, these have mainly gone to individual university units of instructional technology. This strategy has not been very successful and more emphasis now will have to be placed on more centralized sponsorship.

There remains the question of whether the aim should be to develop a separate academic career structure in the new media or whether people in the regular career structure should be tempted into the media on a short-term contract basis. The former has the virtue that it develops media expertise and might attract able people who, in the traditional career structure, would be inevitably attracted to research. On the other hand, it runs the risk of failing to bring into the new media men in touch with the best of current thought. It also involves fewer people *in toto* in the media and thus, while good for supply, may be bad for demand. The Open University is the leading example of an attempt to build up a semi-independent career structure, within which there would yet be substantial time for research. This new emphasis is timely, but the optimal pattern of future recruitment to media activities remains hard to descry. As with the media generally, a thousand forms will bloom — most of them only once; but more and more will, one hopes, prove hardy perennials.

Annex A

Costs of videotape and live lectures

Capital outlays are amortised over seven years at 5 per cent per annum. In the case of master costs this is due to the assumption that course-hours are redesigned every seven years. In addition, all equipment is assumed to have a life of seven years due to obsolescence or 7,000 hours due to wear and tear, whichever is the shorter: organizational factors will however normally prevent more than 1000 hours use per year, and seven years is again assumed here.

I. Videotape

| | £(1970 prices) | |
	Capital cost	Annual cost
Master costs per course-hour		
Lecturer's time (at £1.5 per hour)		
Design of content (10 hours)	15	
Rehearsing, recording and checking (10 hours)	15	
Technician's time (10 hours at £0.75 per hour)	8	
Master tape (1″)	28	

172

Rental value of equipment
(1 videotape recorder (1″) costing £800,
2 cameras costing £600,
and other items costing £700, used to
produce 50 course-hours p.a.)   8
Maintenance of equipment (at an annual cost
of 10 per cent of the original cost of equipment)   4
     78   13.5

Duplicate costs per course-hour per institution
1/3 duplicate tape (½″) at £12 each   4   0.7
Postage of duplicate to an institution   0.1
   0.8

Fixed presentation costs per presentation point
1 videotape recorder (½″)   400
1 T.V. set (23″)   100
   500   88.0
Maintenance of equipment (at an annual cost
of 10 per cent of the original cost of equipment)   50.0
   138.0

Variable presentation costs per presentation
Wear on heads, etc. and variable maintenance   0.2

II. Live lecturer

Master costs per course-hour
Lecturer's time (at £1.5 per hour)
Design of content (10 hours)   15   2.5

Variable presentation costs per presentation
Lecturer's time (assuming a one-hour lecture
needs four other hours of adaptation and   7.5
organization)   10.0

8. The Information Content of Student Evaluation of Faculty and Courses

by Keith G. Lumsden

"At present the universities are as uncongenial to teaching as the Mojave Desert to a clutch of Druid priests. If you want to restore a Druid priesthood, you cannot do it by offering prizes for Druid-of-the-year. If you want Druids, you must grow forests." William Arrowsmith.[1]

Introduction

Student evaluations of faculty and courses in universities are not new. The two universities most often quoted in the history of student evaluations are Harvard and the University of Washington where opinions have been collected and openly published for students, or been made available to faculty, for several decades. While many students and professors enthusiastically endorse the idea of faculty and course evaluations by students many university teachers believe that such evaluations serve no useful purpose and may, in fact, be harmful to the university — asking for student opinion is asking for trouble.

If one considers the large business firm, seeking information from consumers is an obvious method of improving output and services. Many warranties on consumer durables are closely tied in with questionnaires on the characteristics of the commodities purchased. While few firms rely solely on the results of consumers' surveys to determine their output, many argue that such information is important in meeting demand and consequently in maximizing profit. The university, of course, is not a business firm. Its output is ill-defined, it does not always deal in competitive markets and its consumers are constantly changing. The university also is composed of three separable groups of individuals, the administration, the faculty and the student body each often possessing very different goals. Internal conflicts constantly arise not only between any two of the above-named groups but also within the groups themselves; no market rules exist for efficient outcomes.

---

[1] William Arrowsmith, address to the 1966 annual meeting of the American Council in Education quoted in Kenneth G. Eble (1970).

The principal arguments for student evaluations of what they are buying in the university essentially rest on the concept of consumer sovereignty and on the positive effects evaluations can have on the behaviour of suppliers. Potentially student evaluations can provide information about the effects of quality of university inputs on the quantity of output evaluated in terms of student preferences. If these evaluations are correct and faculty advancement is tied to what students say, then improved instruction will take place since rewards will be tied to teaching performance. Critics, however, argue that instead of what students say, what students learn should be measured and rewards should be based on contributions to learning output. Such a system would require pre- and post-tests in each subject and an ability to hold other things equal; in short one would require accurate measurements of students' achievements and characteristics, including ability and background, the possibility of which is viewed with considerable scepticism by those who purport to be in the measuring business. In one attempt at such measurement with which I have been involved, for example, the proportion of variance in measured economics comprehension explained by measured inputs is only 37 percent (Attiyeh and Lumsden (forthcoming)).

Part of this disagreement may stem from the fact that, at university, students receive at least three types of educational services: those that provide higher current consumption, those that provide higher expected lifetime real income and those that reduce the variance in lifetime income. University inputs (facilities, courses and professors) contribute to all three types in varying degrees by subject and by individual student and little attempt has been made to distinguish these components in measuring total educational output. Differences as to how much influence students' opinions ought to have may be based on differences in the weights attributed to each of these components of total output.

If we accept this partitioning of educational output into three component parts we have a framework for analysis within which student evaluations may play a significant role. Consider two institutional arrangements: conventional university and a non-campus institution which uses radio, television, packaged learning systems or whatever, i.e., some institution similar to Britain's Open University.

Assume that the qualities of the degrees from both institutions are indistinguishable on the job market; (in fact one could assume that the non-campus institution is composed of videotaped or live televised lectures from the conventional university and that all students take common examinations; one could also allow some two-way communication with the instructor and the off-campus student but this unnecessarily complicates the issue). Thus the main difference between the two institutions is that the non-campus student is denied many aspects of traditional campus life. This "package of extras" has a price which some students will be prepared to pay to attend the conventional university.

In terms of current consumption the student will be paying for the privileges of being located with his peers, making friends, finding a spouse and in general enjoying many of the spontaneous activities which occur when large groups of people spend lots of time together. Some of these experiences will also provide higher expected lifetime income e.g., the spouse or the ability to explore different fields of study and discover where his own interests and potential lie. Personal contact with faculty members and exhibiting talents not always evident in written examinations can earn advice, letters of recommendation and eventual well-suited employment where the greater informational content of both jobs and job-seekers can result in higher real income and reduced variance in that income because of reduced uncertainty.

The difference in price for the two types of educational services offered should equal the value of additional output of the conventional over the off-campus university. To evaluate each element in this "extra output package" ideally one would require a spectrum of institutions each offering one additional element or service, produced technologically efficiently, and knowledge of how much students would be prepared to pay for each increment. With current institutions and the emergence of open universities and degree-granting continuing education programmes the value that students place on the additional on-campus outputs discussed may be capable of being estimated.

Within the conventional university today, grade point averages and degrees are generally accepted measures of part of the university output and, while a majority of faculty seem to favour student evaluations of courses and instructors, it is not always clear why they

177

favour them or how the student ratings are evaluated and used in the decision-making process in the university. For example a recent study stated its aims thus:

"One major aim of this study is to define and describe effective teaching so that instructors can be helped to improve and graduate students can be better prepared for the teaching function of academic life — the other aim is to find more valid reliable and effective means of incorporating the evaluation of teaching into advancement procedures. We believe this to be the most important single requirement for the improvement of university teaching; the incentive thereby provided will encourage instructors to devote the study, time and effort necessary to do their best, and the status of teaching will increase." Hildebrand et al, (1971). Without being overly critical one would like to see operational definitions of "effective", "improve", "better prepared", "do their best", "status of teaching will increase" since the research which has been done in the field produces little evidence that student opinions are related to grades, other measures of performance in a course or overall grade point average. But this fact does not mean that student evaluation are less important than grades; both may be measuring different university outputs and student opinions may rise in importance in those institutions which favour abolishing grades entirely.

What does seem evident is that students, faculty, alumni, administration and the state government differ — sometimes quite violently — on the weights that ought to be assigned to different university outputs or, in some cases how inputs should be reallocated often without direct reference to output. For example, Governor Reagan appears to be saying that University of California faculty should be spending more time with students and enjoying less leisure; students often appear to be saying the same, perhaps kindly substituting "research" for "leisure". It is certainly not clear that such substitution would mean that students would learn more or even that faculty and courses would be more highly rated by students.

Whose preferences should weigh more heavily is, to a large extent, a matter of value judgment and the political decision-making process is complicated by the lack of known relationships between inputs and outputs. As long as substantial differences exist, however, in the opinion of different groups in university communities as to how resources should be allocated and what weights should be attached to different outputs, research findings hopefully will lead to clarification of some of the issues and will yield empirical results upon which more scientific decision-making can be made.

Amid all the controversy on student evaluations one fact is clear. The recent resurgence of faculty concern with, and student agitation for effective teaching has resulted, on many campuses, in the systematic solicitation of student opinions of their teachers and courses.[2] The prevalence of such evaluation practices may help answer a number of questions broadly raised. Specifically: (1) to what extent do and can the resulting data provide the kinds of information required to achieve the intended objectives? Answering this question involves considering how questionnaires are and should be designed and how their responses are and should be interpreted. It also involves determining what factors students implicitly consider important and what objective factors influence students' evaluations. (2) Do the data generated by the evaluation process provide information about educational production relations? It is possible that student opinions might improve measures of educational inputs and output, and they might permit direct tests of the role of student attitudes as an input in the learning process.

This chapter constitutes an attempt to give preliminary answers to some of these questions and to suggest how a more detailed and extensive research effort might lead to more definitive answers. The results are based on an analysis of questionnaire responses for all students in all courses in Stanford's Graduate School of Business for the academic year 1970/71. The questionnaire is reproduced in the Annex.

---

[2] "Yet in a recent survey of 1000 faculty members at six diverse colleges and universities, 92 per cent stated that teaching effectiveness should be *quite important* or *very important* as a criterion for advancement, whereas only 38 per cent of the sample stated that effectiveness as a teacher actually is *quite important* or *very important*. No less than 72 per cent of the respondents felt that their campuses should have formal procedure for evaluating teaching." Wilson, Gaff and Bauvy (1970).

Determinants of student overall evaluations

One concern that many faculty have in subjecting themselves and their courses to student evaluations is that students may give too much weight to trivial aspects of their efforts. The image of the charismatic but incompetent teacher or the entertaining but contentless course capturing the favour of students is frequently used against granting official status to student evaluations. While there obviously is room for disagreement in the absence of hard empirical evidence as to what attributes of a teacher or course are important for learning, it is of interest to estimate the relative importance that students attach to different attributes in forming overall opinions. Such estimates would not provide a basis for deciding whether students' opinions accurately reflect the contribution of teachers or courses to students' learning but they would provide those teachers who believe in student sovereignty (or who want to up their ratings) with information that will help them "improve" their teaching performance or course design. These estimates would also enable faculty to assess the "reasonableness" of the weights that students give to different attributes.

Another issue involved in appraising the usefulness of student evaluations is the extent to which overall opinions are influenced by student, rather than by teacher or course characteristics. If an overall rating depends largely on what students a teacher has in his course, there is some question as to whether the rating reflects the impact of the teacher and course or the attitudes of those particular students.

To find out which factors students consider important in assessing courses (or course attributes) and their professors, regression analyses were carried out on the 1970/71 student questionnaire data. In this section the 4,996 responses of students in all the GSB courses in 1970/71 are analyzed. In the next section analysis includes additional data collected on the students in the B.201 (Macroeconomics) course for the same year. Unfortunately only one year's data were available for analysis because of "teething" problems in the collection and storage of the student evaluations. The variables in the analysis fall into several categories: student overall evaluations of the course; student evaluations of various educational outputs; student evaluations of various educational inputs, including the overall performance of the instructor; student characteristics; and instructor characteristics.

The first part of the analysis attempts to explain the student's overall evaluation of the course in terms of his evaluations of course inputs. The statistics for these regressions involving these variables are reported in Table 8.1. The regression coefficient for the evaluation of each course input indicates the importance that students implicitly attribute to that input in producing a better course as measured by students' overall course ratings. In effect, each regression can be thought of as a linear approximation to an educational production function where output is measured by the student's overall evaluation of the course and inputs are measured by the student's evaluation of course inputs. In regression (1) all of the inputs have positive coefficients that are significantly different from zero. Nevertheless, there are significant differences in size among the coefficients. The evaluation of lectures had a substantially larger coefficient than any of the other explanatory variables. This means that the effect of improving the rating of lectures would have a larger impact on the overall course rating than an equal improvement in the rating of any other input.

In regression (2) the overall evaluation of the instructor is included as an additional explanatory variable. While inclusion of this variable substantially reduces the size of the coefficients for evaluations of lectures and class discussions, the coefficients on both of these variables remain positive and significantly different from zero. It is striking, however, that the opinion of instructor is by far the most important factor influencing the overall opinion of the course. It appears that the instructor contributes a great deal to the course, as perceived by the student, over and above his influence as reflected in evaluations of lectures, class discussions and other course inputs. One implication of the finding is that students are likely to be substantially less satisfied with courses that substitute other learning media for the instructor. It is not clear, however, how live television (or videotaped lectures) would be evaluated since we have no observations on the instructor on the "tube" compared with in the "flesh".[3]

Regression (3) in Table 8.1 adds student characteristics and time spent studying in the course to the variables included in regression

---

[3] For an attempt to provide an answer to the question see D. Jamison and K.Lumsden (1972).

TABLE 8.1

Dependent variable: overall satisfaction with the course

Independent variable	Regression (1) β	t	Regression (2) β	t	Regression (3) β	t	Independent variable	Regression (3) contd. β	t
Constant term	-2.06	-15.6	-2.13	-17.8	-2.87	13.4	Undergraduate major:		
Evaluation of:							Science	.11	1.2
Reading materials*	.17	13.4	.16	14.0	.16	12.7	Engineering	.15	2.2
Lectures*	.47	32.3	.21	13.5	.46	31.6	Economics	.13	1.7
Class discussions*	.21	14.9	.14	10.7	.21	14.4	Mathematics	.24	2.3
Papers*	.13	.7.6	.10	6.5	.12	7.3	Psychology, sociology, etc.	.05	0.5
Projects*	.06	2.9	.06	3.0	.05	2.4			
Computer exercises*	.06	3.1	.05	3.3	.06	3.1	History, political science, etc.	.06	0.8
Case materials*	.12	7.4	.10	6.7	.11	6.5	Philosophy	.13	0.5
Examinations*	.18	13.1	.15	11.8	.18	13.1	Business administration	.13	1.4
Instructor			.58	32.2			Areas of interest:		
Student characteristics							Accounting	-.01	-0.2
Time spent on course					.19	10.5	Business economics	.10	2.1
Age in years					.01	3.9	Computers & Information systems	.06	1.4
MBA candidate					-.01	-.2			
PhD candidate					-.04	-.4	Finance	.01	0.3
Years in programme					.06	2.1	Marketing	-.10	-2.4
Years of full-time work					-.02	-2.6	Operations Management	.03	0.6
Years in military service					-.01	-1.0	Operations & Systems Analysis	-.10	-2.1
Graduate School of Business grade point average					-.00	-0.3	Organizational Behaviour	.01	0.3
No grade point average					.05	0.3	Transportation & Logistics	-.04	-0.5
R^2		.58		.65					.59

* Note: To control for the fact that some students in some courses did not give a response for these independent variables, dummy variables were included as independent variables in the regressions. When one of variables 2-9 had a value of 0, the corresponding dummy variable took on a value of 1; otherwise the dummy variable took on a value of 0. The mean values for the dummy variables corresponding to variables 2-9 are .04 for 2, .06 for 3, .06 for 4, .43 for 5, .68 for 6, .60 for 7, .31 for 8, and .35 for 9. The regression statistics for these variables are not shown in the table.

(1). The purpose here is to test whether the overall evaluation, given the evaluations of the course inputs, is influenced by the effort and background of the student. A number of these variables have statistically significant coefficients. The more time a student spends on a course, the older he is, the more years he has been in the GSB and

182

TABLE 8.2

Dependent variable: overall satisfaction with the course

Independent variable	Regression (4) β	t	Regression (5) β	t	Independent variable	Regression (5) contd. β	t
Constant term	-.57	-8.0	-.73	-4.0	Undergraduate major:		
Course's contrib. to knowl.	.58	38.4	.56	36.4	Science	°	°
Evaluation of how course helped:					Engineering	.07	.1
To identify problems°°°	.09	4.8	.09	4.7	Economics	.08	1.1
To analyze problems°°°	.19	9.2	.20	9.4	Mathematics	.09	.9
To make decisions°°°	.09	5.3	.09	5.4	Psychology, Sociology, etc.	°	.1
To work with people°°°	.02	1.2	.02	1.5	History, Political Science, etc.	°°	-.4
To do research°°°	.03	2.0	.02	1.6			
To apply techniques°°°	.11	6.6	.11	6.8	Philosophy	-.30	-1.3
Student characteristics					Business Administration	.07	.8
Time spent on course			.03	1.5	Areas of interest:		
Age in years			.01	1.5	Accounting	-.04	-.9
MBA candidate			-.11	-2.0	Business Economics	.05	1.1
PhD candidate			.13	1.4	Computers & Information Systems	°°	-.1
Years in programme			.13	5.1			
Years of full-time work			°	.2	Finance	-.01	-.3
Years in military service			°°	-.6	Marketing	-.03	-.7
GSB GPA			°°	-.5	Operations Management	.06	1.1
No GPA			-.05	-.4	Operations & Systems Analysis	-.10	-2.2
					Organizational Behaviour	-.02	.4
					Transportation & Logistics	-.16	-2.3
R^2	.61					.62	

Notes: ° Between 0 and .005   °° Between 0 and -.005

°°° To control for the fact that some students in some courses did not give a response for these independent variable, dummy variables were included in the regressions. When one of variables 3 - 8 had a value of 0, the corresponding dummy variable took on a value of 1; otherwise, the dummy variable took on a value of 0. The mean values for the dummy variables corresponding to variables 3 - 8 are .05 for 3, .04 for 4, .11 for 5, .48 for 6, .50 for 7, and .17 for 8. The regression statistics for these variables are not shown in the table.

the fewer years of full-time work prior to entering the GSB, the higher the rating of the course. Only the first of these variables has a noticeably large effect, however.

In Table 8.2 the overall evaluation of the course is related to student evaluations of how the course contributed to the develop-

183

ment of different skills. These regressions can be interpreted as relating total output of the course to different dimensions of output. What stands out from these regressions is that students consider the course's contribution to knowledge to be the most important single component of output. In fact, the coefficient on the evaluation of the course's contribution to knowledge is greater than the sum of the coefficients for evaluations of all the other skills. It is also apparent that students consider the course's development of the abilities to work with people and to do research to be of negligible importance.

Table 8.3 shows the results for regressions that attempt to identify the relationship between evaluations of different course inputs and evaluations of individual components of output. As might be expected, the various inputs have different impacts on different components of output. For example, the evaluation of lectures is the most important factor in determining the evaluation of the course's contribution to knowledge, but least important with respect to ability to work with people. There are some irregularities to report, however. For those components of output that students apparently consider important (see Table 8.2), time spent studying and opinion of lectures were the most important explanatory variables. 55 out of 56 regression coefficients were positive and statistically different from zero.

The regressions in Table 8.4 have the same dependent variables as the regressions in Table 8.3. The independent variables in Table 8.4, however, are objective student and instructor characteristics. The purpose of these regressions is two-fold: first to identify systematic differences in the way different types of students rate the various components of output; and, second, to test whether instructors with different characteristics are more or less effective in producing perceived different components of output. While Table 8.4 contains many coefficients which are statistically different from zero, most of these coefficients do not reflect a substantial effect of the independent variable on the dependent variable.

Because the overall evaluation of the instructor is such an important factor in explaining the overall evaluation of the course, this variable should be given more extensive consideration. In Table 8.5, in regression (20) the overall evaluation of the instructor is regressed on the evaluations of individual qualities of the instructor. In regression (21) student characteristics and in regression (22) instructor

184

TABLE 8.3

Independent variable	Mean	Regression (6) Contrib. to knowledge		Regression (7) Ability to identify problems		Regression (8) Ability to analyze problems		Regression (9) Ability to make decisions		Regression (10) Ability to work with people		Regression (11) Ability to do research		Regression (12) Ability to apply techniques	
		β	t	β	t	β	t	β	t	β	t	β	t	β	t
Constant term	1.00	-.70	-5.6	-.28	-1.9	-.48	-3.9	-.49	-3.6	1.06	7.5	.63	4.6	*	*
Time spent studying (substant. below ave. = 1, substant. above ave. = 5)	3.31	.29	17.0	.17	9.7	.20	11.9	.17	9.2	.04	2.3	.05	2.5	.12	6.6
Opinion of:															
Reading materials	4.82	.17	14.8	.12	10.0	.13	11.0	.11	8.4	.04	2.9	.07	5.2	.09	6.9
Lectures	4.98	.31	22.8	.23	16.3	.26	18.9	.22	14.3	.01	0.4	.12	7.8	.25	17.1
Class discussions	4.49	.11	8.3	.17	12.3	.15	11.2	.14	9.5	.17	11.2	.08	5.2	.08	5.4
Papers	3.01	.11	6.9	.13	7.9	.15	9.6	.13	7.4	.02	1.2	.14	8.0	.12	6.9
Projects	1.68	.07	3.5	.07	3.2	.06	3.2	.08	3.5	.17	7.5	.18	8.2	.12	5.6
Computer exercises	1.87	.07	4.4	.07	4.0	.06	3.7	.06	3.1	.06	3.1	.04	2.1	.11	6.3
Case materials	3.55	.14	8.8	.14	8.9	.16	10.0	.18	10.6	.11	6.3	.03	1.9	.12	7.1
No opinion of:															
Reading materials	.04	.45	4.4	.56	5.2	.55	5.3	.56	4.9	.22	1.8	.28	2.4	.20	1.8
Lectures	.06	1.40	13.8	1.23	11.8	1.32	13.0	1.03	9.2	.20	1.7	.64	5.8	1.28	11.5
Class discussions	.06	.42	4.6	.70	7.2	.74	8.0	.64	6.2	.69	6.5	.54	5.3	.52	5.2
Papers	.43	.65	7.2	.68	7.3	.84	9.3	.77	7.7	-.24	-2.4	.56	5.6	.76	7.7
Projects	.68	.37	3.3	.36	3.2	.39	3.5	.47	3.9	.72	5.8	.73	6.0	.62	5.2
Computer exercises	.60	.33	3.8	.33	3.7	.20	2.3	.13	1.4	.33	3.4	.24	2.6	.32	3.5
Case materials	.31	.61	7.1	.53	6.0	.63	7.3	.70	7.3	.54	5.5	.30	3.1	.49	5.2
Dummy**				-4.69	-62.2	-4.70	-55.4	-4.41	-79.3	-3.81	-103.8	-3.99	-114.7	-4.78	-104.0
R^2			.47		.61		.61		.67		.73		.76		.74

Notes: * Between 0 and 0.5

** To control for the fact that some students in some courses did not give a response for the dependent variables a dummy variable was included as an independent variable which took on a value of 1 when the dependent variable took on a value of 0, and 0 otherwise. The mean value of this variable was .05 in regression (7), .04 in (8), .11 in (9), .48 in (10), .50 in (11) and .17 in (12). This procedure serves to measure the R^2 substantially.

185

TABLE 8.4

Independent variables	Mean	Regression (13) Contrib. to knowledge β	t	Regression (14) Ability to identify problems β	t	Regression (15) Ability to analyze problems β	t	Regression (16) Ability to make decisions β	t	Regression (17) Ability to work with people β	t	Regression (18) Ability to do research β	t	Regression (19) Ability to apply techniques β	t
Constant term	1.00	5.1	17.4	5.3	18.9	5.3	18.7	5.1	17.3	39.6	14.8	4.7	17.8	5.8	20.0
Student Characteristics															
Age (decades)	2.46	0.2	5.6	°	1.0	°	0.6	**	-0.7	°	0.4	-0.1	-2.8	°	0.3
MBA candidate (yes=1,no=0)	.82	-0.2	-2.9	-0.2	-2.6	-0.1	-1.6	-0.1	-2.1	-0.1	-2.3	°°	-0.8	-0.1	-1.8
PhD candidate(yes=1,no=0)	.03	-0.2	-1.4	-0.5	-4.2	-0.5	-3.8	-0.3	-2.4	-0.4	-3.5	0.3	2.4	-0.3	-2.8
Year in programme	1.16	0.1	2.2	0.1	1.5	0.1	2.1	*	0.5	*	-0.4	0.1	3.8	0.1	2.3
Years of full-time work	1.88	°	-2.1	*	-0.2	*	-0.2	°	0.7	*	*	*	1.5	*	*
Years in military service	1.37	*	1.6	°	4.2	°	2.8	°	2.2	°	2.9	°	3.5	°	3.4
GSB GPA (D=1, A=4)	1.86	-0.1	-1.9	-0.1	-1.5	-0.1	-1.3	-0.1	-1.4	-0.1	-2.5	-0.2	-3.0	-0.1	-1.8
GPA (no=0, yes =1)	.40	-0.2	-1.2	-0.3	-1.5	-0.2	-0.9	-0.3	-1.6	-0.4	-2.4	-0.7	-4.2	-0.3	-1.5
Instructor characteristics															
Age (decades)	3.70	**	-0.4	**	-0.4	**	-0.7	**	-0.3	0.2	3.1	°	0.9	-0.2	-3.4
Full professor (yes=1,no=0)	.28	0.3	2.8	0.2	1.6	0.1	0.8	-0.1	-1.1	0.2	2.1	0.2	2.3	0.2	1.7
Associate prof. (yes=1,no=0)	.20	**	-0.2	**	-0.2	-0.2	-1.8	-0.3	-2.6	0.2	2.0	°	0.3	-0.1	-1.4
Assistant prof. (yes=1,no=0)	.36	°°	-0.5	-0.2	-2.2	-0.2	-2.7	-0.3	-2.9	**	-0.2	-0.1	-0.7	-0.2	-1.7
Years since PhD	6.60	**	-0.6	*	-0.3	*	-0.2	**	-0.1	**	-0.3	**	-0.9	**	-1.1
Has PhD (yes=1,no=0)	.82	0.2	1.8	0.2	2.6	0.3	3.3	0.3	3.2	0.1	1.8	0.3	3.3	0.1	1.5
Years at Stanford	4.93	**	-3.9	**	-4.2	**	-4.0	**	-2.5	**	-4.7	**	-4.1	**	-0.6
Outside act. (none=0, alot=2)	.49	°	1.2	0.1	2.1	0.1	3.4	0.1	2.3	0.1	3.5	-0.1	-2.7	0.1	3.0
Times taught course before	1.56	0.1	8.2	0.1	6.2	0.1	5.5	0.1	5.9	°	-1.5	*	1.2	°	3.5
Teaching other sect. of same course	.51	-0.3	-5.6	-0.3	-6.7	-0.2	-5.0	-0.2	-3.2	-0.3	-5.8	-0.1	-3.0	-0.2	-4.0
Prop. time on res, last yr.	.28	**	-0.2	°	0.3	°	-0.9	°	2.0	**	-4.1	**	-5.1	°	0.6
Prop. time on res, this yr.	.21	°°	*	**	-0.1	*	-0.2	-1.5		°	2.7	°	0.6	°	0.8
Dummy***		-4.9	-52.8	-5.0	-46.0	-5.0	-46.0	-4.6	-68.6	-3.9	-103.4	-4.0	-108.5	-4.8	-89.8
R²			.06		.40		.33		.51		.69		.72		.64

Notes: * Between 0 and 0.05   ** Between 0 and 0.05

*** To control for the fact that some students in some courses did not give a response for the dependent variable a dummy variable was included as an independent variable which took on a value of 1 when the dependent variable took on a value of 0, and 0 otherwise. The mean value of this variable was .05 in regression (14), .04 in (15), .11 in (16), .48 in (17), .50 in (18) and .17 in (19). This procedure serves to measure the R^2 substantially.

TABLE 8.5

Dependent variable: overall evaluation of the instructor

Independent variable	Regression (20) β	Regression (20) t	Regression (21) β	Regression (21) t	Regression (22) β	Regression (22) t
Constant term	-1.14	-12.5	-1.84	-11.6	-1.05	-6.9
Opinion of extent instruction:						
Imparts enthusiasm***	.24	20.6	.24	21.2	.23	18.8
Knows subject***	.14	8.2	.13	8.0	.14	8.0
Is well prepared***	.12	8.1	.12	8.3	.13	8.3
Has practical know. of subject***	.09	6.6	.09	6.6	.09	6.0
Presents materials clearly***	.26	17.5	.26	18.1	.26	17.3
Speaks clearly***	.03	1.9	.02	1.7	.02	1.3
Uses visual aids well***	.05	4.5	.05	4.6	.06	5.0
Avoids being sidetracked***	.06	6.1	.06	5.9	.06	6.0
Makes useful comments on homework***	.03	2.9	.03	2.9	.02	2.4
Is available outside class***	-.01	-.5	°°	-.3	°°	-.4
Was int. in stud. as person***	-.03	-2.5	-.03	-2.3	-.03	-2.6
Sensitive to stud.'s needs***	.02	1.4	.02	1.9	.02	1.6
Respects student opinion***	.20	16.2	.18	14.6	.21	16.4
Student characteristics:						
Time spent on course	°		.06	4.3		
Age in years			.02	8.4		
MBA Candidate			-.15	-3.6		
R̄²	.73		.73		.73	

Independent variable	Regression (21) contd β	Regression (21) contd t	Regression (22) contd β	Regression (22) contd t
PhD candidate	-.26	-3.5		
Years in programme	.01	0.3		
Years of full-time work	-.04	-7.7		
Years in military service	-.03	-6.1		
GSB GPA	°	.8		
No GPA	.10	.8		
Instructor characteristics				
Age			°°	-.1
Full professor			-.04	-.6
Associate professor			-.05	-.8
Assistant professor			-.13	-2.3
Years since PhD			°°	-.2
Has PhD			.12	2.3
Years at Stanford			-.01	-.5
Outside activities			°°	-.4
Times taught course before				-.1
Teaching other sections			-.07	-2.3
Time for res, last yr.			°	.5
Time for res, this yr.			°	.5
R̄²		.75		.73

Notes: ° Between 0 and .005   °° Between 0 and -.005

*** To control for the fact that some students in some courses did not give a response for these independent variables, dummy variables were included in the regressions. When one of variables 2-14 took on a value of 0, the corresponding dummy variable took on a value of 1; otherwise, the dummy variable took on a value of 0. The mean values for the dummy variables corresponding to variables 2-14 are .01 for 2, .01 for 3, .02 for 4, .02 for 5, .01 for 6, .02 for 7, .07 for 8, .06 for 9, .22 for 10, .41 for 11, .37 for 12, .05 for 13 and .08 for 14. The regression statistics for these variables are not shown in the table.

characteristics are included as additional explanatory variables. In all these regressions, the opinion of how clearly the instructor presents his materials, and the extent to which he imparts enthusiasm have the largest coefficients. Having respect for student opinion, knowing his subject, being well prepared and demonstrating a practical knowledge of the application of course material have sizable and significant coefficients. The instructor's use of visual aids, ability to avoid being sidetracked[4] and willingness to provide useful comments on homework have small but statistically significant coefficients. Speaking clearly, being available outside class and being sensitive to students' needs had no significant effect on the overall evaluation of the instructor, while being interested in the student as a person had a significant negative impact on the overall evaluation.

Regression (21) indicates that given a student's evaluation of the instructor's individual qualities, the more time the student spends on the course, the older he is and the fewer years spent in full-time work or the military, the higher will he rate the instructor overall. Furthermore MBA and PhD students tend to be significantly harsher in their overall evaluation of the instructor. Since a significant number of non-GSB students take GSB courses this finding suggests that teaching performance, as evaluated by these students, is substantially better in the GSB than in the remainder of the University, on average. Regression (22) suggests, again given the evaluation of the instructor's individual qualities, an instructor who is an assistant professor and/or who does not have a PhD and who is teaching more than one section of the same course will fare significantly worse in his overall evaluation.

In the regressions reported in Table 8.6, the individual qualities of the instructor are the dependent variables. The explanatory variables are the instructor characteristics. Here the difference in the effects of particular independent variables on different dependent variables is striking. Age has a significant positive effect on the instructor's practical knowledge of how to apply the course's material, on his ability to make useful comments on homework, and on his respect

---

[4] Interpretation of the coefficient of this variable is ambiguous since some students in several courses maintain that those professors who allow themselves to be sidetracked add to the value of the course; i.e. "poor" at avoiding being sidetracked was a positive attribute.

TABLE 8.6

Independent variable	Mean	Regression (23) Imparts enthusiasm β	t	Regression (24) Knows subject β	t	Regression (25) Is well prepared β	t	Regression (26) Has practical knowledge β	t	Regression (27) Presents materials clearly β	t	Regression (28) Speaks clearly β	t
						Dependent variable — Student opinion of the extent instructor:							
Constant term	1.00	5.91	30.0	6.01	43.6	5.66	33.1	5.01	29.1	5.15	25.5	5.94	34.1
Instructor characteristics:														
Age (decades)	3.70	-.09	-1.7	.01	.2	.03	.5	.22	4.7	.03	.6	.09	-1.9
Full professor (yes = 1, no = 0)	.28	.01	.1	.51	6.6	.44	4.5	.38	3.9	.74	6.4	.08	.9
Associate prof. (yes = 1, no = 0)	.20	-.09	-.9	.34	4.8	.44	4.9	.14	1.6	.63	6.0	-.01	-.1
Asst. professor (yes = 1, no = 0)	.36	-1.27	-13.7	-.04	-.5	.17	2.1	-.52	-6.4	-.16	-1.7	-.43	-5.2
Years since PhD	6.60	-.04	-6.2	-.02	-4.9	-.01	-1.8	-.04	-8.2	-.02	-4.2	°	.2
Has PhD (yes = 1, no = 0)	.82	1.08	12.3	.46	7.5	.27	3.6	.72	9.4	.22	2.5	.55	7.2
Years at Stanford	4.93	-.05	-6.8	-.05	-10.0	-.04	-5.9	-.06	-8.9	-.06	-8.2	-.03	-4.7
Outside act. (none = 0, a lot = 2)	.49	.25	7.7	.11	4.9	.21	7.6	.14	4.8	.42	12.7	.24	8.5
Times taught course before	1.56	.13	9.6	.12	12.8	.17	14.9	.13	11.4	.16	12.3	.12	10.0
Teaching other sections of same course	.51	-.38	-7.9	-.22	-6.6	-.23	-5.4	-.31	-7.4	-.31	-6.3	-.33	-7.7
Proportion of time on res, last yr.	.28	-.62	-5.0	-.38	-4.4	-.35	-3.3	-.49	-4.5	-.72	-5.7	-.46	-4.2
Proportion of time on res, this yr.	.21	-.71	-4.1	-.36	-2.9	-.27	-1.8	-.17	-1.1	-.35	-2.0	-.26	-1.7
Dummy**		-5.43	-24.2	-6.12	-46.7	-5.93	-41.3	-5.74	-40.4	5.29	-28.4	-5.75	-38.1
R²		.26		.37		.32		.34		.25		.31	

Notes: ° Between 0 and .005

    ** To control for the fact that some students in some courses did not give a response for the dependent variable, a dummy variable was included as an independent variable which took on a value of 1 when the dependent variable took on a value of 0, and 0 otherwise. The mean value of this variable was .01 in regression (23), .01 in (24), .02 in (25), .02 in (26), .01 in (27), and .02 in (28).

TABLE 8.6 (contd.)

Independent variable	Dependent variable												
	Student opinion of the extent instructor:												
	Regression (29) Uses visual aids well		Regression (30) Avoids being sidetracked		Regression (31) Makes useful comments		Regression (32) Is available outside class		Regression (33) Is interested in student		Regression (34) Is sensitive to students' needs		Regression (35) Respects student opinion	
	β	t	β	t	β	t	β	t	β	t	β	t	β	t
Constant term	5.72	29.8	5.15	25.7	4.32	21.0	6.03	40.9	5.43	32.2	5.09	24.8	5.08	26.5
Instructor characteristics:														
Age (decades)	-.11	-2.1	-.09	-1.6	.11	2.0	-.16	-4.0	-.05	-1.1	.09	1.6	.12	2.3
Full professor	.38	3.5	.38	3.3	.17	1.5	-.03	-.3	-.13	-1.3	.45	3.8	.52	4.8
Associate professor	.23	2.3	.20	1.9	.11	.9	-.14	-1.9	-.15	-1.7	.24	2.2	.48	4.8
Assistant professor	.05	.6	.01	.1	-.27	-2.8	-.12	-1.8	-.24	-3.1	-.22	-2.3	.10	1.2
Years since PhD	-.02	-2.8	.01	2.1	-.02	-3.0	.01	1.3	-.02	-.5	-.03	-5.0	-.02	-4.3
Has PhD	-.07	-.8	.02	.3	.57	6.3	.15	2.2	.38	5.0	.39	4.3	.26	3.0
Years at Stanford	-.01	-1.9	-.03	3.5	-.05	-6.7	.02	.3	-.01	-2.1	-.06	-7.1	-.05	-6.7
Outside activities	.36	11.5	.10	3.0	.08	2.3	.07	2.9	.15	5.4	.32	9.7	.22	7.1
Times taught course before	.10	7.9	.15	11.5	.15	11.0	.04	3.6	.03	2.6	.08	5.7	.06	4.7
Teaching other sec. of same course	-.29	-6.3	-.15	-3.0	-.46	-9.1	-.08	-2.3	-.22	-5.3	-.25	-5.0	-.23	-4.9
Proportion of time on res. last yr.	-.59	-4.9	-.03	-.2	-.29	-2.2	-.07	-.8	-.12	-1.1	-.48	-3.7	-.48	-3.9
Proportion of time on res. this yr.	-.06	-.3	-.29	-1.6	.09	.5	.23	1.8	.06	.4	-.13	-.7	-.33	-2.0
Dummy**	-5.2	-66.8	-5.1	-53.3	-4.9	-91.0	-5.58	-17.6	-5.28	-14.3	-5.38	-53.3	-5.47	-73.7
R^2	.50		.43		.64		.86		.81		.39		.54	

Note **   To account for the fact that some students in some courses did not give a response for the dependent variable, a dummy variable was included as an independent variable which took on a value of 1 when the dependent variable took on a value of 0, and 0 otherwise. The mean value of this variable was .07 in regression (29), .06 in (30), .22 in (31), .41 in (32), .37 in (33), .05 in (34) and .08 in (35).

for student opinions, but a significant negative effect on his ability to use visual aids and on his availability outside class. Full professors and associate professors are significantly better than assistant professors in all categories except being available outside class and being interested in students as persons and neither of these qualities were regarded by students as being of importance in forming their overall evaluation of the instructor. Having a PhD had a highly significant positive coefficient in all but two regressions, but in most cases, the more recent the degree, the better. Almost uniformly, the more years the instructor had been at Stanford the worse his performance in the eyes of the students. Having outside activities and having taught the course previously enhanced an instructors ratings in most categories by large amounts, while teaching other sections of the same course served to damage his ratings. The latter phenomenon, however, may simply reflect a preference on the part of the students for certain non-required courses, i.e. those courses offered under only one instructor and self-selected by the students. Finally, instructors who spend more time on research tend to generate less enthusiasm, know their subject less well, be less well prepared, have less knowledge of the course materials, practical applications, present course material less clearly, speak less clearly and have less respect for student opinions — not an uninteresting finding since it does suggest trade—offs.

Student evaluations of B.201.

Before we analyze student evaluations of B.201 including additional data it is of interest to compare the regression results for this course as a subset of all courses. In this section we shall also discuss the implications of some of the results. Table 8.7 attempts to explain the student's overall evaluation of the B.201 course. Regression (36) explains the overall evaluation in terms of the evaluations of individual inputs. Of the nine ratings only three had significant coefficients: reading materials, lectures and examinations. The rating of lectures had by far the greatest weight: 0.57 as compared to 0.20 for examinations and 0.16 for reading materials. In comparing the results for B.201 with all courses, it is of interest that class discussions which had the second highest coefficient in the latter does not even have a significant coefficient in B.201. This may reflect the nature of the course (or the manner in which it was conducted by the three B.201 instructors) or the fact that class discussions play a much more significant part in elective courses.

Regression (37) in Table 8.7 shows the results when the rating of the instructor is added to the ratings of inputs as an independent variable. Two effects stand out. First, the R^2 goes up from 0.57 to 0.64. Second, the coefficient on the ratings of lectures is reduced substantially from 0.57 to 0.18, although it remains significantly different from zero. This suggests that students consider the role of the instructor to be critically important and to involve more than just lectures. The same effect was obtained in the corresponding regressions for all courses, though the change was less dramatic.

The third regression reported in Table 8.7 — (38) — relates the overall course rating to the ratings of individual outputs. Only two of the outputs appear to have a significant impact on the overall rating. The course's contribution to knowledge of the subject area had a higher weight (0.46) than all of the other outputs combined and was nearly twice as large as the weight given to the amount by which the course contributed to the ability to analyze problems (0.27).

When inputs and outputs are combined in the same regression (39) some of each remain statistically significant. Reading materials, examinations and the overall teacher rating still have significant weights among the inputs, and contribution to knowledge and help in analyzing problems remain significant among the outputs. (The large and significant coefficient on case materials cannot be regarded as important since 94 per cent of the students regarded this item to be not applicable in this course.) Again the most striking feature of these results is the great importance of the overall rating of the instructor for the overall rating of the course. What the student thinks of his instructor is almost as important in evaluating the course overall as what he gets from the course. This finding might suggest to some that an overall rating of a course is not a good measure of the output of a university course.

Two further regressions with the overall course rating as the dependent variable are shown in Table 8.8. One has student characteristic as the only independent variable and the other student characteristics, evaluations of inputs and evaluations of outputs, as independent variables. In the first of these regressions (40) the

TABLE 8. 7

Dependent variable - overall rating of course

Independent variables	Regression (36) β	t	Regression (37) β	t	Regression (38) β	t	Regression (39) β	t
Reading materials	.16	3..3	.16	3.6			.08	2.1
Lectures	.57	9.2	.18	2.3			.04	0.5
Class Discussions	.04	0.6	.01	0.2			-.00	-0.1
Papers	.10	1.1	.02	0.3			-.01	-0.2
Projects	.05	0.8	.05	1.0			-.02	-0.5
Computer exercises	.01	0.1	.04	1.0			-.01	-1.3
Case materials	.15	0.7	.13	0.7			.35	2.1
Other	.10	0.9	.06	0.6			.00	0.1
Examinations	.20	4.3	.18	4.0			.11	2.6
Overall rating of instructor			.50	6.9			.42	6.2
Contribution to knowledge					.46	6.1	.21	3.0
Helps identify problems					.01	0.5	.03	0.4
Helps analyze problems					.27	3.1	.21	2.9
Helps make decisions					.12	1.2	.12	1.5
Helps work with people					-.12	-1.5	-.09	-1.4
Helps do research					.14	1.7	.12	1.9
Helps apply techniques					.01	0.2	-.01	-0.1
R^2	.57		.64		.57		.73	

student's grade point average, his essay final exam, and his expected grade were significant explanatory variables. The lower a student's GPA, the higher was his overall rating of the course. In the second regression (41), where student evaluations of inputs and outputs are included, only the expected grade remains significant. This suggests that the effects of GPA and subjective final exam score are fully accounted for by the output evaluations, but that expected grade has an effect over and above what students believe they get out of the course.

A comparison of the coefficients on course output ratings in regression (41) in Table 8.8 with the corresponding coefficients in regression (39) in Table 8.7 suggests that students' opinions about what they obtained from the course are something quite different

TABLE 8.8

Dependent variable - overall course rating of course

Independent variables	Regression (41)			Regression (40)		Regression (41) contd.	
	β	t		β	t	β	t
Reading materials	.07	1.7	Undergrad. econ. major	-.42	1.4	-.03	-0.2
Lectures	.02	0.2	ATGSB - verbal	-.10	-1.1	-.02	-0.3
Class discussions	-.03	-0.5	ATGSB - quant.	-.14	-1.7	.01	0.2
Papers	.06	0.8	ATGSB - total	.02	1.4	-.00	-0.2
Projects	-.03	0.6	Grade point average	-.42	-2.0	-.17	-1.3
Computer exercises	-.07	1.6	Final exam - objective	-.01	-0.5	.02	1.6
Case materials	.30	1.7	Final exam - subjective	.02	2.3	.01	1.3
Other	-.04	0.5	Expected grade	.21	3.3	.14	3.5
Examinations	.11	2.8	Age	-.00	-0.1	.03	1.0
Overall rating of instructor	.38	5.4	Years of work experience	-.02	-0.5	-.02	0.8
Contribution to knowledge	.20	2.9	Years of military service	.07	1.9	.01	0.2
Helps identify problems	-.03	-0.3					
Helps analyze problems	.21	2.9	Accounting	.31	1.1	.09	0.5
Helps make decisions	.11	1.4	Business Economics	.90	2.8	.55	2.8
Helps work with people	-.14	2.2	Computers & Information Systems	-.18	0.8	.05	0.4
Helps do research	.17	2.8	Finance	-.56	-2.4	-.19	-1.4
Helps apply techniques	.03	0.5	Marketing	.26	1.1	.21	1.5
			Operations Management	.28	0.9	.15	0.7
			Operations & Systems Analysis	.39	1.3	.07	0.4
			Organizational Behaviour	-.06	-0.2	-.08	-0.4
			Transportation & Logistics	-.81	-2.0	-.57	-2.1
			R^2	.30		.78	

from their "values added" as accounted for by their final exam scores and their status at the beginning of the course as measured by the other student characteristics. The inclusion of these latter sets of variables in the regression does not reduce either the coefficients or the t statistics of the contribution to knowledge. It may be that the students' evaluations are better measures of value added than the "objective" measures included in regression (41) in which case the overall evaluation reflects, even though only in part, the net educational output produced by the course.

The coefficients on the area of interest variables in regressions (40) and (41) indicate that business economics students not only rate the

194

TABLE 8.9

Independent variables	Regression (42) Overall course evaluation		Regression (43) Contribution to knowledge		Regression (44) Ability to analyse problems	
	β	t	β	t	β	t
Final exam - essay	.01	1.9	.01	1.2	.01	1.7
Final exam - short answer	-.02	-0.8	-.02	-0.8	-.05	-1.6
Undergraduate econ. major	-.16	-0.5	-.64	-2.0	-.76	-2.0
Preliminary examination	-.08	-2.5	-.08	-2.6	-.03	-0.8
R^2	.05		.08		.05	

course higher than other students, but do so even after their evaluations of the course's various inputs and outputs are taken into account.

Finance students rate the course significantly lower before, but not after, taking into account the input and output evaluations. And, transportation and logistics students rate the course lower both before and after.

In considering how good student evaluations are as possible measures of educational output it is of interest to test for relationship between those evaluations and the net output of the course implicit in the final examination test scores and the measures of initial understanding. Unfortunately the latter, which include whether the student was an undergraduate economics major and his score on an examination at the end of the first week in the course, are not very good. The evaluations considered as possible measures of output are the overall evaluation of the course, the student's opinion of how much the course contributed to his knowledge of the subject and the student's opinion of how much the course improved his ability to analyze problems. The statistics for regressions relating these evaluations to the test measures of output are shown in Table 8.9.

The results of these regressions indicate that there is not a high correlation between the student evaluations as measures of output and the examination results. This low association suggests that if one believes the test results capture what a student obtained for the course, then the evaluations are not good measures of output. The

TABLE 8.10

Dependent Variable - Total Final Exam Score

Independent variables	Regression (45)		Regression (46)	
	β	t	β	t
Undergraduate econ. major	2.89	0.7	2.85	0.7
Hours spent studying	2.75	1.8	3.01	1.8
ATGSB - verbal	3.07	2.8	2.87	2.6
ATGSB - quant.	3.47	3.5	3.21	3.2
ATGSB - total	-.41	3.0	-.39	-2.8
Grade point average	4.81	1.9	5.18	2.0
Age	-.05	-0.1	-.09	-0.2
Race	-11.50	-1.9	-12.60	-2.1
Years of work experience	.94	1.5	.92	1.5
Years of military service	-.44	-0.9	-.34	-0.7
Accounting	-3.34	-0.9	-4.42	-1.1
Business Economics	-2.24	-0.5	2.64	0.6
Computers and Inf. Systems	-1.74	-0.6	-.24	-0.1
Finance	3.21	1.1	3.81	1.3
Marketing	-1.01	-0.3	-2.78	0.9
Operations Management	.10	0.0	.61	0.1
Operations & Systems Analysis	-11.30	-2.8	-12.72	-3.1
Organizational Behaviour	-3.34	-0.8	-4.37	-1.0
Transportation & Logistics	2.99	0.5	1.41	0.3
Overall course evaluation	2.36	2.0	2.56	2.1
Overall teacher evaluation	-.89	-0.7	-1.41	-1.1
Section A			-2.41	-0.6
Section B			-2.95	-0.6
Section C			5.19	1.3
R^2	.26		.27	

opposite possibility, that the test scores give poor information about what students get from the course, should not be excluded from consideration, however.

Regardless of whether student evaluations are good measures of output it is possible that they are in themselves inputs in the educational process. A student who likes the course and/or teacher may well do better as a result of this positive attitude. To test for this, the total final examination score was regressed against variables reflecting initial understanding, general aptitude, other student characteristics and overall teacher and course characteristics. The results are shown in Table 8.10.

Regressions (45) and (46) show some large regression coefficients but not very large "t" statistics. Nevertheless, it does appear that the opinion of the course did have a significant effect on the final

TABLE 8.11

Dependent variable - Overall rating of instructor

Independent variables	Regression (47) β	t	Regression (48) β	t	Regression (49) β	t	Regression (50) β	t
Imparts enthusiasm	.21	5.4	.17	4.4			.18	4.2
Knows subject	.21	3.8	.18	3.4			.17	3.1
Is well prepared	.03	0.5	.03	0.6			.04	0.9
Knows applications	.04	0.7	.04	0.8			.04	0.8
Presents materials with clarity	.41	8.3	.37	7.3			.34	6.6
Speaks clearly	-.07	-1.3	-.05	-1.1			-.06	-1.2
Uses visual aids well	.07	1.4	.06	1.4			.07	1.6
Avoids being sidetracked	.10	2.6	.07	1.9			.06	1.8
Provides helpful comments	.10	2.6	.07	2.0			.10	2.6
Is available outside class	-.01	-0.3	.01	0.3			-.00	-0.0
Is interested in me as a person	-.06	-1.5	-.06	-1.5			-.06	-1.5
Responds to students needs	.09	2.0	.07	1.6			.07	1.4
Respects student opinions	.03	0.8	.03	0.6			.03	0.7
Overall rating of course			.15	3.6			.18	4.1
Undergrad. econ. major					.14	0.5	.15	1.0
ATGSB - verbal					-.11	1.3	-.05	1.0
ATGSB - quantitative					-.13	-1.6	-.04	-0.9
ATGSB - total					.02	1.4	.01	1.1
Grade point average					.45	2.2	.09	0.7
Final exam - short answer					-.02	0.8	-.00	-0.2
Final exam - essay					.01	1.8	-.00	-0.6
Expected grade					-.05	-0.9	.04	1.4
Age					-.04	0.9	-.03	-1.3
Race					-.30	-0.7	-.31	-1.4
Years of work experience					-.04	-0.8	.03	1.2
Years of military service					.00	0.1	-.03	-1.8
Accounting					.70	2.6	.17	1.2
Business Economics					.20	0.7	-.15	-1.0
Computers and Inf. Systems					-.49	-2.1	-.14	-1.2
Finance					-.60	-2.7	-.04	-0.3
Marketing					.04	0.2	-.16	-1.4
Operations Management					.49	1.6	.25	1.7
Operation & Systems Analysis					.27	0.9	-.12	-0.8
Organizational Behaviour					.23	0.8	.12	0.8
Transportation & Logistics					-.56	-1.4	-.06	-0.3
R^2	.81		.82		.31		.84	

examination score. Other things being equal, an extra point on the course evaluation scale was worth 2—1/2 points on the final. Separate regressions (not shown here) replacing the total final exam score with the short answer exam score, in one case, and the essay exam score in the other, show that this effect is concentrated entirely on the essay exam score.

Also in B.201, as before, the overall ratings of the instructor was

197

TABLE 8.12

Student weights, (actual), (predicted by faculty) and faculty weights

Characteristics	Implicit student weights[a] (1)	Expected student weights (2)	Average faculty weights (3)
Imparts enthusiasm	.18	.12	.08
Knows his subject	.18	.07	.15
Is well prepared for class	.03	.11	.13
Demonstrates practical knowledge about the application of course material	.03	.09	.07
Presents his materials with clarity	.35	.11	.10
Speaks clearly and distinctly	-.06	.06	.06
Uses visual aids (including blackboard) without interfering with a coherent presentation	.06	.05	.05
Avoids being sidetracked	.09	.04	.05
Provides helpful comments on homework assignments	.09	.05	.06
Is available outside class	-.01	.06	.05
Is interested in individual student as person	-.05	.07	.03
Is sensitive to students' understanding of subject matter and responsive to students' questions	.08	.10	.10
Has respect for student opinions	.03	.07	.04
Sum			
[a] normalized to add to 1.00	1.00	1.00	1.00

regressed on the ratings of the individual instructor attributes. The results are shown in Table 8.11, regression (47). The regression coefficients indicate as they did for all courses that the most important attribute is clarity of presentation followed by imparting enthusiasm and knowledge of subject.

A brief survey of a group of economists not in the Graduate School of Business was made in which they were asked to weight each of the characteristics according to importance and to indicate what weights they expected students, on average, would give to each. The results are shown in Table 8.12. One implication which emerges from Table 8.12 is that if the implicit student weights are accurate, and relatively constant for some given course and if the faculty weights are used by instructors wishing to "maximize golden opinions," improvements in instructor ratings might be achieved by a change in emphasis and/or attitude. For example instructors appear to underestimate the effects on student opinion of presenting materials with clarity and imparting enthusiasm and over-rate the effects of speaking clearly and distinctly, being well prepared for class, being interested in an individual student as a person and being available outside class. Thus a re-allocation of effort, not necessarily involving any increase in objectively measured total input, might result in a substantial payoff in terms of student opinion and possibly even in salary and promotion.

Regression (48) in Table 8.11 shows the statistics for a regression which is identical to regression (47) except for the addition of the overall course rating as an independent variable. The hypothesis is that the quality of the course as perceived by students is a factor influencing their opinion of the teacher. While there undoubtedly is some simultaneous equation bias in the estimates, these statistics indicate that the hypothesis is correct. Inclusion of this variable, however, reduces the sum of the weights of other factors by only 0.07 and makes little change in the relative weight assigned to each. Thus, in evaluating an instructor in B.201, students appear to give some, but not very much, weight to the quality of the course as they perceived it.

Regression (49) in Table 8.11 relates the overall instructor rating to the student characteristics for which data were available. Here the results are striking. Most variables did not have a statistically significant regression coefficient, although this might be explained in part by the high correlation among the independent variables. Except for dummy variables representing areas of study in which students expressed a particular interest, only the coefficient for a student's grade point average was statistically significant. This coefficient indicates that, other things being equal, the higher a student's GPA, the higher his rating is likely to be. It will be necessary to test for the joint effect of the various measures of intelligence and aptitude to determine whether brighter students tend to give higher or lower ratings. It is clear, however, that the expected grade does not have an effect that differs significantly from the student's actual performance as measured by his final exam score.

Several of the coefficients and the dummy variables that indicate whether a student has a particular interest in different subject areas are statistically significant. A student's having an interest in accounting· added significantly to his overall opinion of his economics instructor, while having an interest in computers or finance significantly reduced the rating.

The statistics shown in regression (50) of Table 8.11 are for a regression containing the independent variables from regressions (48) and (49). The questions here are whether the student characteristics have an effect on the overall instructor rating that is not reflected in the ratings of the separate instructor attributes and whether the inclusion of the student characteristics alters the implicit weights given to the instructor attributes. The answers to both questions are negative. None of the student characteristics have statistically significant coefficients and none of the implicit weights was significantly affected by holding constant the student characteristics.

Apart from the conclusions we have already discussed regarding possible changes in instructors' behaviour several others suggest themselves.

As a practical matter, since filling in evaluation forms and having them processed for computer handling is neither costless to students nor the administration, the existing GSB evaluation form could be reduced somewhat without much loss of information. Second, this research is based on only one year's data and several questions have not been answered satisfactorily. For example, in a few variables large differences exist in student overall evaluations of the same instructor by section (two of the instructors taught two sections each).[5]

While some of the difference can be explained by different average student characteristics by section, much of the difference remains. It may be the case that factors such as the time of day when teaching occurs affects student ratings. It is also possible that if, with some given group of students, an instructor in one subject is teaching alongside other instructors who are rated highly by students, the students may rate that instructor on a relative rather than absolute basis and that this fact may explain why one instructor receives substantially different ratings in the same course in different sections. This implies that the poor instructor will be rated even lower than he deserves to be and the better instructor higher than he

---

[5] Full details of mean scores and standard deviations for each variable are available for each section from the author on request.

deserves to be. Preliminary results based on data from multi-section courses suggest, however, that student opinion of any one instructor is independent of the student ratings given to other sectional instructors but that such a conclusion does not hold for the opinion of the course. One possible explanation is that students have had sufficient exposure over time to many instructors to enable them to evaluate a teacher on an absolute basis but that new courses are subject to within-section comparisons. This area appears to be worthy of further research. Third, the academic community as a whole with access to such results, might want to reconsider how to evaluate a course and its teacher — by examination results, by student opinion of the course, by student opinion of the faculty member or by some other method during the course, immediately after its completion or some time much later in the student's life. Finally, the GSB's policy of continuing to store student evaluation data yields an opportunity for different fields in the GSB, or an enterprising Ph.D. student, to undertake more thorough research than has been attempted in this initial effort.

STANFORD UNIVERSITY

GRADUATE SCHOOL OF BUSINESS

COURSE EVALUATION QUESTIONNAIRE

Quarter (F=1, W=2, S=3)	☐	(1)
Year	7 ☐	(2-3)
Course Title_____; Number	☐	(4-6)

Section (A=1, B=2, C=3, D=4, E=5, F=6, leave blank if no section.) ☐ (7)

1. How would you compare the amount of time you spent on this course with the amount spent on the other courses you took this quarter? (Check one)

Substantially above average	☐ 5	
Above average.	4	
Average.	☐ 3	(9)
Below average	2	
Substantially below average	☐ 1	

2. How helpful did you find each of the following? (Circle your answer.)

	Check if not applicable	Detracted						Helpful	
(a) Reading Materials	☐	1 2 3 4 5 6 7							(10)
(b) Lectures	☐	1 2 3 4 5 6 7							(11)
(c) Class Discussions	☐	1 2 3 4 5 6 7							(12)
(d) Papers	☐	1 2 3 4 5 6 7							(13)
(e) Projects	☐	1 2 3 4 5 6 7							(14)
(f) Computer Exercises	☐	1 2 3 4 5 6 7							(15)
(g) Case Materials	☐	1 2 3 4 5 6 7							(16)

3. How well do you think the course examinations given thus far (if any) covered the more important aspects of the course? (Circle your answer.)

Not Applicable ☐

Covered Poorly   1 2 3   4 5 6 7   Covered Well   (18)

4. How much do you feel this course has contributed to your knowledge of the subject area?

No contri-bution   1 2 3 4 5 6 7   Great con-tribution   (19)

5. How much has this course improved your ability to:

	Check if not applicable	No improvement						Great improvement	
(a) Identify problems	☐	1 2 3 4 5 6 7							(20)
(b) Analyze problems	☐	1 2 3 4 5 6 7							(21)
(c) Make decisions	☐	1 2 3 4 5 6 7							(22)
(d) Work with people	☐	1 2 3 4 5 6 7							(23)
(e) Do research	☐	1 2 3 4 5 6 7							(24)
(f) Apply techniques	☐	1 2 3 4 5 6 7							(25)

202

6. Evaluate the extent to which the instructor -

		Check if not applicable or you have no basis to judge	Poor						Excellent	
(a)	Imparts enthusiasm	☐	1	2	3	4	5	6	7	(26)
(b)	Knows his subject	☐	1	2	3	4	5	6	7	(27)
(c)	Is well prepared for class	☐	1	2	3	4	5	6	7	(28)
(d)	Demonstrates practical knowledge about the application of course material	☐	1	2	3	4	5	6	7	(29)
(e)	Presents his materials with clarity	☐	1	2	3	4	5	6	7	(30)
(f)	Speaks clearly and distinctly	☐	1	2	3	4	5	6	7	(31)
(g)	Uses visual aids (including blackboard) effectively in presentation	☐	1	2	3	4	5	6	7	(32)
(h)	Avoids being sidetracked	☐	1	2	3	4	5	6	7	(33)
(i)	Provides helpful comments on homework assignments (whether his own or those of a reader)	☐	1	2	3	4	5	6	7	(34)
(j)	Is available outside of class	☐	1	2	3	4	5	6	7	(35)
(k)	Was interested in me as a person	☐	1	2	3	4	5	6	7	(36)
(l)	Is sensitive to student's level of understanding of subject matter and responsive to student's questions	☐	1	2	3	4	5	6	7	(37)
(m)	Has respect for student opinions	☐	1	2	3	4	5	6	7	(38)

7. Knowing now what you do about this course would you have taken this course if it were not required?

☐ Yes   ☐ No
(39=2)   (39=1)

8. What was your over-all satisfaction with this course?

Dissatisfied   Satisfied
1 2 3 4 5 6 7   (40)

9. Over-all how would you rate the instructor of this course?

Poor   Excellent
1 2 3 4 5 6 7   (41)

10. What two aspects of the course and/or the instructor did you like best? Least?

Liked best: _____

Liked least: _____

11. Other comments (if any)_____

203

12. Tell us something about yourself but do not sign this form.

a. Your age (in years) ☐☐ (43-44)

b. Program in which you are enrolled. MBA ☐ PhD ☐ Other ☐
   (45=1)   (45=2)   (45=3)

   (Specify if other program)_____

c. Your year in the above program (1 or 2). ☐ (46)

d. From the below list of fields select the one which best describes your undergraduate field of study. (47-48)

   - biology, chemistry, physics, and related fields . . . . ☐ (=01)
   - engineering . . . . ☐ (=02)
   - economics . . . . ☐ (=03)
   - mathematics . . . . ☐ (=04)
   - psychology, sociology, and related fields . . . . ☐ (=05)
   - history, political science, and related fields . . . . ☐ (=06)
   - philosophy . . . . ☐ (=07)
   - art, music, and related fields. . . . . ☐ (=08)
   - business administration. . . . . ☐ (=09)
   - other (specify) _____ (=10)

e. How many years, if any, have you spent in full time employment? In military service? (Note: Do not count employment or service in the military during the summer of the school year.)

   Full Time Employment ☐☐ (49-50)

   Military Service ☐☐ (51-52)

f. In what area(s) of study within the business school are you most interested?

   - Accounting. . . . . ☐ (53)
   - Business Economics . . . . ☐ (54)
   - Computers & Information Systems . . . . ☐ (55)
   - Finance . . . . ☐ (56)
   - Marketing . . . . ☐ (57)
   - Operations Management (OM) . . . . ☐ (58)
   - Operation & Systems Analysis (OSA) . . . . ☐ (59)
   - Organizational Behaviour (OB) . . . . ☐ (60)
   - Transportation and Logistics . . . . ☐ (61)
   - Other (specify) _____ ☐ (62)

g. Where would you most like to work on your first job? Where would you like to work after 10 years? (Check one of each)

	First job		After 10 years	
Government	☐	(63)	☐	(70)
Large company	☐	(64)	☐	(71)
Small Company	☐	(65)	☐	(72)
Self	☐	(66)	☐	(73)
University or school	☐	(67)	☐	(74)
Non-profit organization	☐	(68)	☐	(75)
Other (specify)	☐	(69)	☐	(76)

h. What is your approximate GSB grade point average to date? ☐☐☐ (77-79)
   If not applicable (i. e. , no GSB grades previously received)
   check here ☐ (80)

Part V
Financing University Education

9. A Suggestion for Increasing the Efficiency of Universities

by Melvin W. Reder

As I use it, "efficiency" is something that varies directly with a ratio of output to input. Accordingly, its application must be restricted to situations where agreement can be reached on techniques of measuring the elements of this ratio. Notoriously, university output is not a quantity whose measure reflects wider agreement. Attempts to define the "output" of a university always founder on such rocks as "teaching versus research," subject i versus subject j, etc. For many reasons appeal to market prices will not advance agreement in this case.

Accordingly, any consideration of university efficiency must proceed output element by output element. By an output element I mean an activity of such characteristics that agreement can be reached on when more or less of it is being performed and when the quality of what is performed is better, worse or the same as that performed elsewhere. For example, consider the teaching of a specified body of subject matter as an output element of two dimensions: quantity and quality. Let the quantity measure be "students of specified initial endowment processed per year" and let "quality" be reflected in one or more student performances, observed at the end of the academic year and/or later. The quality measure may conveniently be thought of as the score on one or a battery of tests, but this is not essential; it is enough that there be agreement among relevant parties on quality rankings.

Where there is agreement on rates of trade-off between quantity and quality of output, statements about efficiency can be made much stronger. However, in general, such agreement cannot be obtained; i.e. there is not general agreement on how much of (say) minimum quality should be sacrificed to get more students per annum through an educational process, or whether a university should strive to contribute "a little" to a given number of students with superb natural gifts, or much more to an equal number of less fortunate students who, despite all efforts, will not quite reach the heights of the former group, etc. To avoid issues like these, I shall address myself solely to cases where quantity of output per input unit can be raised and an agreed upon measure of quality not lowered.

In the education industry, an output measure often reflects some aspect of student performance. In all such cases, it is imperative that variations in student endowment — knowledge and learning ability at the start of the teaching process to be monitored — be allowed for in measuring output. Barring an explicit university production function that permits calculation of rates of substitution between inputs of initial student endowment (ability) and university training inputs the best (only?) way to proceed is to hold constant initial student endowment (e.g. by studying matched pairs of students with identical initial endowments) and observe performance of comparable individuals under alternative methods of instruction. Apart from student ability, in the following discussion inputs will be measured in (real) dollars expended. Problems may arise from this assumption, but I do not expect them seriously to affect the argument.

In short, the efficiency with which a university produces a given output element is an increasing function of the number of students per year who attain not less than (or surpass) some specified level of performance per dollar spent in the process. "Specified level of performance" may be set to suit the convenience of the investigator: "attain" or "surpass" implies that no trade-off between quantity and minimum quality is permitted. Minimum quality may be defined as an absolute level of examination performance; or as a frequency distribution of examination scores, each percentile of which equals or exceeds some preassigned level, etc. As measured here, efficiency will vary with quantity, quality constant, but not vice-versa. While joint costs of various output elements might present difficult practical questions, for the moment I assume them to be solved; they do not involve important issues of principle.

The basic course and extra cost options

In virtually every department of a university, there is a basic or elementary course. The content of these courses is greatly influenced and sometimes completely determined by the textbook used. Perusal of the frequency distribution of textbook sales indicates that in most fields there is heavy concentration among a small number of these books. Not surprisingly, this results in a great deal of duplicated teaching effort, i.e. a goodly number of teachers are doing more or less the same thing in a number of different institutions.

The use of video-tape surely should make it possible to reduce this duplication. At the very least, the authors of the texts or — better still — specialized lecturers could tape the lectures that are normally supposed to accompany the texts. This would obviate the necessity for building the large lecture halls required for "live performances;" eliminate schedule conflicts (the tapes could be re-run at will); minimize the bad performances that result from sub-par condition of lecturer, listener or both; permit editing of tapes to preserve only the best parts of a performance, etc. It could also permit use of complicated visual aids not readily available in a lecture hall or classroom. All of these suggest improvement of *quality* of instruction.

But the gains on which I wish to concentrate are in efficiency. While the situation varies from one subject to another, in Elementary Economics, most instructional tastes could be satisfied by selection from among, say, a half dozen courses, each associated with a leading seller among current textbooks. (Where there is demand for a new type course — perhaps a "Radical" course — one could be developed.) Enterprises could easily be developed to produce and sell "packaged" courses — tapes, textbooks, workbooks, examinations and possibly mechanical grading services — to universities. The potential saving in instructional time would be very substantial.

The saving in cost would depend critically upon (a) the price charged for the packaged course and (b) the amount of supplementary instruction provided. Since freedom of entry into the field of "packaged courses" will be virtually unrestricted save for copyrights, the prices charged could not long exceed competitive levels; the production of close substitutes would be too easy. The packaged course producers would no doubt try to prevent reproduction of tapes; but their success in this would be uncertain.[1] The fees and royalties paid to authors, editors, etc. would have to equal the going value of their time but there would seem little opportunity for returns greater than those currently earned by authors of textbooks with accompanying instructor's kits, workbooks, etc.

But video-tape or no, a packaged course is correspondence school education, and subject to all the limitations thereof. Granted, with sufficient maturity and motivation, a great deal of training can be absorbed from a well designed correspondence course. But, at the bare minimum, section leaders are needed to answer questions, and even more to stimulate discussion and arouse intellectual curiosity. The quality of these instructors and their ratio to students (instructor hours/student hours) is a major determinant both of the cost and quality of educational activity.

Clearly, many students neither desire nor obtain more educational contact than would be afforded by a packaged course. Others desire such contact only in a limited number of subjects. Consequently, offering packaged courses with one or more options for participation in a supervised discussion group would expand the options now available to students[2]. Moreover, by requiring students to pay extra for "high participation" options that involve heavy use of instructional time, a university could induce students to use this valuable resource economically.

Quality of training for students of packaged courses could be measured by standard examinations, possibly given on a national basis. If, after standardizing for initial student endowment, it appeared that examination performance was no worse (and hopefully better) than among students taught by conventional methods, the cost saved by use of a packaged course would count as an increase in efficiency.[3]

As a partial offset to this (alleged) increase in efficiency it would

---

[1] The producers might refuse to sell the tapes and insist on having them run only by their own employees. The ramifications of this need not be pursued here.

[2] That is, a student might opt for varying degrees of course participation above a "packaged course" minimum.

[3] Measuring the quality of instruction in a high participation option might be more difficult than in a packaged course, but I shall beg this question.

be necessary to weigh two sources of potential loss: not all students would opt for a packaged course; some would select one of the high participation options that involved (say) tutoring, additional reading, preparing a term paper, etc. These options might be no better than what is presently available to eager students who seek out instructors. Moreover, the extra cost of the high participation option to the student would represent a pecuniary loss to him relative to the present situation where high participation involves no additional out-of-pocket cost to the student.

In other words, charging two-part tuition for a course (one part for the packaged "basic" course, the other for a high participation option) would probably involve an income redistribution (relative to the present situation) from earnest (i.e. instructionally time-intensive) students to other users of university resources and possibly from the faculty.[4] If the putative cost savings are reflected in lower tuition the non-earnest students will benefit; to the extent that the cost-savings are diverted to other uses, others will gain. These distributional considerations must obviously enter into any judgment as to the propriety of seeking improved efficiency via changes in pedagogical technique.

Beyond redistributing the benefits of education, instituting a two-part tuition scheme will affect allocative efficiency. By putting a price upon the use of valuable instructional time, the scheme may make the price of instructional activity more nearly approximate its marginal cost, but the practical difficulties of estimating the latter suggest that claims on this count should be made modestly.

In addition to the two groups of students with stable preferences as between a packaged course and a high participiation option, there is yet a third group: those whose interest in a subject is awakened during a course. The size of this group is increased by good — and time-intensive — instruction. If students from this group mistakenly opt for a packaged course, they may (literally) miss the chance of a lifetime.

---

[4] The incidence of the burden placed upon instructional time facilities by the unusually earnest student is a moot point. Depending upon faculty response to student demands for attention, it may fall upon other less importunate students, upon other uses of faculty time, or some combination of the two. Also it depends upon the characteristics of the time-using students; if they very able and/or seriously interested in the subject, their importunities cause less loss of utility to an instructor than if they are mere grade-seekers.

Educators rejoice in the process of intellectual awakening, and much of the inevitable opposition to packaged courses will stem from (or be rationalized by) reluctance to sabotage this important teaching function. I do not wish to minimize the importance of awakening intellectual interest nor the capacity of good teachers to contribute to the process. But surely this process is very costly (especially when one considers the overwhelming ratio of failures to successes), and I doubt that its cost-effectiveness is sufficient to contribute much to defence of the current time-intensive teaching methods except for a very small segment of the student population.[5]

Let me summarize the argument thus far. The seemingly homogeneous "output" of a given course consists in reality of (at least) three separate components: students who learn the equivalent of a packaged course and seek no more; students who desire a more intimate and critical knowledge of the subject (high participators) and students who change from the latter group to the former during the course. It is alleged that in a good many courses, substantial increases in efficiency could be achieved by catering solely for the first group whose members comprise the great majority of students.[6] Students desiring the more (instructor) time-intensive, and therefore more costly, high-participation options should be charged an additional fee sufficient to cover the prime cost of producing the options.[7].

The effect of implementing this recommendation would be to change the output-mix of a course, eliminating the third group and increasing the first group relative to the second. As there are no readily available market prices to use in weighting these output components, any claim of increased efficiency from introduction of packaged courses may be rejected by a given evaluator if he places a sufficient value upon the learning of the second and third groups

---

[5] This statement implies that the traditional form of higher education is not cost-effective for more than a small part of the population, and that a packaged mass-produced course is a "good enough" substitute for most people, considering the extra cost of the (superior) version.

[6] Even the best students are, in some courses, mere passive absorbers of academic material.

[7] I am avoiding the difficult problem of preventing non-payers from participating in high-participation activities.

relative to the learning of the first group. I suggest that for many large (non-elite) universities, the appropriate weights are such as to make a substitution of packaged courses for present elementary courses a movement toward increased efficiency.

Utilization of packaged courses could be extended well beyond the first level. Indeed, wherever there is a market big enough to support a textbook, there is a *prima facie* case for considering use of a packaged course. This covers much of undergraduate, and a considerable part of graduate course work as well.

I have no desire casually to estimate the potential savings in cost and improvement of instructional quality resulting from substitution of packaged courses for those conventionally taught. However, the following analogy may be suggestive: traditional classroom methods of instruction are like "live" entertainment, while packaged courses are like the cinema or phonograph records. The cost saving per hour of entertainment resulting from substitution of the latter for the former is obvious, and the improvement of *average* quality even more obvious. The loss of spontaneity and, perhaps, of intimacy is also obvious. The problems of valuing losses and gains in the two cases (entertainment and instruction) would appear to have many common elements.

Packaged courses are inappropriate in situations where either the individual interpretation of the instructor is essential (and scale small), or live discussion is essential. However, large numbers of sparsely attended courses in esoteric fields (notably in the humanities) are terribly costly and (in the judgment of many students of university finance) are taught in too many places and on too small a scale in each. Use of closed circuit television in courses such as these might make possible substantial increases in efficiency, although a critical variable (about which I must plead ignorance) is the cost of television facilities.

Pedagogical efficiency and research activity

Thus far, I have not mentioned the employment effect of increasing teaching efficiency. That is, I have not taken into account that most cost saving of the kind discussed above arises from saving instructional salaries by reducing employment of teachers. Fear of the economic consequences for university teachers of reduced (or slackened growth in) demand for their services has almost certainly been an important source of opposition to schemes — such as the above — to increase output per pedagogical hour.

In this opposition, teachers are treading a path long followed by craftsmen faced with reduced employment prospects as a result of technical progress; i.e. they stress the superior virtues of the output of the hand (or mouth) craft process, and the defects of the mass produced item. But though our arguments may be self-serving, it does not follow that they are wrong. Indeed, there is a very good rationale for fostering the employment of (university) academics that does not rest on guild self-interest.

This rationale is based on the fact that, *inter alia*, the university produces teaching and research jointly. Faculty concern with expanding the numbers of their colleagues and students does not stem from interest in the teaching programme but from the desire to promote research. This is not usually acknowledged because outside the physical sciences there is a deep — and possibly well-grounded — fear that the research-teaching mix desired by the faculty would not attract as much funding as one with a larger teaching component. Consequently, research programmes desired mainly for their own sake, are often rationalized by their (alleged) contribution to teaching, community service, national defence or otherwise. Similarly, faculty members desired for their talents as researchers are pressed into service as course teachers, an activity for which (often) they are not particularly well suited or interested.[8]

This is not to contend that too much is being put into research. On the contrary, my own (self-serving) judgment is that too little is being directed into this activity. However, funding sources do not now accept — and have rarely in the past accepted — the faculty consensus on this point, so that research support must be diverted from other uses. Chief among these (other) uses are university funds supposed to promote teaching and research jointly.

A research community or subculture consists of a group of individ-

---

[8] These remarks are not intended as a denial of the close relationship between teaching and research at the advanced graduate level — the research project-dissertation stage. At this level, good teaching and good research are almost inseparable. However, teaching advanced graduate students is very different from teaching basic courses or tutoring undergraduates who are technically unsophisticated and/or uninterested.

214

uals whose attention is focussed on expanding and developing knowledge of a particular subject matter. In the sciences, these communities are organized around the activity of developing and testing the paradigm (or paradigms) that constitute the subject.[9] In the humanities, paradigms do not exist in the same sense as in the sciences. Nevertheless, even there, one finds research communities of specialists in particular areas, periods and combinations thereof, who share a common language and body of expertise into which an outsider can be initiated only with considerable time and trouble. Full-time members of these intellectual communities must be financially supported, and university appointments are a prime source of such support. These appointments are usually conditional upon a certain amount of teaching; hence the tension between the demands of teaching and research at the margin.

An obvious and appropriate question for an economist to ask is why markets for the product of research activity do not generate adequate (profit-seeking) support for members of research communities. The principal answer is that the difficulty of appropriating its output leads to systematic private underinvestment in research.

However, when a national or international body needs technical information or immediate short-range research bringing the best available knowledge to bear upon some immediate problem, it calls upon members of the appropriate community of (full-time) specialists who charge relatively modest consultant fees for their services. These fees would never cover the overhead cost of maintaining these specialists; accordingly, said maintenance must be provided in some other way.

Conceivably, private firms might invest in stocks of such specialists, contracting for exclusive use of their services, and then retailing them for whatever the market would bear when they were needed. What prevents this from happening is the cost of contract enforcement i.e. after years of maintenance by a firm, a specialist might leave (or threaten to) and obtain all the quasi-rent afforded by a market made tight by an emergency. Even if the firm could collect damages for breach of contract (specific compliance being prevented by the 13th amendment and the difficulties of getting good performance from a reluctant worker) the costs and uncertainties of doing so would

---

[9] The notion that scientific communities are organized around paradigms (roughly theories and their testing) is developed by T.S. Kuhn, (1970).

seriously reduce the expected value of any claim to the future services of a specialist. Moreover, it is very doubtful that a government would allow a private employer to charge the full rental rate for the services of its employees that a very tight labour market would permit. For these reasons, private firms would hold a sub-optimal quantity of scientific experts.[10] This argument applies, *a fortiori*, to the humanities.

Granting, then, that much of the social inventory of intellectual specialists must be held outside the profit-seeking sector, it does not follow that it must be located within universities. Research institutes, centres for studies of one kind or another also can — and do — serve as *loci* for intellectual subcultures. While these institutions exhibit a strong (mutual) attraction to universities, they can survive without such affiliation.

Nevertheless, it is doubtful that any substantial withdrawal of university support for research activity could quickly be replaced. And there is good reason for fearing that freeing university resources from support of teaching would lead to a reduction in the joint product, research. This is because university resources are under heavy pressure to do social work, improve the environment, etc. and it is quite possible that resources saved in teaching would go to promote these objectives rather than research. Any valuation of the change in the *overall* efficiency of the university resulting from an increase in the efficiency of its teaching arm must depend upon how the freed resources are used; upon the valuations placed upon these uses, and, finally, upon the effect of the overall reallocation upon the ability of the university to attract further resources.

In fine, despite the presence of guild-like motivations, there is a defensible rationale for resisting improvements in teaching efficiency if one is pessimistic about the ability of pure research activities to obtain adequate support. Frank discussion of this matter may not be altogether prudent, but the duty of intellectual honesty is compelling.

---

[10] Looked at in a slightly different way, private firms tend to invest in applied research (whose product is more easily predicted and appropriated) and permit in-house researchers to engage in pure research only to a limited degree. Of course, scientists who opt for this type of career may not be very desirous of doing pure research, but that does not gainsay the difficulty of placing (would-be) pure researchers in the private sector.

216

10. Economic Organization and Inefficiency in the Modern University
by Paul H. Cootner

It is widely believed that university education is economically inefficient. Whether this is in fact true is an empirical question, not one for abstract argument. Unfortunately, empirical testing of such a proposition is not likely to be very convincing without a model of the educational firm that will permit us to formulate testable hypotheses and to isolate the data that are relevant to the test.

This chapter is a first, faltering step along these lines. It is far from a complete analysis of the educational process. What it does do, however, is to apply some basic economic principles to some rather elementary facts about the economic organization of the industry and its competitive structure. Given the assumptions of the analysis, it yields a set of observations about where an economist might expect to find inefficiencies in this industry and, by implication, indicate which levers might have to be changed if we hope to remove those inefficiencies. Neither the model nor the analytic techniques I use are new. In what follows I will draw heavily on papers by A. Alchian and H. Demsetz (1972) and Henry Manne (1971). Nor do I, by using the economist's word of art – model – mean to imply that the view presented here is really an abstract and tightly woven analytical presentation. In the strict sense a model is a logically self-contained statement which can be attacked only because its assumptions are false or its predictions untrue. The investigation of the model's empirical validity *can* be quite separate from its statement. The view I present here is one that I believe accurately represents and elucidates some of the problems of educational efficiency, and I have not always been as careful as I might to separate the pure model from the casual empiricism supporting it. Nevertheless, there is a common analytic foundation to this view of the educational industry which I hope makes it somewhat more than a collection of more or less accurate observations about the university of today.

217

The argument of this chapter is presented in three sections, which overlap somewhat in content. The first presents the key elements of educational organization which I feel underly the problems of economic efficiency in the modern university and a capsule indication of their probable impact. In the second, I sketch out some casual empirical observations which I feel tend to support the view expressed in the first section. Finally, in a painfully brief section, I try to indicate some possible directions for reform and change which might be enhanced by changes in the internal pricing system. With regret, I have abandoned completely my initial objective of formulating some clear and careful statement of testable hypotheses. That will have to await another opportunity.

The Model

There are certain key features of the education industry on which this model draws. First, it is a "non-profit" industry. Actually, while almost everyone believes he knows what is meant by a non-profit organization, the term in common usage covers a wide variety of organizational forms. On the one hand, it includes both units which are merely conduits for spending gifts and which have no revenues of their own, and huge self-contained cooperatives which carefully balance revenue and expenditure and which differ from ordinary firms only in the fact that they are organized without a class of proprietors or stockholders investing in the hope of a pecuniary return on their investment. The case of the university generally falls between the extremes. There is a range of revenue producing products: college educations are "sold", research activities are produced for sponsors, etc. These revenues, however, typically fall far short of covering current costs, nor are they expected to recompense the capital costs of the firm's physical assets. The capital is supplied free of any expected monetary return and indeed some capital is provided to cover expected current deficits. Although I will dwell on this point at greater length later, I will simply observe at this point that one implication is that there is no explicit contractual "stockholder" group in control of the considerable physical assets involved, leaving an important degree of ambiguity about the goals of the educational firm.

218

The absence of a proprietary group with the customary contractual prerogatives of shareholders is an invariant aspect of non-profit institutions. It is less invariant that the firm sell its products at less-than-full-cost. Nevertheless, the *university* does so, and it leads to an easily predictable economic phenomenom. With a college education priced below cost, we not surprisingly find demand usually in excess of supply and available admission slots rationed among applicants. The result is that a valuable prerogative – matriculation – can be granted on the basis of non-price considerations, and control over the disposition of this right will fall to whomever can control the admission process.

The third characteristic of the university which is important to my model is the difficulty of monitoring the output of the employees, in particular the faculty. A university faculty typically produces two major products: teaching and research. In both of these fields quantitative measures of output are unusually inadequate indications of the quantity or value of input. When we speak of hours of teaching or pages of research output, we exclude important qualitative aspects of production. A class can be large or small, the students well-prepared and intelligent or mediocre and of diverse background, the lecture carefully annotated or off-the-cuff, the instructor readily available after class or not, etc. In the same fashion, a published article can be brief and seminal, or long and mediocre or any intermediate gradation. This is not an exclusive property of education. Many of the outputs of our professions – medicine, and law, for example – have similar characteristics, but the importance of this characteristic increases when the services are engaged by a large employer rather than a self-proprietorship. The issue in the university is that the educational firm monitors a large number of employees producing a product for which it is difficult to measure either input or output accurately. This is not to say that such measurement is impossible. In fact, universities engage in a cumbersome but largely effective process for evaluating the research of their faculty members,[1] but the costs of such evaluation usually mean it cannot be accomplished at regular frequent intervals, and the imprecision of the measures admit of a large possibility of error. In the teaching area, the issue is more

---

[1] When I say this process is effective I do not mean that it always leads to good decisions; only that it usually succeeds in acquiring relevant information.

clouded. It is impossibly expensive to get readings from outside observers on teaching quality, and there are a number of problems with relying on consumer (student) opinion. The most often cited problem is whether students are qualified to judge the quality of their education, but as I will stress below, the structure of the university creates an adversary relationship between students and faculty that hampers the use of student opinions.

Now let me tie these three strands together. Alchian and Demsetz (1972) argue with considerable cogency that the ubiquity of the "firm" as a unit of economic activity arises from the cost of monitoring efficient production. Abstractly, one can envision even the most complex and capital-intensive industries operating under quite decentralized conditions, with expensive machine tools being rented to individual worker-entrepreneurs who each turn out some small component of a product along an assembly line, just as some "department stores" are, in effect, assemblies of individual leased proprietorships within a common building. For the university, the analogous picture would be one of a cluster of buildings in which individual faculty-entrepreneurs would rent facilities to teach students at independently determined tuition rates, and class sizes. From this view, they argue that the existence of firms cannot be simply explained as an artifact of economies of scale in production, as narrowly construed, but must rest on a particular class of administrative problems.

Take first the industrial process. The problem with the scheme of individual entrepreneurships is that in a complex productive process there is a continuing opportunity and incentive for each individual to shirk as his task. If any one such individual were to reduce the quality of his output or to work at a more leisurely (and expensive) pace, the impact of his reduced efforts would be marginally negligible and virtually indetectable and thus impossible, in practice, for someone to resist. Once it is established that this shirking is taking place somewhere in the system, it is irrational for it not to be undertaken everywhere in the system. The only way to restrain this spreading inefficiency is to appoint a "manager", whose compensation depends upon the entire process, to monitor the process and supervise the activities of the individuals. To make such supervision effective the manager must have the power to hire and fire and set standards, etc. – in other words to create a firm with an ability to appropriate (a share of) residual profits.

220

This capsule version of the Alchian-Demsetz argument hardly does it full justice, but it does indicate the key issue for education and the university: the problem of monitoring the efficiency of the production process. In other service industries where output measurement is important, we tend to get, wherever possible, some form of individual entrepreneurship. A doctor or lawyer or accountant generally operates as a proprietor or small partnership where his own efforts are directly rewarded by his own revenues and there is minimal need for anyone else to see if he is pulling his weight.[2] There remains the difficulty of the client-patient in determining the quality of the service rendered, but within the (sometimes wide) limits imposed by the costs of gathering such information, the potential for productive efficiency is increased by that form of organization.

The modern educational industry is not organized in this fashion, although it apparently was something like a collection of proprietors in classic times. Presumably, in modern education the valuable output is "an education" – a degree [3] – which means that the educational services provided must be of coordinate quality among the many suppliers, both because of the dependence of later instruction on prior learing and because of the costs to potential employers of determining the quality of an unstandardized education. We should note, however, that it is a moot question as to whether a university form of organization is essential to an education so long as the industry is marked, as it is now, by subsidized tuition policies. It would be extremely difficult for a system of proprietorships to compete with existing institutions short of the point where the inefficiencies of such institutions just offset the subsidies.[4]

---

[2] For a study which suggests that group medical practice tends to create real monitoring inefficiencies, see Joseph Newhouse (1972).

[3] Although the empirical evidence is not clear. Some studies suggest that there is a discretely higher value to a degree than to three years of education, but others show differently.

[4] Not only the subsidies of philanthropy and governmental appropriations but also that of non-profit tax treatment. If it is true that there is a growing, though small, private profit-seeking university industry, it could be the basis of an estimate of university inefficiency, assuming of course that one could correct for quality, and that the accreditation process does not create unfair bias against such universities which cannot earn such accreditation.

Given that post-secondary education must be dispensed in university format, we must face the problem of producing an efficient output despite the difficulty of measuring input (and output) quality. In the case of many similar service or professional activities, the monitoring process is aided by consumer sovereignty. In dealing with individual proprietorships the customer directly measures the output in his own calculus and, within his information limitations, assesses its quality. In dealing with service *firms*, he assesses the quality and costs of the entire firm and a firm that does not adequately monitor its employees will lose revenues to its competitors. For universities, this process is impeded by the factors I outlined earlier: the rationing of student applications and the lack of a formal shareholder class with property rights to the residual "profits" of the university. With student applications rationed, it will not necessarily follow that an inefficiently-produced education will cause a university to lose student *admissions*, and possibly not even *applications*. As long as the inefficiency is less than the subsidy there will continue to be excess demand for matriculation, although to the extent that the effective subsidy is reduced by inefficiency, the amount of the excess demand may be trimmed. What has gone before is not an argument that universities must be inefficient — only that, if they prove to be so because of the difficulties of monitoring faculty inputs, the underpricing of tuition will prevent consumer sovereignty from correcting the inefficiency. There is no reason in principle, for example, why universities might not choose to value very highly the opinion of its customer-students independently of their unwillingness to "vote with their feet", so that consumer choice might play an important role in monitoring teaching output. Even without getting involved in issues of consumer sovereignty, there are some other institutional mechanisms for improving organizational efficiency which are not currently used. To lay the final foundation for our model of educational inefficiency we must pass on to the last of our three organizational facets.

In a profit-seeking firm, legal control of its operations is vested in the suppliers of equity capital — the stockholders. In the standard economic model, these owners seek to maximize their return from the enterprise. If, at the same time, the firm operates in a competitive environment free from certain market imperfections, these "maximum" profits will prove to be only the minimum required to reimburse the contributors of capital. But while the standard economic analysis turns on returns to the productive factors, from the Alchian-Demsetz view of the firm the stockholders also turn out to be the ideal place to vest management control. Since their capital cannot "shirk" and its efficient utilization is disciplined by impersonal market forces, it will be economically efficient to have this group monitor the other inputs. The owners of the rights to the residual profits have an interest in the overall profit of the enterprise that is not shared by other human factors.

This is clearly an ideal picture. There is obvious scope for inefficiency that might arise from stockholders' interest in improving profits by eliminating competition. There may be external economies or diseconomies which make the private calculus socially inefficient. In widely-held corporations, there is a need to delegate management authority and with it the need to coordinate the interests of management and shareholders and the "transactions costs" of overturning a management once established in control. These costs of separating ownership and control may substantially impair this picture of economic efficiency. These are, of course, empirical questions.

For our purposes, however, we are interested not in the implications of the profit-maximizing model, but the implied forecast of the "non-profit" model. In non-profit firms, the contribution of capital funds does not carry with it the same sort of property right to residual profits as in the normal firm. Capital contributions are either by gift or by association with a purchase of services. A depositor contributes capital out of the earnings on his deposit, the insurance policy-holder out of his premium. Once the funds are contributed, the equity supplier retains no interest in his equity when he ceases to be a customer and even while a customer his control is not usually related to the size of his contribution and his rights to a return on capital are severely restricted. A philanthropist has the same sort of control over a gift: he may extract some sort of *quid pro quo*, including even some temporary management control, but the control is not a right which can legally be sold or bartered and a return on his "investment" is necessarily indirect.

The issue of management control in a non-profit firm is, therefore, subject to the vagaries of power, sometimes economic, sometimes legal, sometimes extra-legal. All participants in the process have some interest in control: the philanthropists, the employees, the customers, and the suppliers. The degree of concern with control turns in considerable part on the opportunities for gain, if one thinks of gain as including "utility" benefits as well as cash. Outside the educational field, where there is considerable competition between profit and non-profit firms, there is an opportunity to earn a "profit" on the capital which has been contributed, and the distribution of that profit will fall to whoever controls the enterprise. There are numerous assertions that in such organizations as mutual savings and loan associations, banks or insurance companies such profits are seized by management or suppliers in either the form of money or an easier life. Manne (1971) has stressed the interest of religious denominations in setting up the early universities to produce ministers and parishioners alike, and Manne (1971) and Veblen (1899) have both spoken of the interest, at a later date, of the upper (leisure) classes in training their sons in the canons of taste. Manne has gone on to suggest that a substantial part of the *current* control rests with the faculty, a point of view that has a special connection with the difficulty of monitoring faculty performance, but before we turn to that argument, it would be helpful to indicate why the process or seizure of control is likely to lead to economic inefficiency no matter who maintains that effective control.

Whether or not there are positive economic profits to be seized, the inability to maintain legal property rights to any potential profits will produce inefficiency. The benefits of control can only be appropriated by the currently existing control group. If the students were in control, they would have an incentive to maximize current benefits without concern for future endowment, or research reputation, or faculty development. The current donors would, during their life and for as far into the future as their trusts can control, have an incentive to maximize whatever they desired — their self-esteem or their field of interest — but unless their goal was itself the maximization of economic efficiency it would be unlikely to achieve such efficiency. Non-academic employees might have the best incentive for economic efficiency if their compensation was limited by the amount of the inefficiency, but their own attempts at appropriating the residual would probably militate against efficiency.

When the legal rights to an asset are unclear, the acquisition of the assets is likely to depend on a variegated combination of sources of power — economic, political, and chance. All we need say is that the faculty has perhaps the greatest economic interest in university control since its tenure in office is longer and its opportunity for benefit is greater than most other participants. Still, the degree of faculty control in university management has probably shown considerable variance. It has probably increased over time in the private university (1) as the costs of schooling have risen past the point where a few donors could account for the bulk of funding, and (2) as a college education has increasingly become viewed as a capital good rather than a consumer good, so that the content of education became less a matter of taste and more a matter of technical competence. Faculty participation has probably fluctuated in both directions with the scarcity or surplus of personnel relative to demand and, for public universities, with the ebb and flow of legislative concern with the cost or content of education.

Faculty control over the management of universities, whatever its magnitude, leads to a situation where the group with the greatest potential for benefitting from imperfect monitoring is also the group chosen to help perform the task. Under the best of circumstances ensuring efficient use of faculty resources would require careful and continuing evaluation of their inputs where such evaluations would have to be particularly intrusive because of the measurement difficulty. Without such monitoring, the opportunity for one teacher to shirk would be the incentive for his neighbour to do the same or bear an extra burden. Close control would be highly expensive if it did not use the market test: the continuing supervision by the student. (Note that there is no easily tapped counterpart group of consumers to evaluate research.) I do not mean to understate the problems that are often asserted in having those who are not yet educated evaluate the educators: I simply point out how difficult it is to do the job without them. With faculty having an important voice in university management, it becomes increasingly difficult to institute controls which, if imposed, would constrain established practices of comfort and laxity. The usefulness of student sovereignty, or labour-saving innovation in teaching, or enforced attendance at the university, or restraint on outside employment opportunities will always seem to have a little less merit to a management which can see an immediate benefit from the *status quo* and only an uncertain and indirect benefit from experimentation. The real test of this issue is not how many controversial, potential innovations in university management practice are introduced, but how strong is the resistance to the most tentative experiments.

It is only fair to note that while faculty control may discourage attempts at economic rationalization which might reduce shirking, it does not imply that there are huge faculty benefits from the practice. Like the inefficiencies produced by monopolistic competition, employee control is likely to distort resource use without net profit to the faculty. Since teachers are produced in a competitive market, the advantages produced by shirking are merely reflected in faculty supply and salaries. While a professor sees his salary as low, he is unlikely to see the relationship between his salary and his productivity. Low teaching loads are seen as barely adequate compensation for a small paycheque. The ability to take time off from his university duties to consult with outside firms is not seen as a fraud on his students, but as the only thing that enables him to resist the attraction of offers outside the university. Those teachers who value most highly the nonpecuniary advantages of teaching stay in the field and those most concerned about the compensating pecuniary disadvantages leave. As a result, when economic reform is contemplated we find that it would result in a reduction in utility for many faculty members even if it results in a compensated increase in marginal productivity. If, in particular, the ability to shirk on teaching effort is pronounced at some university, that school will attract those faculty members who most value research relative to teaching. Competition for those jobs may even depress monetary salary below that in other schools, but it will nevertheless create an aversion to any reform which values more highly teaching performance among those currently employed. With outside control, a reform could be undertaken which could improve efficiency, change the structure of rewards and possibly result in a turnover of teaching staff. Without outside control, the transactions costs of the shift would not be willingly borne.

Some implications

Under present systems of compensation the faculty member has no self-motivation for improving the efficiency of education. He has no financial incentive for teaching more students or more hours a

226

week or during hours which would increase the utilization of physical facilities. He has no incentive to devise new techniques for teaching except insofar as they may be commercially saleable outside the university (and these techniques must be sold — either directly or indirectly — to other faculty members who similarly have little incentive to buy them). He is not self-motivated to make himself available for office hours or to spend more than a minimum amount of time on grading. To prevent utter choas, the incentives must be supplied by administrative fiat — a load is X courses, class sizes will be Y students, and will be scheduled at *these* hours, etc. Because the faculty have the incentive to evade these rules, they are usually defined on the easily quantifiable and enforceable variables indicated in the previous sentence. Rules about "the quality of teaching", the number of office hours, or exams, or term papers, or the care taken on grading are stated in much more general terms and the degree of evasion is evidenced by the universality of student complaints of the non-observance of these standards. (Of course, student complaints are themselves encouraged by the absence of any charge for the disputed services. Since they are nominally free, the student is encouraged to demand them to excess, while the faculty member endeavours to supply as little as possible.) The enforceability of these rules is further hindered by the absence of a formal workday. The standard reason for the lack of a formal workday is the expectation that faculty members will produce research as well as teaching services and that such research effort is best achieved in a location free from casual student or administrative interruption. The lack of a formal workday, in turn, is encouraged by the awareness that if some faculty members shirk, those who do not will bear a disproportionate load of student contact and be particularly penalized with respect to research output.

The measurement of research output poses its own problems of quality as does teaching, but for most faculty the time spent on research (whatever the productivity of such research) is a relatively enjoyable effort akin to leisure so that the inability to meter time spent on research does not produce a corresponding degree of evasion. However, since it is so hard to meter accomplishment and the relationship between time input and page output is so variable this may not be a testable proposition. In view of the greater enjoyment typically accruing to "research" (i.e., non-contact hours with students) any trade-off between teaching and research that is permitted will typically be utilized and where the terms of the trade-off are not (or cannot be) stated with precision, the faculty member is encouraged to supply more research and less teaching than desired. In particular, wherever authority or personal obligations can be brought to bear, they will be used to "buy" more research time, so that senior professors with rank or prestige will typically teach less than their (less skilled?) junior colleagues.

The ultimate discipline for the establishment, let alone enforcement, of the rules stems from the outside market rather than the administration *per se*. The rules must be sufficiently observed to maintain a satisfied alumni, a sufficient generous group of donors, and an adequate pool of student applicants. The adequacy of the applicant pool is measured not simply by its ability to pay tuition, but also by its quality.

There are two aspects to this "outside market" discipline. One is purely financial in the customary sense. Funds must be forthcoming to operate the school and the ability to attract funds must be maintained at some equilibrium level. This is analogous to what in normal competitive markets we think of as consumer sovereignty. In the university, however, there are many consumers and funds come from many sources only imperfectly related to the educational product. Many charitable contributions are, in fact, purchases of educational services designed to shift the basket of outputs in one direction or another – foundation support for public management programmes or research on sickle cell anaemia or cancer, or minority education; corporate giving which is directly related to employment of graduates, etc. However, with student tuition falling short of full costs and applications far in excess of enrolment, the grant of admission is a valuable privilege. In a normal market economy, this value would be extracted by the selling university. That this is not done is due to a mixture of reasons. In part, of course, with imperfect capital markets, poor applicants would not be able to secure a socially (and privately) valuable education if forced to pay full educational costs. This, however, is less an argument for low tuition than for fellowship subsidies for the economically disadvantaged, but intellectually competent, student. The most cogent argument is the hypothesized existence of external economies which warrant private underpricing supplemented by public funds. Note that regardless of the virtue of

228

the basic argument, the underpricing of tuition does not necessarily produce the desired result because it does not grarantee that a greater quantity of the socially valuable service is *produced* than would be produced with full cost pricing. The reduced price may be a stimulant of the right level of demand, but to achieve the external economies it should be accompanied by a supply of services adequate to meet the demand stimulated by the right price. I will return to this argument later, but for now I need only point out that with little empirical information on the size of the external economies available, the general solution is to underprice tuition by the same amount for each student no matter what his ability or his course of study, so the social subsidy is only imperfectly related to the type or characteristics of the student admitted.

In part, the continued underpricing of tuition despite its inadequacy as a means of achieving any social economies is merely a case of doing what one can, even if it is not the "right" thing. But we should not overlook that the resultant rationing creates a valuable right which could increase university revenues but does not. Nor should we overlook the fact that a major if not dominant role in granting that right is maintained by university faculties. The faculties have no means for extracting direct cash value for this right, although they sometimes grudgingly grant some influence in the process to potentially generous alumni. For the most part, however, faculties utilize the admission process to ease their teaching and research "loads". The student selection process is oriented toward admitting the brightest students − those easiest to teach − and expanding the graduate educational facilities of the universities. (It is rewarding to observe economics professors scorn engineers who overdesign bridges, in one voice, and defend the admission of only the best educated students, with the other. It is also worth noting the bias of graduate admissions committees toward low-risk admittees from standard high-quality undergraduate schools whose training is most like the faculty and that are easier to teach.) Since we know very little about the economics of the education process it *may* very well be that the greatest net value-added accrues to the education of the smartest students. It *may* even be that the economic optimum is to devote even more total resources to the teaching of a bright student who could reach any given attainment with a smaller investment of resources. The point is that present admissions policies appear to be based on a canon of faith, and one that is unlikely to be subjected to much testing so long as it coincides with the economic motivation of admitting bodies. In short, underpricing tuition leads to an economic rent which is at least partially captured by the university faculties. Another aspect of the same phenomena is seen in the allocation of stipends to doctoral students. The competitive process among faculties allocates funds not to the needy or to those with greatest potential for producing social benefits in excess of private benefits, but to those who will furnish the greatest utility to the faculty, either as consumption or production goods. (To be sure, the graduation of superior PhDs redounds to the benefit of a university's reputation and through that to the augmentation of philanthropic funds and possibly a premium tuition closer to costs. It may also enable a university to reduce its wage bill by improving the non-wage benefits of the faculty. In view of the motivations, however, it is only by chance that it will not reduce the net benefits of the university and the education process.)

The impact of the incentive structure pervades the university in the field of education and tuition. Given resource expenditures it is reasonably clear that graduate tuition is subsidized by undergraduate. Not only are faculty and physical facilities supplied in greater amounts but, as I mentioned above, the tuition subsidies supplied by the university bear little or no relationship to the potential external economy involved. In particular, they bear little relationship to the likelihood that the student would not be able to receive the presumed socially valuable education in their absence.

The impact of the absence of positive incentives in the university extends into seemingly unrelated fields. Two different factors leading to faculty overinvestment in administration should be distinguished.

I have already noted Manne's argument that the faculty exercises the real control of the university. Whatever one's empirical evaluation of the argument any power held by the faculty would have to be exercised by pervasive participation in the administrative process. Since the faculty has no *formal* power over the university president, the exercise of authority must take place by arrogating to themselves specific areas of decision-making and staffing those bodies with its own members. This part of the administrative process does not, however, require large-scale participation: conceivably, the faculty could select relatively few members to represent it in these

230

decisions subject to recall. In fact, in a wide range of decisions, usually at the university level, this is the procedure utilized in substance if not always in form. Either there is a select faculty "senate" or university-wide faculty meetings which are *de facto* attended by a small group of interested faculty so long as there is no critical controversy. On a departmental or school level, however, this delegation of power may be less feasible because of the lack of a price system or currency to allocate the "tax burden" of decisions. A hiring or tenure decision, a change in course requirements, an alteration of admission standards, a proposed new programme – all these impinge on the "equity" of each faculty member in an immediate way in which it is currently virtually impossible to construct a calculus to agree on benefits or costs. Even a faculty committed to "research excellence" at the expense of teaching is likely to differ on which field will be benefitted or injured by a decision to hire or a change in admissions policy.

There are some other aspects of university organization that have economic implications through the operation of political power in a system without well-defined economic power. As in our national government where the boundaries of authority have been carefully made diffuse, one must be careful of exercising formal power for fear that the attempted exercise will demonstrate weakness rather than strength. A "strong" president or dean may exercise considerable "power" so long as he does not excessively alienate his constituency. The result of these forces (spelled out more carefully in Manne 1971) is to make the administration of a university more like that of a legislature than that of a formal business organization. The particular feature I would like to stress is that of logrolling, where issues important to one group can be achieved by trading votes on other issues to other groups.

This effect seems to play a particularly important role in such diverse issues as tuition at the university level and "core curriculum" at the degree level. Assume for example that we wished to price tuition at a level consistent with profit-maximization. It seems reasonable to believe that, on both the graduate and undergraduate level, a degree in philosophy, or classics, or anthropology is likely to be less "cost-effective" than one in engineering, or geology, or business. Even at present levels of tuition many fields are considerably constrained in number of students by the perceived poor remuneration, and a substantial element of "consumption utility" is credited to the student enrolment. It is also likely that the elasticity of demand is noticeably lower in those fields, so that general tuition increases would have a greater impact on humanities enrolment in general than in applied or technological fields. On the other hand, the operation of outside market demand has already had an impact on the salaries and other compensation of faculties in various academic departments, so that professors in business or engineering commonly receive higher salaries, lower teaching leads and more luxurious offices than do faculty in the humanities. Based on these higher personnel costs, a cost-based tuition would tend to create a differentially higher tuition for some departments than for others.

While there is no evidence of explicit collusion that I have ever seen, we see universities ending up with a below-cost tuition structure which implicitly subsidizes the less applied sectors of university education, and a flat tuition structure which permits the more costly departments to avoid differential tuitions. That this practice is created by the historical form of university organization can best be seen in the recent trends that have developed in some universities as a result of limited decentralization policies. As the budget squeezes have tightened on many universities, they have introduced the concept of placing various schools – particularly the professional ones – on a semi-independent budget basis. With tight budgets, it has become particularly attractive for the professional schools, with their increased ability to attract funds and charge higher tuitions, to opt out of the old arrangements. They have been *willing* to raise tuitions differentially under a regime where the increased profits accrue to the school rather than the university, while the humanities faculties have been forced to acquiesce in view of the importance of the financial difficulties to the entire institution.

A similar sort of logrolling seems to explain the pervasive phenomenon of "core" curricula. While the ostensible rationale usually is the efficiency of citing a common set of prerequisites so that all students will be prepared for advanced courses, or for professional competence, in fact the "core" usually ends up including a subset of courses which students would not take unless required to and which are not prerequisites in any strict sense for the subsequent course the student desires. The "cores" become a mechanism for ensuring the breadth of an education and generally include aspects of the subject matter for which enrolment is expected to be arguably inadequate to support the current staff levels if not required. It may be, of course, that the ubiquity of the phenomenon simply reflects widespread ignorance, by the student, of the requisites of an adequate education. Nevertheless, some suspicion may be entertained in light of the death of past prerequisites (languages, history of economic doctrine, philosophy) as pressures unfold and as influential members of departments with specialties in the required areas depart.[5]

The preceding issue — the exercise of authority — is one reason for extensive administrative participation — even by those who decry it. The other issue — quite different in principle — is the need for faculty participation in administration to achieve a consensus in order to prevent excess "shirking". Since the opportunity for evading rules is so widespread — even for those rules which it would be advantageous for all to obey if only it were advantageous for each — an important part of good organizational procedure is the involvement of faculty in university administration. All university decisions must be ratified by the faculty as a whole or by subcommittees as a form of participatory democracy, to insure enough of a consensus to make the rules effective.

Using the price system to improve efficiency

If there turns out to be substantial empirical support for the preceding views of the sources of ecomomic inefficiency in higher education, these views have the advantage of indicating the direction which productive reform might take. Since I argue that the source of the difficulty is a counter-productive incentive system, any reform should alter those incentives. There is no single way that this need be done, since different proposals will have different income redistribution implications and on that subject the economist offers no special wisdom. At one extreme, we could probably improve efficiency by permitting a "shareholder class" to "buy out" the existing *de facto* control group — a procedure which would transfer all the potential benefits of economic efficiency to the existing control group. Alter-

---

[5] A not inconsiderable issue in tenure decisions seems to turn, in reality, on this kind of logrolling about department balance compared to issues of competence.

natively, one can imagine a price system which would appropriate those benefits for students, trustees, or government. In practice, any system would have to meet the test of practicality — of dealing with the political art of the possible.

Still, without developing a complete programme on incentives, one can indicate some of the desirable features. We cannot expect an optimum level of educational innovation unless we give faculty and students the incentives to make such innovations. If monitoring performance is difficult for management, then it is more efficient to create the incentive for the worker to do what it is desirable to have him do. This means, for example, that a faculty member must have some opportunity to benefit from an improvement in his individual productivity, preferably in some clearly defined way so that the additional remuneration is not subject to an administrator's whim. Furthermore, while this kind of incentive could be introduced even with the present tuition system, full economic efficiency would require some more realistic method for evaluating the *value* of the increased efficiency, and it is difficult to see how such a valuation could be reasonably effected without a change in the pricing of university services.

The present-day university is a multi-product firm which prices its output in a relatively uniform and inflexible manner. A student pays the same tuition whatever courses he studies, whether he uses much or little of the faculty time or the physical plant facilities, whether his classes are lectures or seminars, etc. He has no incentive to accept cost-saving educational innovations since he does not share in the benefits, or even to take classes in off-period hours to increase physical plant utilization. He pays the same tuition whether all he needs to pass a course is the reading list or whether he needs to attend classes, ask questions, and see the professor in non-classroom situations as well. The tuition is also the same (typically) if he is a student in the first economics course who has little need of his professor's research capabilities or if he is a PhD candidate who is vitally concerned with the faculty's research competency.

This is not to say that it is essential that every cost differential must be reflected in price: in many cases the cost of ascertaining and billing the differences would exceed the benefits. There certainly are, however, broad areas where pricing could open up opportunities for change. In particular, of course, the possible opportunities for innovation in teaching, whether in introducing new technologies or in utilizing currently optimal production techniques are not encouraged — indeed, are discouraged — by the lack of a price scheme.

There is, however, a well recognized — perhaps even over-emphasized — potential for distortion from using price mechanisms. While the absence of a price mechanism creates incentives to favour research at the expense of efficient teaching, the use of market-based prices could create incentives to under-invest in research if research has substantial social benefits that cannot be privately appropriated. Actual academic discussion of this issue is often quite ambivalent reflecting the strong faculty self-interest in maintaining at least the current level of research on the one hand, and the dubious income distribution implications of financing it under current procedures, on the other. Thus we encounter one justification for the level of re-search which is based on the putative improvement in the quality of education produced by having faculty who are expanding the fron-tiers of their fields. To argue this erodes at least some of the validity of the public good issue — to the extent that research improves teaching it can be captured by a market price mechanism. The argu-ment for subsidizing research is valid only to the extent it does not result in appropriable benefits, whether from students, consulting clients, special-purpose foundation grants or other charitable grants directly tied to the quantity or quality of research output. The ex-isting non-price mechanism creates the incentive for the faculty to extract much of the research subsidy indirectly by skimping on its teaching contribution. Regardless of the social value of the research and the desirability of maintaining a given level of output, a taxation policy which tried to balance benefits and costs would not be likely to operate the way the current "tax policy" does.

Actually, the degree to which research benefits are non-appropri-able is probably overstated and a good part of the perceived diffi-culties are due as much to a problem of distribution of the benefits as they are to the inability of private parties to reap the benefits. Clearly, the level of research currently achieved is being currently financed. To some extent it may come from tuition payments, even though tuition does not cover full costs, because full costs already include much of the costs of research through inclusion of plant costs and the higher faculty costs of lower teaching loads. But that which does not come from tuition — the part supplied by various

235

grants and other funds — is often directly related to the volume of research output. The most striking case is that of sponsored research — Department of Defense contracts, National Institutes of Health grants, industrially financed research, etc., where the specific research is clearly "purchased". Slightly less direct is the foundation grant which is more likely to be a reward for perceived research excellence instead of the purchase of specific pieces of work. Although this is less clear to many, much research is directly saleable through private consulting contracts: in effect, some of the research can be viewed as "speculative investment" which is sold after its usefulness is made clear. In other ideal cases, the privately contracted research turns out to be an area of legitimate academic inquiry which can be published.

However, even the most indirect research finance still constitutes a payment for services. General philanthropy or even the alumni contribution are frequently the product of the school's prestige — and the prestige often stems from research results. (It was often an occasion for bitterness among fund-raisers at MIT prior to the late 1960s that although a very large number of Nobel Prize winners had been trained at that institution, no member of the faculty had won such an honour — to the presumed detriment of contributions.) This is not to deny that many contributions seem either stochastic or to be based on other considerations: it is only to point out that a university's research accomplishments often have economic benefits.

Many of these different methods of finance have different and important implications for university finance. In some cases the funds go directly to the university; in other cases they are seized by the faculty member. (The whole treatment of patent rights in universities offers some interesting case studies of this distribution process.) Of course, even in cases where the initial distribution goes to the faculty, prestigious universities have been known to pay lower salaries in part *because* of the acknowledged greater opportunity for increased consulting fees. And no matter how dedicated the university is to research in all fields, the differences between departments in salary, teaching loads, and research funds clearly reflects differences in the "marketability" of research in the different subject areas.

This does not settle the question of whether research is, or is not, maintained at the appropriate level of activity . The present system

236

may still provide an inadequate social level of research but if so that deficiency should not be chalked up to any incentive pricing system. The relevant issue for instituting a price mechanism is to determine whether that system would alter the current level. There are two alternatives. First, that the level of research does produce direct private benefits either through improvement in education or through the collection of university donations or private faculty rewards, in which case nothing need be lost by going to a market-type price system for education. Second, that the current research level does not produce enough direct private benefits to finance itself, and as a result it is financed by funds diverted from tuition payment or philanthropic contributions which were ostensibly given for other purposes. The optimality of this latter "tax" procedure is open to some doubt.

Of course, even if the present level of research output can be "sold" by the university to the present group of "consumers", it may not necessarily be easy to price research on a per-unit basis in a manner which is easily adaptable to a decentralized price system. Much philanthropic benefaction directly or indirectly traceable to research is not further traceable to any specific output, leaving a great deal of discretion to the administration as to how to create a satisfactory research "image". Indeed, this flexibility is likely to be part of the constant logrolling that must go on in the process of creating an effective "legislative majority" in running the university. As in other aspects of this process, a vote in the decision-making councils can be "sold" for research funds or other prerequisites and create distortions in optimum allocations. Nevertheless, the main point here is that a more consumer-responsive price system need not damage the *status quo* even if the actual pricing of research has to continue on an *ad hoc*, administrative basis much as it does now.

The real threat to research posed by a price system would come if the marginal value of a faculty member's time in teaching were raised to the point that he privately had an incentive to cut back on socially desirable research. In other words, even though research funds continued to be available at the old level, the professor's opportunity costs were such as to make him unwilling to supply the old level of services under the new conditions. If the supply of faculty is perfectly elastic this will at most be a temporary effect, but investigation of the full equilibrium effects would need more study than I have been able to give them. If it turns out to be true that tuition has been subsidizing research and that subsidy can be avoided under a flexible price system the effect would undoubtedly be adverse. One thing a price system would do, however, is make it easier to measure just what subsidy is required to establish a given research level and focus on whether the output is worth it. One cannot help feeling that most academics — like most farmers or oil men — would prefer leaving the question unresolved.

Summary

The bulk of this paper has been devoted to spelling out some of the inefficiencies and obstacles to innovation that stem from the form of organization employed by educational institutions. While one or another of these imperfections may not have been perceived before, the general picture is well-known and does not require such a lengthy exposition. What I am going to try here is to draw some implications from the preceding.

First, let me start with a negative conclusion. The structure of the university has such a pervasive distorting effect on resource use that data based on past operations will form a poor basis for the kind of empirical investigations that one might like to undertake. Such a simple concept as establishing cost-based tuition makes little economic sense when the costs themselves are distorted. The concept of a production function implies the use of optimal technology to produce a given combination of outputs from a given set of inputs. If this definition is not to be a tautology, there must be some objective measure of the inputs, so that one can distinguish between faculty time or effort inputs of varying amounts produced by different organizational patterns even when the numbers of faculty remain constant or the utilization of classroom space that is truly committed to education under different incentive schemes, etc.. As long as we cannot specify the relative prices of different inputs supplied by the same person or building we cannot measure the *quantity* of inputs really supplied. Then, beyond the production function we have surprisingly little data on the quality of output, or data to allocate costs to the different outputs especially given the incentives for misreporting. We know precious little about what the demand for univer-

238

sity services would be if price or quality were varied, and even the data on the benefits from education will not stand too much scrutiny. We have, apparently, almost no information on what characteristics of a university are associated with its charitable receipts or the size of its legislative appropriations. The point is not simply to say that nothing can be done, but only to point out that many of the data we have available for use do not correspond to the numbers that fit our theoretical models, and caution in using the data is well-advised.

Another conclusion that might be drawn is that to have any reasonable chance of adoption, sophisticated transfer pricing schemes must take into account existing distributions of power and income if they are to have any chance of voluntary acceptance. Every proposal for instituting change must not only pass the test of economic efficiency but must also appeal to a significant power base of the parties concerned as not unduly impairing their economic welfare, unless we have serious expectations that a solution can be imposed by external force, such as legislation. The possibility of such voluntary solutions is enhanced to the degree that the inefficiency of the existing techniques offers a social bonus from change that can be redistributed, but the mere proof that an optimal price system could make everyone better off is not enough. The problem exists in all welfare economics: it is worse here only because the mechanisms for redistribution are so fraught with subterfuge due to the divergence of real and ostensible purposes.

If one is concerned about creating an incentive for faculties to support labour-saving technological innovation in teaching one can imagine a royalty scheme for inducing support for such change just as dock workers can collect royalties for containers. If, however, a market-oriented tuition scheme has the property of revealing that education has been subsidizing research, it is unlikely to be adopted voluntarily by a research-oriented faculty, for the same reasons that US farmers prefer price-support programmes to direct subsidy plans. Not only do we have the question of maintaining something close to the existing income distribution but the problem is amplified so long as we have so much uncertainty above the impact of any change.

Working on the side of change, however, is another phenomenon: the difficulty of perceiving the full effects of relatively innocuous steps. Some of the "purely administrative" changes that universities have adopted recently in a period of tight finances have potentially attractive consequences. The divisionalization of universities, mentioned before, is one of these. If we recall that part of the university's organizational problem is the lack of a formal shareholder class, divisionalization recreates that class. With the narrow base of accounting and increased pressure against resource availability, many incentives for efficiency appear. A closer attention to the discrepancy between tuition and costs is attractive because the benefits accrue more narrowly to the group making the decision. Once the tuition is raised and the rents to accepted students reduced, there is a need to pay a greater attention to consumer sovereignty and with that a myriad of further ripples. This is not to argue that this whole process is necessarily uniformly good or satisfactorily rapid: simply that the process once inaugurated may contemplate more far-reaching consequences than would have been acceptable when it started.

The growing expense of our educational system is creating pressures for change in the financing and organization of the modern university. The optimists among us argue that this will create increased incentives for improving efficiency. It seems to me at least equally likely for these pressures to create a movement toward quantitative restrictions and increased bureaucracy, a trend that I think I already perceive in the state institutions. Any movement toward improved management of our current university system could help to stem that trend.

11 Private and Social Risk and Return to Education[1]

by William C. Brainard

Introduction

Most discussions of divergences between private and social returns on education focus on differences between the costs and benefits to the individual and to society as a whole. The divergences most frequently mentioned are these. Individuals do not bear the full costs of their education. Their education carries important positive externalities. Returns to education are taxed without allowing "depreciation" of the investment. Education is partially a labelling or screening process which identifies, and therefore benefits, high productivity individuals without necessarily increasing their productivity.[2]

In the absence of these divergences, and in a competitive world with perfect loan markets, individuals would tend to drive the rates of return on education to the social discount rate. In fact, however, the capital markets faced by a typical individual are far from perfect and the opportunities for diversifying labour or educational endowments are almost non-existent. This provides still another reason why the value of the costs and benefits of education may be quite different for an individual and for society. In this chapter I will explore the importance of capital market imperfections as a source of divergence between private and social returns. The analysis will be broken, somewhat artificially, into two parts. First, I will analyze the

[1] I am grateful to James Tobin and the participants in the La Paz conference for useful comments and suggestions, and to Hugh Tobin and Michael Coiner for able research assistance.

[2] The importance of this characteristic of education is explored by K. Arrow in Chapter 3.

241

importance of access to perfect loan markets in a world of certainty. How is the private "profitability" of education reduced by constraints on the amount of borrowing an individual can obtain? How effective are various types of "educational loans" in increasing the attractiveness of educational investment? In order to answer these and related questions I have constructed a life cycle model of the consumption and saving decisions of the individual within which it is possible to model various market imperfections. Needless to say, the quantitative importance of borrowing restrictions cannot be obtained without some empirical presumption about life-time income profiles, with and without education. In order to get some sense of the possible quantitative importance of loan restrictions I have made use of some rough estimates of life-cycle income profiles for different kinds of occupations and households.[3]

The second and more difficult part of the analysis attempts to deal with the effects of uncertainty on the attractiveness of investment in education. In a world with a complete set of contingent commodity markets we might expect the uncertainty in the return to an individual's education to be "diversified" away and to have little effect on the level of investment undertaken.

In the last section, I draw together some casual evidence on the variability of income, and its relationship to level of education. I also discuss briefly the relevance of such uncertainty for the comparison of various loan programmes.

Private and social returns in a world of certainty

The life-cycle model with perfect loan markets

One indication of the importance of capital market imperfections to educational investment decisions is the extent to which individuals use capital markets when they are perfect. In order to get a sense of the importance of capital markets for various types of households, and to provide a basis of comparison with the case where markets are

---

[3] The approach of this part of the chapter follows that of Tobin (1967) and Tobin and Dolde (1972). The latter paper considers in detail the aggregate implications of individual life-cycle behaviour in response to capital gains, interest rates and liquidity constraints.

imperfect, I have calculated optimal consumption and borrowing paths in a model where individuals can borrow and lend at the social discount rate r. In that case the budget constraint is given by

$$\sum_0^T (c_i - Y_i) \frac{1}{(1+r)^i} - W_0 = 0$$

where c_i and Y_i are consumption and earned income in period i respectively, and W_0 is initial wealth. The actual consumption path chosen will of course depend upon the individual's utility function. In the discussion which follows I will make the standard assumption that an individual's prospective utility is the discounted sum of the utility associated with consumption in each period.

$$U = \sum_0^T u(c_i) \frac{1}{(1+\delta)^i}. \tag{1}$$

One objection to this specification is the fact that the utility derived from consumption in one period is independent of previous rates of consumption. In particular (1) rules out rate-of-change or ratchet effects, which might explain the differences in short- and long-run consumption behaviour and also explain, without the subjective discount factor, why consumption is relatively low early in the life-cycle.

In some of our calculations the decision unit will be a household comprising more than one individual. In that case, we will assume that the household's utility function will be simply a weighted sum of utilities of its members. An individual aged 18 or over is given a weight of 1, a child aged 0–13 is given a weight of 0.31, a child of 14–17 a weight of 0.62.[4] It is assumed that consumption is allocated "efficiently" across members of a household, i.e. there is equality in consumption per adult equivalent. This is also a device for modifying equation (1) to allow age-specific effects on consumption. It would be possible to place weight on "terminal" wealth in the utility function to reflect a bequest motive, but throughout this paper I will

---

[4] These weights, based on differences in the consumption of households with different age composition, were obtained from Walter Dolde's doctoral dissertation (1973).

assume that individuals die at age 70 and leave zero bequests. For simplicity of exposition here I will discuss the household as if it consists of a single individual.

In most of the numerical calculations I will assume that $u(c_i)$ is a member of the class of the iso-elastic or constant relative risk averse functions:

$$u(c_i) = \frac{1}{\gamma} c_i^\gamma; \gamma < 1.$$

From such utility functions, the optimal consumption path with a perfect loan market may be easily found from the first order conditions

$$\frac{1}{(1+\delta)^i} c_i^{\gamma-1} = \lambda \frac{1}{(1+r)^i} \tag{2}$$

where λ is the lagrangian multiplier associated with the wealth constraint. Hence,

$$c_i = \frac{(1+\delta)}{(1+r)}^{i/\gamma-1} \lambda^{1/\gamma-1}, \quad i = 0, \ldots, T. \tag{3}$$

Equation (3) indicates that consumption grows, falls at a constant geometric rate, or is constant, depending upon whether the discount rate is less than, greater than, or equal to, the rate of interest. $\lambda^{1/\gamma-1}$ is easily found from the wealth constraint:

$$\Sigma \, Y_i \frac{1}{(1+r)^i} + W_0 = \Sigma \, c_i \frac{1}{(1+r)^i}$$
$$= \lambda^{1/\gamma-1} \Sigma ((1+\delta)^{1/\gamma-1}(1+r)^{-\gamma/\gamma-1})^i$$

or

$$\lambda^{1/\gamma-1} = \left(\Sigma \, Y_i \frac{1}{(1+r)^i} + W_0 \right) \Sigma [(1+\delta)^{1/\gamma-1}(1+r)^{-\gamma/\gamma-1}]^i.$$

How much borrowing is associated with the optimum consumption path? The answer obviously depends on both the level and timing of income receipts. In order to get a concrete idea of the extent to which borrowing is necessary in order to pursue an optimal consumption path, I have calculated the time paths of income, consumption, borrowing, and debt for a number of stylized households.

244

The basic inputs of these calculations are the income profiles calculated by Robert Stearns (1971) for a number of different occupational groups.

Stearns' profiles are derived from regression estimates of the time paths of mean income for various demographic groups (identified by age, education and occupation) represented in the Surveys of Consumer Finances 1951–64. Stearns assumed that for a given occupation-education group the income of individuals of different ages grew at the same rate. With information from these regressions, Stearns was able to construct "typical" income profiles for individuals of a given education and occupation. The profiles vary, of course, with the vintage of an individual. In Figure 11.1, I have reproduced Stearns' real wage profiles for two occupation classes. Stearns makes these calculations for a number of different income concepts. In all my calculations I use his profiles for real disposable wage income in 1960 dollars. Since Stearns actually reports income by ten-year age brackets, I have interpolated his data to get profiles by year of age.

In perfect capital markets, the only relevant thing about an income stream is its present value. I have calculated the present value of real disposable wage income for three different interest rates (0.03, 0.06, 0.09) which I assume bracket most people's estimates of the "social rate of return" (Table 11.1). Although these calculations were not intended to provide a serious estimate of the returns to education (increase in present value of income associated with obtaining an education) they are essentially the same as those made by a number of authors, and like other studies they show the great sensitivity of quantitative estimates of the profitability of education to the interest rate.

I have reported two other numbers in Table 11.1. The average present discounted value of income (ADY) provides another indication of the consumption opportunities of an individual. For an individual with a log utility function ($\gamma = 0$) and a zero rate of time preference the optimal consumption path would be constant in present discounted value and hence equal to ADY. The "average arrival time" (AT) is the age such that if all the income (undiscounted) were to arrive at that time, it would have the same present value as the actual stream. It is meant simply as a rough indication of whether income arrives early or late. Obviously, the present value of income varies less with the discount rate for low, as compared to high, AT.

245

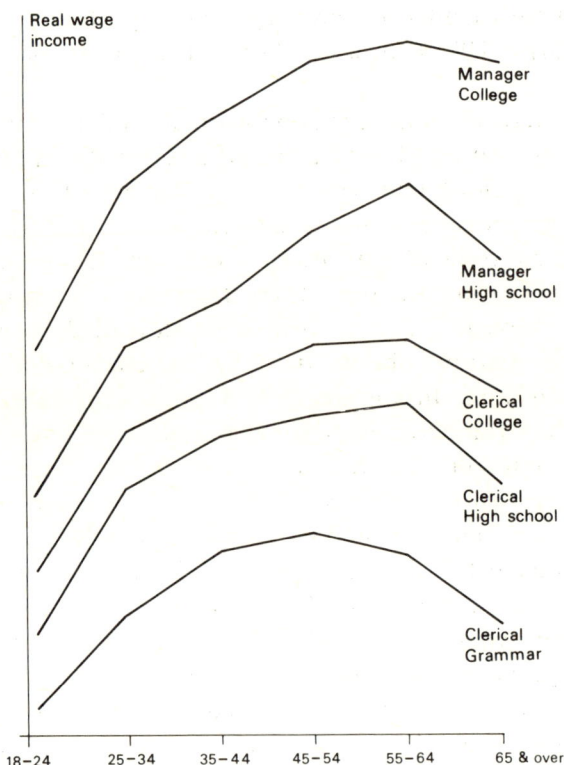

Fig. 11.1. Typical historical income profiles for spending units, aged 45–54 in 1960, managerial and clerical occupational groups.

For each occupation, I have calculated the optimal consumption path for a number of stylized households. The purpose of these simulations is to gain some impression of the sensitivity of the borrowing requirements of a household to the household's composition. Three types of households were simulated. In the first, a male leaves home and enters "life" at age 18, gets married two years later, has his first child two years after that, followed by another child two years later. The wife works until childbirth, earning one-half of the husband's wage, and the children leave home when they reach 18. The second type of household has the same timing of events, but

246

TABLE   11.1

Present value of income for households age 25-34 in 1960 (US dollars)

Occupational Group	Education	R = .03			R = .06			R = .09
		PDY	ADY	AT	PDY	ADY	AT	PDY
Labourers	Grammar	60,775	1,146	40	35,507	669	38	23,516
	H. S.	95,081	1,793	42	52,635	993	40	33,168
Clerical	Grammar	141,377	2,667	42	79,126	1,492	40	50,608
	H. S.	160,714	3,032	43	86,484	1,631	41	53,322
	College	271,908	5,130	46	133,934	2,537	44	76,110
Craftsmen	Grammar	144,242	2,721	43	77,949	1,470	41	48,537
	H. S.	184,757	3,485	43	100,027	1,887	41	62,130
	College	233,415	4,404	45	119,472	2,254	43	70,588
Professional	H. S.	285,507	5,386	48	135,333	2,553	45	75,431
	College	307,106	5,794	47	150,038	2,830	44	84,977
Managers	H. S.	340,760	6,429	49	157,306	2,968	46	84,994
	College	428,013	8,075	49	197,237	3,721	46	105,751

PDY   = Present discounted value of income

ADY   = Average discounted income

AT   = Average arrival time of the income

displaced four years, the male entering "life" at 22. Parents are assumed to receive their children's income and pay for their consumption and tuition while they attend college. Households formed at age 18 are assumed to earn their own way. The third type of household is an individual who stays single throughout life.

Representative consumption, borrowing and debt paths for the "clerical" occupation with college education are shown in Table 11.2. This household was formed at age 22, with marriage occurring at age 24. The γ in the utility function was assumed to be -0.5. The interest rate used was 6 percent. The household's behaviour is typical of most simulations for other occupational and educational groups. The household depends heavily on the capital market, borrowing for very substantial periods of its lifetime. Not surprisingly, the timing of its consumption is highly sensitive to the presence or absence of children. In the illustrative example, where the children are assumed

TABLE 11.2

Clerical, college, leaving home at 22, married at 24

(R = .06)

Age	Income	Consumption	Borrowing	Debt
22	3562.541	2969.349	-593.191	-593.191
23	4077.363	3046.481	-1030.882	-1659.665
24	6888.276	6251.232	-637.044	-2396.289
25	7660.509	6413.612	-1246.896	-3786.963
26	5754.527	7600.144	1845.617	-2168.564
27	6402.048	7797.564	1395.516	-903.162
28	7049.569	9073.720	2024.151	1066.800
29	7697.089	9309.417	1612.328	2743.136
30	8344.610	9551.237	1206.627	4114.351
31	8992.131	9799.338	807.207	5168.419
32	9639.652	10053.884	414.232	5892.756
33	10287.173	10315.042	27.869	6274.190
34	10934.694	10582.984	-351.710	6298.931
35	11582.215	10857.885	-724.329	5952.537
36	11886.798	11139.928	-746.870	5562.820
37	12191.382	11429.296	-762.086	5134.503
38	12495.965	11726.182	-769.783	4672.790
39	12800.548	12030.779	-769.769	4183.389
40	13105.132	13803.754	698.622	5133.014
41	13409.715	14162.318	752.603	6193.597
42	15217.554	16067.520	849.966	7415.178
43	16036.959	16484.886	447.928	8308.016
44	18359.619	18896.729	537.111	9343.608
45	19904.695	19387.587	-517.107	9387.117
46	17887.230	21979.223	4091.993	14042.335
47	18917.486	22550.151	3632.665	18517.539
48	16385.199	17351.932	966.733	20595.324
49	16900.633	17802.662	902.030	22733.072
50	17416.067	12176.734	-5239.332	18857.725
51	17931.500	12493.035	-5438.465	14550.725
52	18446.934	12817.552	-5629.382	9794.389
53	18962.367	13150.498	-5811.869	4570.185
54	19477.801	13492.093	-5985.708	-1141.309
55	19141.654	13842.561	-5299.092	-6508.878
56	18805.506	14202.133	-4603.373	-11502.782
57	18469.359	14571.045	-3898.314	-16091.260
58	18133.211	14949.540	-3183.671	-20240.406
59	17797.064	15337.866	-2459.198	-23914.026
60	17460.916	15736.280	-1724.636	-27073.502
61	17124.769	16145.043	-979.726	-29677.638
62	16788.621	16564.423	-224.198	-31682.493
63	16452.474	16994.698	542.224	-33041.218
64	16116.326	17436.149	1319.823	-33703.868
65	14926.813	17889.067	2962.254	-32763.847
66	13737.300	18353.750	4616.450	-30113.229
67	12547.786	18830.504	6282.718	-25637.308
68	11358.273	19319.642	7961.369	-19214.182
69	10168.760	19821.485	9652.725	-10714.311
70	8979.247	20336.364	11357.117	-0.059

TABLE 11.3

Family formation and the life cycle

(R = .06)

Occupation/ Education	PDY	ADY	AT	Max **D**	Age Max D	Age O Debt
Clerical						
H. S. -Actual	86,500	1,632	41	7,176	56	62
College-Actual	133,900	2,527	44	25,020	44	62
H. S. -18	89,900	1,696	41	4,044	23	25
College-18	137,000	2,586	43	30,911	45	54
College-22	132,929	2,508	44	22,733	49	54
Craftsmen						
H. S. -Actual	100,000	1,887	41	9,942	36	60
College-Actual	119,472	2,254	43	16,423	34	64
H. S. -18	103,159	1,946	41	177	41	42
College-18	122,365	2,308	43	816	45	46
College-22	116,900	2,206	44	26	31	32
Managers						
H. S. -Actual	157,356	2,968	46	50,265	48	64
College-Actual	197,237	3,721	46	49,258	46	65
H. S. -18	161,000	3,038	46	118,232	47	63
College-18	200,251	3,778	46	114,760	45	64
College-22	194,875	3,676	47	108,607	49	65

Note: See Table 11.1

to attend college, consumption falls by approximately $10,000 per year between the time in which children are in college and the time they leave home. This household starts borrowing when the first child arrives, does some debt repayment before the children reach their teens, and goes heavily into debt during their college years. The household then saves at a high rate, getting out of debt between the ages of 53 and 54, and accumulates wealth until the early 60s. Table 11.3 reports summary statistics for a number of different types of households. The simulations labelled "actual" assume the consumption profiles estimated by Stearns; the other simulations assume the calculated optimal consumption paths. The income paths in the optimal calculations differ from those in the "actual" because of the difference between an actual and assumed wage income for the wife. Table 11.3 also reports the maximum debt position, the year in which the household is in maximum debt, and the age at which it finally repays all debts.

"Imperfect" loan markets

There are a number of reasons why credit markets may be imperfect — why the rate at which a person can borrow, if he can borrow at all, may be substantially greater than the rate at which he can lend. Most of these trace back to transactions or information costs and the difficulty in an uncertain world of using human wealth, or future wage income, as collateral without encountering "moral hazard".

What are the implications of credit market imperfections for the attractiveness of educational investment? In fact, with imperfect credit markets, how do we evaluate the return to educational investment? Although it may still be appropriate to discount the returns to education by the social discount rate to assess the social desirability of educational investment, changes in the present discounted value of income are an unreliable indicator of the changed consumption opportunities education makes available to an individual. Even knowing the (various) rates the individual faces in credit markets would not enable us to compute a simple measure of his consumption opportunities.

A related complication is that the value of a given stream of returns to education is dependent upon the time profile of the income stream it augments. As far as private returns are concerned, therefore, it is inappropriate to estimate returns by calculating the increment a college education makes to the *average* income stream of high school graduates (as virtually all studies do).

In this section I will analyze the consequences of credit market imperfections by the simple device of placing an individual with a given income profile in different credit market environments and having him compute an optimal consumption path for each. It is then possible to compare the impact of different credit arrangements on his utility level and on his consumption and borrowing paths. Differences in utility levels themselves can be translated into "cash equivalents" to provide a more intuitive measure of the importance

250

TABLE 11.4

Clerical, college, single, borrowing at 6 per cent, no limit

Age	Income	Consumption	Net worth	Interest rate
18	518.256	5398.889	0.	0.060
19	1033.077	5539.130	-5173.471	0.060
20	1547.898	5683.013	-10260.295	0.060
21	2062.720	5830.634	-15259.135	0.060
22	3562.541	5982.090	-20168.671	0.060
23	4077.363	6137.479	-23943.512	0.060
24	4592.184	6296.906	-27563.846	0.060
25	5107.006	6460.473	-31024.681	0.060
26	5754.527	6628.289	-34320.836	0.060
27	6402.048	6800.464	-37306.273	0.060
28	7049.569	6977.112	-39966.970	0.060
29	7697.089	7158.348	-42288.183	0.060
30	8344.610	7344.292	-44254.408	0.060
31	8992.131	7535.066	-45849.334	0.060
32	9639.652	7730.796	-47055.805	0.060
33	10287.173	7931.610	-47855.764	0.060
34	10934.694	8137.640	-48230.212	0.060
35	11582.215	8349.022	-48159.146	0.060
36	11886.798	8565.895	-47621.509	0.060
37	12191.382	8788.401	-46958.641	0.060
38	12495.965	9016.687	-46168.999	0.060
39	12800.548	9250.903	-45251.103	0.060
40	13105.132	9491.202	-44203.543	0.060
41	13409.715	9737.744	-43024.990	0.060
42	13714.298	9990.690	-41714.199	0.060
43	14018.882	10250.207	-40270.026	0.060
44	14323.465	10516.464	-38691.430	0.060
45	14838.898	10789.638	-36977.494	0.060
46	15354.332	11069.908	-34903.927	0.060
47	15869.766	11357.458	-32456.673	0.060
48	16385.199	11652.477	-29621.026	0.060
49	16900.633	11955.160	-26381.602	0.060
50	17416.067	12265.705	-22722.296	0.060
51	17931.500	12584.317	-18626.250	0.060
52	18446.934	12911.205	-14075.810	0.060
53	18962.367	13246.584	-9052.486	0.060
54	19477.801	13590.675	-3536.905	0.060
55	19141.654	13943.704	2491.234	0.060
56	18805.506	14305.903	8150.535	0.060
57	18469.359	14677.511	13409.145	0.060
58	18133.211	15058.771	18233.052	0.060
59	17797.064	15449.935	22585.941	0.060
60	17460.916	15851.260	26429.053	0.060
61	17124.769	16263.010	29721.031	0.060
62	16788.621	16685.455	32417.757	0.060
63	16452.474	17118.873	34472.177	0.060
64	16116.326	17563.550	35834.124	0.060
65	14926.813	18019.778	36450.113	0.060
66	13737.300	18487.857	35358.577	0.060
67	12547.786	18968.094	32444.500	0.060
68	11358.273	19460.806	27585.644	0.060
69	10168.760	19966.316	20652.097	0.060
70	8979.247	20484.958	11505.813	0.060

TABLE 11.5

Clerical, college, borrowing up to $8,000 at 6 per cent, 18 per cent beyond

Age	Income	Consumption	Net worth	Interest rate
18	518.256	2923.811	0.	0.060
19	1033.077	2999.759	-2549.888	0.060
20	1547.898	3077.680	-4787.564	0.060
21	2062.720	3157.626	-6696.387	0.060
22	3562.541	3479.754	-8233.726	0.180
23	4077.363	3834.744	-8658.107	0.180
24	4592.184	4225.950	-8970.277	0.180
25	5107.006	4657.064	-9192.770	0.180
26	5754.527	5132.159	-9356.537	0.180
27	6402.048	5655.721	-9346.319	0.180
28	7049.569	6232.695	-9187.991	0.180
29	7697.089	6868.530	-8917.918	0.180
30	8344.610	7569.229	-8585.443	0.180
31	8992.131	8341.412	-8255.873	0.180
32	9639.652	9174.173	-8015.464	0.177
33	10287.173	9733.049	-7978.409	0.115
34	10934.694	9985.872	-7869.742	0.060
35	11582.215	10245.264	-7336.175	0.060
36	11886.798	10511.393	-6359.177	0.060
37	12191.382	10784.435	-5282.799	0.060
38	12495.965	11064.570	-4108.403	0.060
39	12800.548	11351.981	-2837.628	0.060
40	13105.132	11646.858	-1472.404	0.060
41	13409.715	11949.395	-14.978	0.060
42	13714.298	12259.790	1532.062	0.060
43	14018.882	12578.248	3165.764	0.060
44	14323.465	12904.979	4882.782	0.060
45	14838.898	13240.196	6679.344	0.060
46	15354.332	13584.121	8774.728	0.060
47	15869.766	13936.980	11177.634	0.060
48	16385.199	14299.005	13897.045	0.060
49	16900.633	14670.433	16942.233	0.060
50	17416.067	15051.510	20322.779	0.060
51	17931.500	15442.485	24048.575	0.060
52	18446.934	15843.617	28129.845	0.060
53	18962.367	16255.168	32577.151	0.060
54	19477.801	16677.409	37401.411	0.060
55	19141.654	17110.619	42613.910	0.060
56	18805.506	17555.081	47323.641	0.060
57	18469.359	18011.089	51488.508	0.060
58	18133.211	18478.942	55063.584	0.060
59	17797.064	18958.947	58000.923	0.060
60	17460.916	19451.422	60249.381	0.060
61	17124.769	19956.688	61754.407	0.060
62	16788.621	20475.081	62457.835	0.060
63	16452.474	21006.937	62297.657	0.060
64	16116.326	21552.609	61207.785	0.060
65	14926.813	22112.457	59117.790	0.060
66	13737.300	22686.846	55048.074	0.060
67	12547.786	23276.156	48864.438	0.060
68	11358.273	23880.773	40424.231	0.060
69	10168.760	24501.096	29575.835	0.060
70	8979.247	25137.532	16158.109	0.060

TABLE 11.6

Clerical, college, borrowing up to $1,000 at 18 per cent, 30 per cent beyond

Age	Income	Consumption	Net worth	Interest rate
18	518.256	1377.132	0.	0.060
19	1033.077	1598.370	-1000.008	0.275
20	1547.898	1878.911	-1914.892	0.300
21	2062.720	2208.691	-2799.676	0.300
22	3562.541	2596.353	-3709.340	0.300
23	4077.363	3052.056	-3446.098	0.300
24	4592.184	3587.743	-3027.028	0.300
25	5107.006	4217.451	-2509.363	0.300
26	5754.527	4957.684	-1985.751	0.300
27	6402.048	5827.841	-1425.581	0.300
28	7049.569	6680.013	-993.963	0.251
29	7697.089	7361.481	-736.800	0.180
30	8344.610	8110.234	-473.211	0.180
31	8992.131	8739.193	-272.493	0.141
32	9639.652	9481.695	-22.541	0.153
33	10287.173	10100.328	151.860	0.121
34	10934.694	10362.692	359.028	0.060
35	11582.215	10631.371	986.892	0.060
36	11886.798	10908.043	2053.470	0.060
37	12191.382	11191.388	3214.158	0.060
38	12495.965	11482.094	4467.000	0.060
39	12800.548	11780.351	5809.724	0.060
40	13105.132	12086.355	7239.716	0.060
41	13409.715	12400.308	8754.002	0.060
42	13714.298	12722.417	10349.213	0.060
43	14018.882	13052.892	12021.560	0.060
44	14323.465	13391.952	13766.803	0.060
45	14838.898	13739.819	15580.215	0.060
46	15354.332	14096.721	17680.052	0.060
47	15869.766	14462.896	20073.922	0.060
48	16385.199	14838.582	22769.639	0.060
49	16900.633	15224.026	25775.231	0.060
50	17416.067	15619.482	29098.947	0.060
51	17931.500	16025.211	32749.263	0.060
52	18446.934	16441.479	36734.884	0.060
53	18962.367	16868.560	41064.758	0.060
54	19477.801	17306.736	45748.078	0.060
55	19141.654	17756.292	50794.291	0.060
56	18805.506	18217.527	55310.431	0.060
57	18469.359	18690.742	59252.314	0.060
58	18133.211	19176.249	62572.786	0.060
59	17797.064	19674.368	65221.531	0.060
60	17460.916	20185.426	67144.879	0.060
61	17124.769	20709.759	68285.590	0.060
62	16788.621	21247.712	68582.635	0.060
63	16452.474	21799.640	67970.955	0.060
64	16116.326	22365.902	66381.215	0.060
65	14926.813	22946.875	63739.536	0.060
66	18737.300	23542.940	59062.642	0.060
67	12547.786	24154.487	52212.420	0.060
68	11358.273	24781.920	43042.061	0.060
69	10168.760	25425.651	31395.518	0.060
70	8979.247	26086.103	17106.944	0.060

TABLE 11.7

Effect of loan market imperfections - single individual

Occupation/ education		r_{B1}	r_{B2}	Utility level	Years in debt r_{B1}	Years in debt r_{B2}	Maximum debt	Age at Max D	Equivalent
Clerical									
H.S.	∞	.06	.06	14.3	15		$9,853	25	
H.S.	$8,000	.06	.18	14.3	13	0	8,000	23	
H.S.	5,000	.10	.18	13.5	9	1	5,178	23	
H.S.	1,000	.10	.18	12.8	0	8	3,703	23	
H.S.	1,000	.18	.30	12	2	5	1,898	22	
College	∞	.06	.06	30.3	36		48,230	35	0
College	8,000	.06	.18	27.5	10	13	9,408	28	$10,000
College	5,000	.10	.18	25.7	6	12	8,421	26	17,000
College	1,000	.10	.18	24.3	0	17	8,165	27	21,000
College	1,000	.18	.30	22.5	5	8	3,709	22	26,000
C + $1,000	1,000	.10	.18	25.3	3	14	6,700	26	---
Managers									
H.S.	∞	.06	.06	36.5	44		$103,800	48	
H.S.	$8,000	.06	.18	34.5	26	8	8,948	25	
H.S.	5,000	.10	.18	32.0	20	8	6,971	24	
H.S.	1,000	.10	.18	31.0	12	13	6,200	24	
H.S.	1,000	.18	.30	30.0	5	6	2,505	22	
College	∞	.06	.06	42.8	47		120,600	46	0
College	8,000	.06	.18	37.7	18	14	15,700	30	$32,000
College	5,000	.10	.18	36.3	9	15	14,900	30	40,000
College	1,000	.10	.18	35.3	6	19	14,300	31	45,000
College	1,000	.18	.30	34.1	10	6	1,805	22	50,000
C + $1,000	1,000	.10	.18	36.0	2	19	12,852	30	---

of varying the credit arrangements. This procedure has been followed for households consisting of a single individual leaving his parents at age 18, for three occupations and for income profiles corresponding to high school and college graduates. In all of the simulations it was assumed that an individual can lend at 6 per cent, but that the rate he must pay on loans varies from 6 to 30 per cent. In addition some simulations are made where the individual can borrow from special programmes described in the next section. In all "college" simulations it is assumed that full tuition is paid for four years. Tables 11.4–11.6 give a sample of the actual simulation results for the clerical group. The loan environments actually used are shown in Table 11.7. "Debt limit" indicates the maximum amount that can be borrowed at r_{B1}, there is no limit on borrowing at r_{B2}. Table 11.7 also gives some summary statistics including the number of years in debt, maximum debt and utility levels for both the clerical group and managers. In order to calibrate the utility differences I have reported the utility increase associated with a $1000 "bequest" received at the beginning of the life-cycle.

The quantitative impact of loan market stringency differs substantially across occupational and educational groups. A typical individual in the "craftsmen" occupation does very little borrowing, for either income profile, even at a borrowing rate of 6 per cent. Consequently even the most stringent loan market conditions have no significant effect. Similarly, the mildest of the loan restrictions has slight effect on the utility of a "clerical" with high school education.

In contrast, credit restrictions have a significant effect on the borrowing and utility levels of "clericals" with college education and managers of either educational level. The last column of Table 11.7 gives the "cash equivalent" of the loan restriction, i.e. the amount of cash an individual could give up at the beginning of his life, if he were able to borrow at 6 per cent and be no worse off than he is with a given loan restriction. For example, placing a limit of $8,000 on borrowing at 6 per cent reduces the utility of the college income stream for "clericals" by as much as the loss of $10,000. In the case of managers the cash equivalents range from $32,000 to $50,000.

For the "average" individual for whom the calculations are made, market imperfections never alter the relative attractiveness of the various educational and occupation groups. However, the magnitudes involved may well be large enough to be decisive to individuals on the margin. Whether or not there are more "craftsmen" and fewer college educated "clericals" and "managers" than would be optimal, these results suggest that the social return to the reduction of credit market imperfections may be substantial.

There are several ways in which related generations may arrange their affairs so as to minimize the consequences of imperfect loan markets. A tradition of parents supporting children through college, for example, is likely to decrease the amount any single generation needs to borrow over its life-cycle. Each generation receives an "inheritance" at the time it would otherwise be heavily dependent on the loan market, incurring an obligation to "pass it on" at a more propitious time in the life-cycle. As can be seen from Table 11.3, the maximum amount borrowed by the clerical and manager groups

TABLE 11.8

Effect of inheritance

(Debt limit \$1,000, $r_{B1} = .10$, $r_{B2} = .18$)

Occupation/ education	Inheritance	Utility	Years in debt r_{B1}	Years in debt r_{B2}	D Max	Age at D Max
Clerical- College	0	24.3	0	17	8,165	27
	5,000	27.5	3	10	2,967	27
	10,000	29.1	5	5	1,205	28
	15,000	29.9	5	2	1,064	29
	20,000	30.2	3	0	397	29
	25,000	30.3	0	0	0	--
No limit on debt at 6%	0	30.3	36		48,230	35
Manager- College	0	35.3	6	19	14,300	31
	5,000	37.9	2	15	8,283	30
	10,000	39.5	2	12	5,880	30
	15,000	40.6	2	9	3,551	30
	20,000	41.4	1	7	2,204	31
	30,000	42.3	2	4	1,239	31
	40,000	42.7	3	0	642	32
	50,000	42.8	0	0	0	--
No limit on debt at 6%	0	42.8	47		120,600	46

decreased substantially (from \$6,000–8,000) with such an arrangement, but they still made considerable use of perfect loan markets. I have made some calculations which suggest that with imperfect markets the gains from this reduced demand are substantial relative to the cost of education.

In the same way, families which accumulate wealth and pass it on generation after generation can avoid the use of imperfect loan markets. They effectively "earn" a rate of return greater than the market lending rate by lending to themselves. In Table 11.8 I have reported the effect of varying the size of the "inheritance" on the extent to which individuals use the loan market, and on their utility. In order to focus on the interdependence of inheritances and imperfect loan markets, an individual is required to pass on to his or her heirs a capital sum equal in present value to the inheritance received at age 18. Thus, with perfect loan markets, the inheritance would not affect the individuals' consumption possibilities. As indicated in the table, even quite modest inheritances have a substantial effect on an individual's welfare. However it takes an inheritance of approximately $25,000 for clericals, and $50,000 for managers to make an individual as well-off as with perfect markets.

Educational loans and imperfect loan markets

The lack of perfect loan markets is one of the major justifications for various student loan plans. But the natural remedy is to improve loan markets in general, not just those which finance investment in education. Some existing student loan programmes, e.g. National Defense Education Act, (NDEA), involve what must be a very substantial rate of subsidy (NDEA charges a maximum of 3 per cent) and the usual arguments against specific egalitarianism seem as appropriate here as elsewhere.

Setting aside the question of whether it is a good idea to "subsidize" education via a loan plan, it is interesting to ask how effective the NDEA plan is as a subsidy. In most of our simulations (at 6 per cent interest) the household would have chosen to be in debt for a great many years after graduation. In such cases, the NDEA plan, which requires (amortized) repayment in 10 years, is not as attractive as a scheme which would allow an individual to repay the loan during a period when he would have been saving anyway. Simulation provides a way of estimating the extent to which this poorly timed repayment schedule affects the desirability of the loans. In Table 11.9 I have reported the effects of an NDEA loan, and "contingent repayment loans" (CRP) of two different maturities. In each case the individual was loaned $1,000 for each of four years of college. The NDEA loan charges interest at 3 per cent starting at graduation, and amortizes the principal over 10 years. The contingent loans are stylized versions of the contingent loan plan adopted by Yale (the Tuition Postponement Option). In these plans an individual pays back his loan on the basis of the actual income he earns, the "tax rate" being sufficient so that when applied to the average income of borrowers it will eventually repay the principal and interest (in these cases assumed to be 6 per cent). The primary motivation for the contingent repayment plan, of course, is the elimination of the risk that an individual will be saddled with a great deal of debt in the event that his income turns out to be low. Even for the individual

TABLE 11.9

Effect of NDEA and Contingent Repayment Loans ($4,000)

Occupation/ education	Plan	Debt limit	r_{B1}	r_{B2}	Utility
Clerical-College	---	∞	.06	.06	30.3
	NDEA	∞	.06	.06	30.5
	---	$8,000	.06	.18	27.5
	NDEA	$8,000	.06	.18	28.3
	CRP-20yr.	$8,000	.06	.18	28.5
	CRP-40yr.	$8,000	.06	.18	28.6
	---	$1,000	.10	.18	24.3
	NDEA	$1,000	.10	.18	26.2
	CRP-20yr.	$1,000	.10	.18	26.4
	CRP-40yr.	$1,000	.10	.18	26.5
Manager-Clerical	---	∞	.06	.06	42.8
	NDEA	∞	.06	.06	42.9
	---	$8,000	.06	.18	37.7
	NDEA	$8,000	.06	.18	38.4
	CRP-20yr.	$8,000	.06	.18	38.6
	CRP-40yr.	$8,000	.06	.18	38.75
	---	$1,000	.10	.18	35.3
	NDEA	$1,000	.10	.18	36.6
	CRP-20yr.	$1,000	.10	.18	36.9
	CRP-40yr.	$1,000	.10	.18	37.0

who turns out to be average however, these plans have the advantage that repayments are most heavily concentrated in high income years.

As indicated in the table, the advantage of the low rate on the NDEA loan is outweighted by the more advantageous maturity structure of the CRP loans in either of the imperfect loan environments (with perfect markets of course, the NDEA loan is preferable). In the case of managers, the advantage of the 40-year CRP plan over the NDEA plan appears to be comparable to a gift of approximately $400 at age 18. In the absence of perfect markets the amount an individual is allowed to borrow is also a crucial variable. It appears that both managers and clerical households, for example, would prefer the opportunity to borrow $7,000 at 6 per cent to a $4,000 NDEA loan at 3 per cent.

Private and social risk

Few will disagree with the assertion that social risk on investment in education is less than private risk. As long as there is some in-

258

dependence in the rate of return on educational investment to different individuals, the variance in the rate of return to society's investment in education will be less than on a typical individual's. Indeed if the returns are independent, the variance in the rate of return for society will be close to zero. Even if there is substantial correlation in the returns to education of different individuals, so that the total returns to education for society are quite variable, still there may be little social risk to educational investment. In particular, if the total investment in education is sufficiently small, and the returns are independent of the returns on other investments in the economy, education's contribution to the variation in the total output of the economy may be negligible. If perfect markets existed in this situation, the risk premium required for investment in education would be zero.

In general, with perfect markets, the risk premium charged on a particular investment reflects its contribution to variation in total output. Elsewhere I have argued that the social risk on a typical investment is not negligible (Brainard and Dolbear, 1971). I see no strong *a priori* reason to think that the returns to education are untypically correlated with other components of national output, one way or the other, and hence I do not believe *a priori* the social risk on education is zero. Whatever one believes about this magnitude, however, it is clear that private risk is much greater.

This discrepancy results, as usual, from the absence of markets which enable efficient risk distribution. In the case of the returns to labour or education the absence of such markets undoubtedly reflects, in addition to the usual costs of running markets and conducting transactions, the difficulty of establishing financial instruments or contracts which meet the twin problems of adverse selection and moral hazard.

In this section I will analyze the effect of private risk on investment in education. As the above discussion indicates, for an individual, as for society, what is relevant about the return on an investment is not variation in its return *per se*, but rather its contribution to the uncertainty in the total income receipts of the individual. First I discuss the extent to which there are important differences in the private risk to income of different occupations and educational groups and then briefly discuss the implications of risk for the design of loan plans.

Certainty equivalent income

How much difference does uncertainty in income make? In particular, if most of the risk facing an individual is private, and not social, how great is the loss from the absence of markets which efficiently distribute the risk? In a simple, one-period model, it is a straightforward exercise to compute the riskless income which would have the same (expected) utility as the uncertain income prospects of an individual, given a specific utility function. Suppose an individual is "constant relative risk averse", i.e. his preferences can be represented as in the first section of this paper by:

$$u(c) = \frac{1}{\gamma} c^{\gamma}, \gamma < 1.$$

As a first approximation it is probably not implausible to assume that income is distributed log normally. In that case, since in the one period model consumption is simply income,

$$E.U. = \frac{1}{\gamma} \int_0^{\infty} Y^{\gamma} f(Y) dY = \frac{1}{\gamma} \int_{-\infty}^{\infty} e^{\gamma X} g(X) dY \qquad (4)$$

where $X = \ln Y$ and $g(X) : N(\mu, \sigma^2)$.

Then,

$$E.U. = \frac{1}{\gamma} e^{\gamma \mu + \gamma^2 \frac{\sigma^2}{2}}. \qquad (5)$$

Suppose we define $\hat{Y}$ as the certainty equivalent to the distribution of Y given by $f(Y)$:

$$\frac{1}{\gamma} \hat{Y}^{\gamma} = E.U. = \frac{1}{\gamma} e^{\gamma \mu + \gamma^2 \frac{\sigma^2}{2}} \qquad (6)$$

or

$$\hat{Y} = e^{\mu + \gamma \frac{\sigma^2}{2}}.$$

Since, for the log-normal, expected income $(\overline{Y})$ is given by

$$\overline{Y} = e^{\mu + \frac{\sigma^2}{2}}, \qquad (7)$$

TABLE 11.10

Educational Production Relationships

Table 2 – Means and standard deviations* of log earnings, IQ and background variables by education level (Rogers)

Education Level	Sample Size N	LE65	LE60	LE55	LE50	LDE4%	IQ	SCH	SCL	RC	RJ	PS	NM
E_1	60	8.857 (.326)	8.708 (.281)	8.664 (.279)	8.569 (.335)	11.836 (.221)	95.9 (11.8)	.033	.917	.750	-	.033	.050
E_2	117	9.001 (.392)	8.764 (.336)	8.662 (.320)	8.550 (.338)	11.872 (.324)	102.3 (11.1)	.034	.829	.650	.017	.094	.077
E_3	51	9.262 (.557)	9.057 (.439)	8.900 (.428)	8.668 (.478)	12.070 (.429)	107.8 (9.59)	.196	.529	.431	.039	.235	.039
E_4	70	9.434 (.599)	9.244 (.481)	9.004 (.429)	8.692 (.528)	12.204 (.521)	115.6 (11.0)	.429	.414	.314	.043	.471	.067
E_5	47	9.640 (.574)	9.414 (.607)	9.061 (.502)	8.525 (.624)	12.262 (.445)	117.3 (10.0)	.446	.319	.298	.170	.383	.042

* Numbers in parentheses are standard deviations. Source – data tape of D.C. Rogers. Sample is based primarily on male eight graders (most from Connecticut) who were given IQ tests in 1935. Earnings are based on questionnaire responses in 1966. Earnings from 1965 are reported annual earnings plus imputed self-employment income from personal labour services. Earnings for 1960, 1955, and 1950 are full-time annual earnings based on reported monthly or weekly salary. Lifetime discounted earnings were obtained by Rogers through an involved smoothing and extrapolation procedure.

Source: Hause (1971)

261

we have:

$$\frac{\hat{Y}}{\overline{Y}} = e^{(\gamma - 1)} \frac{\sigma^2}{2}.$$

What is the σ^2 faced by a typical individual? To apply this simple model one has to imagine that an individual lives his life one "period" at a time — there is no way for him to borrow and lend between periods — or alternatively that there are perfect markets between periods but he gets only a single random draw of the present discounted value of his income when he enters the job market. The estimate of σ^2 is, one would think, dependent upon the length of period. Surprisingly, what casual data I have uncovered suggest that although there is substantial variation in σ^2 across different educational classes, there is relatively little variation as between single years and "lifetime income". An indication of the range of estimates of σ^2 for earned income can be obtained from Hause (1971) (see Table 11.10). He finds a range from a low of approximately 0.05–0.09 for high school drop-outs to approximately 0.18–0.36 for college graduates. Hause also reports the variance in income for different individuals who were high school juniors in 1960. In that sample he finds the variance of log income for high school graduates is close to that of college graduates–approximately 0.16.

Houthakker (1959) provides another source of information on variation in income. Houthakker reports a coefficient of variation of income estimated from the 1950 census (unfortunately inclusive of unearned income). He finds that the coefficient of variation (v) rises slowly with age after age 22–24. He also finds that in the early years of a life-cycle, there is mildly greater variation in income for college graduates than for individuals with only a high school education, but that the variability for a college graduate increases less with age and that the coefficients of variation are approximately equal at age 60. If it is assumed that the underlying data are log-normally distributed, Houthakker's results can be used to give an estimate of σ^2:

$$v^2 \equiv \frac{var\ Y}{E(Y)^2} = (e^{\sigma^2} - 1); \sigma^2 = ln(v^2 + 1).$$

Typically these calculations give an estimate of σ^2 somewhat greater than those of Hause. For example, the lowest coefficient of variation reported by Houthakker is 0.58, which gives an estimate of σ^2 of approximately 0.30. A more typical coefficient of variation is 0.9, which gives σ^2 equal to 0.6. Some preliminary calculations I have made on the 1960 census seem to give σ^2 in the order of 0.25.

With estimates of σ^2, it is trivial to compute out the "loss" associated with various γ's.

$$\frac{\overline{Y} - \hat{Y}}{\overline{Y}}$$

	$\gamma = 0(\log)$	$\gamma = -0.5$	$\gamma = -1$
0.07	0.035	0.05	0.07
$\sigma^2 = 0.25$	0.12	0.16	0.22
0.50	0.22	0.31	0.39

The income uncertainty confronting a particular individual at the time he is contemplating an educational investment, of course, may be quite different from the population variance reported in the first columns of Hause's Table 2. Some of the observed variation in income undoubtedly reflects characteristics of the individual (IQ, motivation, etc.) about which he has some estimate. What is relevant to him is the distribution of income conditional on all the things he knows about himself. If he doesn't know more things about himself relevant to his future earnings than the various researchers who have studied this question have found out about their subjects, he doesn't know a great deal. The best regressions, including attribute variables, leave 60–80 per cent of the variance in income unexplained. Since a number of variables are typically included which an individual will not know about himself when he contemplates college (occupation, whether he will be employed full time, grades) even these regressions overstate what could be known in advance statistically.[5]

Given the inadequacies of the empirical studies which do exist and

---

[5] To use the regressions to calculate forecast error, one would need the variance-covariance matrix of sample coefficient estimates. With such information a direct calculation could be made for particular variables which an individual knows about himself, assuming a distribution for the other variables. Unfortunately, none of the studies I have uncovered report such information.

the apparent difficulties of doing better, it would not be surprising if many individuals operate with quite inappropriate expectations. The only survey I know which explores expectations of future income was designed to determine whether students would join the Yale Tuition Postponement Option. The most striking findings of the survey were that roughly 66 per cent believe they will fare worse than average after graduation, and that eventual membership in the plan does not seem correlated with these income expectations.

How would a high school graduate, contemplating going to college, be affected by the differences in risk indicated in Hause's table? Suppose the degree of relative risk aversion is 0.5. Then, the ratio of certainty equivalent college income to the certainty equivalent high school income would be roughly 96.5 per cent of the ratio of the expected incomes for the two groups. If we can regard an individual as choosing among the income distributions associated with different educational and occupational groups, this ratio is an indication of the extent to which the risks facing individuals may distort their private decisions.

Risk, borrowing and investment in education

How does the presence of risk affect investment in education? It is not obvious that uncertainty in the returns to education itself decrease its attractiveness. There is, for example, some slight evidence for the frequent allegation that returns to education may be negatively correlated with returns to other factors. Education increases an individual's ability to adapt to changes in job requirements, make job switches, etc. In that case, the variations in the return to education may actually decrease the total income risk facing an individual; he may require a lower rate of return on educational investment than on "riskless' bonds. Indeed it is possible for the private risk on educational investment to be less than the social risk, if an individual does not have a way to diversify his other sources of income. Whatever the correlation of returns to education and other factors, I believe that the major risks faced by a typical individual are a reflection of his inability to diversify his combined labour and educational "investment". The implication of this view is that what is needed are credit instruments which enable more efficient distribution of risk in general, rather than instruments designed to co-insure the returns on education *per se.*

A loan plan which insures income rather than simply the returns to education, will, for a given cost (and risk) to the lender be more attractive to the borrower. In my view, then, it is a virtue not a sin, that the various contingent repayment loan plans use income, rather than the returns to education, as the base for repayment. This view conflicts with Vickrey (1962) and with the authors of some CRP plans (Shell, *et al.*, 1968) who seem slightly embarrassed by their practical inability to design a scheme which would tax only the returns to education.

References

Chapter 3

Arrow, Kenneth J. (1972A), "Models of Job Discrimination", chapter 2 in A.H. Pascal (ed.)

Arrow, Kenneth J. (1972B), "Some Mathematical Models of Race in the Labor Market," chapter 6 in A.H. Pascal (ed.)

Berg, Ivar (1970), *Education and Jobs: The Great Training Robbery* (New York: Praeger)

Griliches, Zvi and William M. Mason (1972). "Education, Income, and Ability," *Journal of Political Economy*, 80:S74—S103

Hause, John C. (1972), "Earnings Profile: Ability and Schooling," *Journal of Political Economy*, 80:S108—S138

Hirshleifer, J. (1971), "The Private and Social Value of Information and the Reward to Inventive Activity," *American Economic Review*, 61:561—574

Pascal, A.H. (ed.) (1972), *Racial Discrimination in Economic Life* (Lexington, Mass., Toronto and London: D.C. Heath)

Spence, A. Michael (1972), "Market Signalling" (Harvard University, Department of Economics, unpublished PhD Thesis)

Chapter 4

Frisch, R. (1965), *Theory of Production* (Dordrecht: Reidel Publishing Company)

Chapter 5

Taubman, T.J. and Wales, T.J. (1973) "Higher Education, Mental Ability and Screening," *Journal of Political Economy*, vol. 81, January-February

Chapter 6

Attiyeh, R. and Lumsden, K.G. (1971), "University Students' Initial Under-standing of Economics: The Contribution of the 'A' Level Economics Course and of Other Factors," *Economica*, February

Attiyeh, R. and Lumsden, K.G. (1972), "Some Modern Myths in the Teaching of Elementary Economics," *American Economic Review*, May

Attiyeh, R. and Lumsden, K.G. (forthcoming), "The Production of Economics Understanding: An Analysis of the First Year Course," *Economica*

Committee for Economic Development (1961), *Report of the National Task Force on Economic Education* (New York: CED)

Economics Education Project (1969, 1970, 1971), *Test of Economics Com-prehension* (Edinburgh: Heriot-Watt University)

Joint Council on Economic Education (1967), *Test of Understanding in College Economics* (New York: The Psychological Corporation)

Jorgenson, D.W., Christensen, L.R. and Lau, L.J. (1970), "Conjugate Duality and the Transcendental Logarithmic Production Function." Paper presented at the Second World Congress of the Econometric Society, Cambridge, England

Lumsden, K.G. and Attiyeh, R.E. (1971), "The Core of Economic Analysis," *Economics*, Summer

Rubinfeld, D. (1972), "Credit Ratings on General Obligation Municipal Bonds" (Cambridge, Massachusetts: MIT, unpublished PhD thesis)

Chapter 7

Attiyeh, R.E., Bach, G.L. and Lumsden, K.G. (1969), "The Efficiency of Pro-grammed Learning in Teaching Economics: The Results of a Nationwide Experiment," *American Economic Review*, May

Baldwin, L.V., Davis, P., and Maxwell, L.M. (1972), *Innovative, Off-campus Educational Programs of Colorado State University*, Special Report to the President's Science Advisory Committee, April (Denver: Colorado State University)

Bartlett, C.C. (1970), "Mathematics for Undergraduates by Television" in A.C. Bajpai and J.R. Leedham (eds.) *Aspects of Educational Technology*, vol. IV (London: Pitman)

Bates, A .W. (1973), "Broadcasting and Multi-Media Teaching" in J. Tunstall (ed.) *The Open University Opens*

Bottomley, J.A. *et al.* (1972), *Cost-effectiveness in Higher Education* (Paris: OECD, Centre for Educational Research and Innovation)

Bright, L. (1970), "Educational Technology — Practical Issues and Implica-tions," Committee for Scientific and Technical Personnel, Conference on Policies for Educational Growth (Paris: OECD, mimeo)

British Computer Society (1971), *Educational Yearbook 1971–2* (London: British Computer Society)

268

Carnegie Commission on Higher Education (1972A), *The More Effective Use of Resources* (New York: McGraw Hill)

Carnegie Commission on Higher Education (1972B), *The Fourth Revolution: Instructional Technology in Higher Education* (New York: McGraw Hill)

Chu, G.C. and Schramm, W. (1967), *Learning from Television: What the Research Says* (Stanford: Institute for Communications Research)

Commission on Instructional Technology (1970), *To Improve Learning. A Report to the President and the Congress of the U.S. by the Commission on Instructional Technology*, Committee on Education and Labor, House of Representatives, March 1970, reprinted with papers prepared for the Commission in S. Tickton (ed.) *To Improve Learning. An Evaluation of Educational Technology*, vols. I and II (New York: R.R. Bowker and Co.)

Committee for Economic Development (1968), *Innovation in Education: New Directions for the American School*. A statement on national policy by the Research and Policy Committee, July (New York: CED)

Committee of Vice-Chancellors and Principals of the Universities of the U.K. (1972), *Report of an Enquiry into the Use of Academic Staff Time* (London: CVCP)

Committee on Higher Education (1963) (Robbins Report), *Higher Education, Appendix Two (B), Students and their Education*, Cmnd. 2154 II—I (London: HMSO)

Dubin, R. and Hedley, R.A. (1969), *The Medium may be Related to the Message. College Instruction by T.V.* (Eugene, Oregon: University of Oregon Press)

Dubin, R. and Taveggia, T.C. (1968), *The Teaching-Learning Paradox* (Eugene, Oregon: University of Oregon Press)

Gagné, R.M. (1970), *The Conditions of Learning*, 2nd ed. (London: Holt.)

Gordon, S.D. (1969), "Organizing the Use of Televised Instruction," *Journal of Economic Education*, Fall

Jamison, D., Suppes, R. and Butler, C. (1970), "Estimated Costs of CAI for Compensatory Education in Urban Areas," *Educational Technology*, September

Laidlaw, B. and Layard, R. (1973) "Traditional versus Open University Teaching Methods: A Cost Comparison" (Higher Education Research Unit, London School of Economics: mimeo.)

Layard, R., and Jackman, R. (1973), "University Efficiency and University Finance" in M. Parkin (ed.) *Essays in Modern Economics* (London: Longmans)

McConnell, C.R. (1968), "An Experiment with Television in the Elementary Course," *American Economic Review*, May

McConnell, C.R. and Lamphear, C. (1969), "Teaching Principles of Economics without Lectures," *Journal of Economic Education*, Fall

McKeachie, W.J. (1963), "Research on Teaching at the College and University Level," in N.L. Gage (ed.) *Handbook of Research on Teaching* (Chicago: Rand McNally)

MacKenzie, N., Eraut, M. and Jones, H.C. (1970), *Teaching and Learning — An Introduction to New Methods and Resources in Higher Education* (Paris: UNESCO/IAU)

Oatey, M. (1972), *Effectiveness and Costs of Instructional Media* (London: Air Transport and Travel Industry Training Board)

Oettinger, A.P. (1969), *Run, Computer, Run. The Mythology of Educational Innovation* (New York: Collier-Macmillan)

Office of Educational Communications (1970), *Assembling the Revolution* (New York: State University of New York, mimeo)

Paden, D.W. and Moyer, M.E. (1969), "The Relative Effectiveness of Three Methods of Teaching Principles of Economics," *Journal of Economic Education*, Fall

Perry, W. (1972), *The Early Development of the Open University, Report of the Vice-Chancellor* (Bletchley: Open University)

Schramm, W. (1964), *The Research on Programmed Instruction: An Annotated Bibliography* (Washington, D.C.: U.S. Government Printing Office)

Suppes, R. and Morningstar, M. (1969), "Computer-assisted Instruction," *Science*, 17 October

Wagner, L. (1972), "The Economics of the Open University," *Higher Education*, vol. 1, no. 2

Chapter 8

Attiyeh, R. and Lumsden, K.G. (forthcoming), "The Production of Economics Understanding: An Analysis of the First Year Economics Course," *Economica*

Eble, K.G. (1970), *The Recognition and Evaluation of Teaching* (Washington, DC: American Association of University Professors)

Hildebrand, M., Wilson, R.C. and Deinst, E.R. (1971), *Evaluating University Teaching* (Berkeley: University of California, Center for Research and Development in Higher Education)

Jamison, D. and Lumsden, K. (1972), "A Proposal for Increasing Efficiency in the Graduate School of Business," (Stanford University)

Wilson, R.C., Gaff, J.G. and Bauvy, J.L. (1970), *Manual of Information, Faculty Characteristics Questionnaire* (Experimental Form I) (Berkeley: University of California, Center for Research and Development in Higher Education)

Chapter 9

Kuhn, T.S. (1970) *The Structure of Scientific Revolutions* (Chicago: University of Chicago Press)

Chapter 10

Alchian, A.A. and Demsetz, H. (1972), "Production, Information Costs and Economic Organization," *American Economic Review*, vol. LXII, no. 5 (December), pp. 777–795

Manne, H. (1971), "Political Economy of Modern Universities" (Stanford University: mimeo)

Newhouse, J. (1972), "The Economics of Group Practice," Rand Corporation Research Memorandum P-4478/1 (Stanford: The Rand Corporation)

Veblen, T. (1899), *The Theory of the Leisure Class* (New York)

Chapter 11

Brainard, W.C. and Dolbear, F.T. (1971), "Social Risk and Financial Markets," *American Economic Review*, vol. LXI, no. 2 (May)

Dolde, W. (1973), "Capital Markets and the Relevant Horizon for Yale Consumption Planning" (Yale University, unpublished PhD thesis)

Hause, J.C. (1971), "Ability and Schooling as Determinants of Lifetime Earnings or If you're so smart, why aren't you rich? ", *American Economic Review*, vol. LXI, no. 2, (May)

Houthakker, H.S. (1959), "Education and Income," *The Review of Economics and Statistics*, vol. XLI, no. 1, (February)

Shell, K., Fisher, F.M., Foley, D.K. and Friedlander, A.F. in association with Behr, J.J. Jr., Fischer, S. and Mosenson, R.D. (1968), "The Educational Opportunity Bank: An Economic Analysis of Contingent Repayment Loan Programs for Higher Education," *National Tax Journal*, vol. XXI, no. 1, (March)

Stearns, R. (1971), "Life-Cycle Earnings and Consumption Evidence from Surveys" (Yale University; unpublished PhD thesis)

Tobin, J. (1967), "Life Cycle Saving and Balanced Growth" in *Ten Economic Studies in the Tradition of Irving Fisher*, Cowles Foundation Paper No. 272 (New York: John Wiley)

Tobin, J. and Dolde, W. (1972), *Wealth, Liquidity and Consumption* (Yale University: Cowles Foundation Paper No. 360)

Vickrey, W. (1962), "A Proposal for Student Loans Repayment to be Computed as Share of Future Earnings' in Selma Mushkin, ed., *Economics of Higher Education* (Washington: Department of Health, Education and Welfare)

Author Index

273

Subject Index

Ability, 8, 17, 52, 69, 208; *see also* Students
Academic freedom, 12, 29, 43, 44, 128*ff.*
Administration, as inside pressure group, 43
    consumption, 44
    perquisites, 44
Allocation
    internal, of university, 11
    of resources, 3, 4, 10, 18
    teaching vs. research, 6
Alternative investment, 3

Benefit—Cost, 9, 15—16, 21, 30
Black Studies, 38
Business
    recruitment of professionals and
        executives, 33

Capital
    and firm, 223
    consumption capital, 23
    educational, 3
    physical, 3
    production capital, 23
Capital market, 28, 86, 241—265
Committee for Economic Development, 138
Committee on Higher Education, 167
Competitive markets, *see* Market
Computer-assisted instruction, 155, 162—
    163
Consumer sovereignty
    and efficiency, 222
    and student evaluations, 176
    in university, 228
Consumption, 35, 44
    as a component of education, 23, 34,
    115, 177

Cost
    and technology, 5
    differences of instructional media, 155—
        158
    marginal, of educating a student, 136
    of education, 64, 131
    of educational capital, 3
    of educational filtering, 60
    of videotape and live lectures, 172—173
Cost—Benefit, 26; *see also* Benefit—Cost
Credit rationing and higher education, 59;
    see also Capital market

Degree, 115
    market value, 116
    output measure, 177, 221
    screening device, 115, 177

Economics Education Project (EEP), 119*ff.*,
    127, 137, 144
Economies of scale
    and instruction, 152, 156, 158
    external and internal, of university, 157
Education
    adult and extension, 93
    free, and filter, 65
    general, 23
    opportunity, 13
    output of universities, 7
    primary and secondary, 88
    production and human capital formation,
        131—145
    technology, 98
    undergraduate, 6
Educational attainment, 3
Educational policy, 4

275

distrust of, 6, 12
and education level, 68
failure, 13, 119
forces, 9
and price of education, 13, 15
and public good, 12
for research, 215
system, 9, 18
Maturation hypothesis, 23, 33, 34

National Defense Education Act, 257

Occupational categories, 3
On-the-job filtering, 69
Open University, 165, 172, 176
Output
disaggregation, 116
gain from filtering, 60
measurement of, 4, 6, 113–130
quality of university, 26
research, 5
of universities, 4, 5

Packaged courses, 213
Political
activity of students, 35
interference in university, 12
planning of higher education, 10
Preference
of education's consumers, 5, 10
functions of university interest groups,
48; *see also* Utility function of
household
Pressure groups, 9, 30–31; *see also* Interest
groups
Price(s)
of academic inputs, 211
internal price, 218
system, 27, 233
of university output, 4, 5, 7, 9, 11, 12,
207
Production, 7, 98
Production function, 59, 109, 113–114
for economics teaching, 142
of education, 3, 32, 181
optimal technology, 238
Productivity, 8, 25, 60, 74
and incentives in higher education, 11
increases from higher education, 17

Professional
associations, 30, 32
schools, 25, 52
teaching, 32
training, 23, 30, 31, 34, 36
Profit, 9, 10, 11, 17
maximization of university as a firm, 77,
101
monopoly profits of professionals, 32
and public goods, 13
social profit, 133
Programmed text, 149
Public good; *see also* Externalities
aspect of the university, 40, 48
component of human capital, 88–89
nature of research, 12
and profit, 12

Rate of return
and higher education, 3, 8
and human capital, 69, 86
private vs. social, from education, 242
Redistribution of income, 28, 30, 31, 113,
135
Research, 6, 7, 9, 15, 16, 21, 31, 41, 89*ff.*,
96
applied, 22, 24, 120–122, 191
evaluating, 5, 6, 12, 219
facilities, 33, 39
financing, 21, 235
incentives, 39
institutes, 13, 48, 216
market for products of, 215
and pedagogical efficiency, 213
and promotion of faculty, 39, 41
as public good, 12, 22, 97
pure, 24
scale of, 22
Risk and uncertainty
of investment in higher education, 15
private vs. social in higher education, 15,
241–265

Salaries, 226
Scholarships, 29, 136
Screening, 25, 35, 51–74, 116, 130, 241;
see also Filter
Service staff of university, 47
Social welfare, 21–49
function, 30, 49

277

Books from the
Higher Education Research Unit

Elsevier Scientific Publishing Company — Amsterdam,
Studies on Education

The Practice of Manpower Forecasting: A Collection of Case Studies by B. Ahamad,
M. Blaug and others (1973)
Returns to Education: An International Comparison by George Psacharopoulos
assisted by Keith Hinchliffe (1973)
The Academic Labour Market by Gareth Williams, Tessa Blackstone and
David Metcalf (1974)
*A Fresh Look at Higher Education: The European Implications of the Carnegie
Commission Reports* by Jack Embling (1974)
Efficiency in Universities: The La Paz Papers edited by K.G. Lumsden (1974)

In preparation

Demand for Social Scientists
Costs in Universities and Polytechnics

Published by Allen Lane The Penguin Press
'L.S.E. Studies on Education'

Decision Models for Educational Planning by Peter Armitage, Cyril Smith and
Paul Alper (1969)
The Causes of Graduate Unemployment in India by Mark Blaug, Richard Layard
and Maureen Woodhall (1969)
Paying for Private Schools by Howard Glennerster and Gail Wilson (1970)
Policy and Practice: The Colleges of Advanced Technology by Tyrrell Burgess and
John Pratt (1970)
A Fair Start: The Provision of Pre-school Education by Tessa Blackstone (1971)
*Qualified Manpower and Economic Performance: An Inter-plant Study in the
Electrical Engineering Industry* by P.R.G. Layard, J.D. Sargan, M.E. Ager and
D.J. Jones (1971)

Published by Penguin Books

The Impact of Robbins: Expansion in Higher Education by Richard Layard,
John King and Claus Moser (1969)

Published by Oliver and Boyd

Graduate School: a Study of Graduate Work at the London School of Economics
by H. Glennerster with the assistance of A. Bennett and C. Farrell (1966)
The Utilization of Educated Manpower in Industry by M. Blaug, M. Peston and
A. Ziderman (1967)
Manpower and Educational Development in India (1961—1986) by Tyrrell Burgess,
Richard Layard and Pitambar Pant (1968)
Educational Finance: its Sources and Uses in the United Kingdom by Alan Peacock,
Howard Glennerster and Robert Lavers (1968)
Education and Manpower: Theoretical Models and Empirical Applications by
Tore Thonstad (1969)

Published in collaboration with the
Directorate for Scientific Affairs, O.E.C.D.

*Statistics of the Occupational and Educational Structure of the Labour Force in
53 Countries* (1969)

Published by Her Majesty's Stationery Office, London

Education for Management: A Study of Resources by Deborah Jones,
Kay Ball and Michael Shellens (1972)